About the Author

G. FRANCO ROMAGNOLI, an accomplished chef and restaurateur, was born, raised, and educated in Rome, and moved to the United States in 1955. From 1974 to 1976, he and his late wife, Margaret, wrote and starred in *The Romagnolis' Table*, a television series on Italian cooking. Their cookbook of the same name and its sequel, *The New Romagnolis' Table*, have sold nearly 400,000 copies, and for ten years they owned three four-star restaurants in the Boston area. Romagnoli is the author of numerous cookbooks, a frequent contributor of articles on food and travel to newspapers and magazines, and a culinary arts professor at Boston University. Widowed in 1995, he remarried in 1998, and now lives in Boston with his wife, Gwen, a lawyer and writer.

A Thousand Bells at Noon

A Roman Reveals the Secrets and Pleasures of His Native City

G. Franco Romagnoli

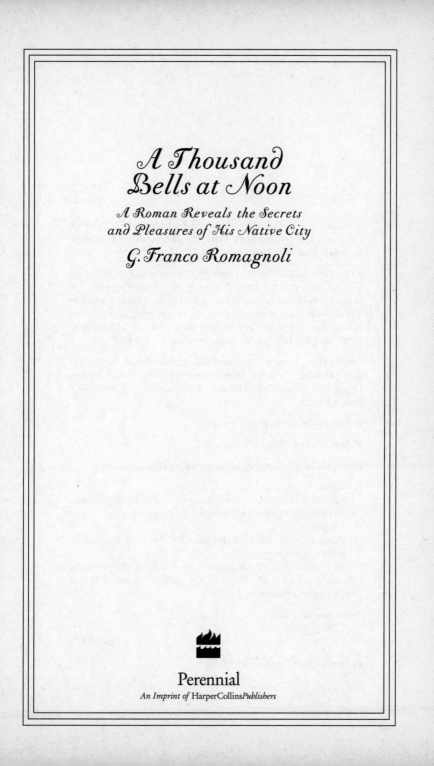

Perennial

An Imprint of HarperCollinsPublishers

First Perennial edition published 2003.

Photographs by G. Franco Romagnoli

Library of Congress Cataloging-in-Publication Data

Romagnoli, G. Franco.
  A thousand bells at noon : a Roman reveals the secrets and pleasures of his native city / G. Franco Romagnoli—1st Perennial ed.
    p. cm.
  Originally published: South Royalton, Vt. : Steerforth Italia, 2002.
  ISBN 0-06-051920-7 (pbk.)
    1. Rome (Italy)—Description and travel. 2. Rome (Italy)—Social life and customs—20th century. 3. Romagnoli, G. Franco—Homes and haunts—Italy—Rome. I. Title.

DG806.2 .R634 2003
945'.63093—dc21

2002192685

03 04 05 06 07 ❖ / RRD 10 9 8 7 6 5 4 3 2 1

To all my Roman Friends
who never allowed me to forget
how Roman I am.

❖

Quest'aria nun è aria de villani,
noi nun semo facchini, io ve l'ho detto!
Noi, pe' grazia de Dio, semo Romani.

This air is not for rubes,
I am telling you: we are not riffraff!
We, by the grace of God, are Romans!

— Trilussa, twentieth-century vernacular poet

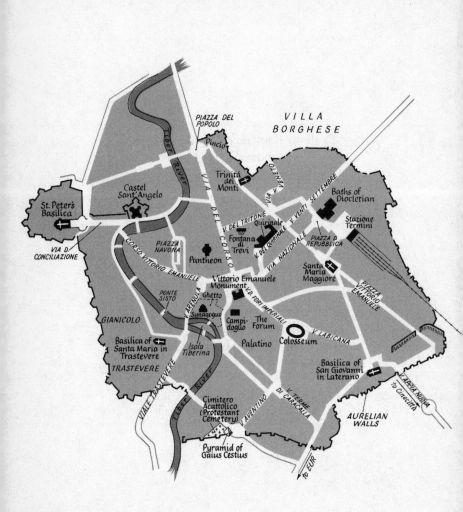

CONTENTS

Civis Sum

I WAS BORN AND raised in Rome. I was privileged, perhaps lucky, to be born within the Roman walls, almost a Roman: to be *a Romano de Roma*, a Roman of Rome, a real Roman, you have to have behind you at least seven generations of Romans on both mother's and father's side. My mother was a Roman: that was lucky. The real privilege was my father: he loved Rome, perhaps as only non-Romans do, and his love was contagious. He passed that love on to me, and I wish I could say this also of his knowledge: of Rome he knew everything there was to know about everything. During the many long walks — since I was barely able to walk, it seems to me now, and until I took along my own child — he spoke of Rome, he sang of Rome. He taught me — in the Tiber — how to swim. . . . From him I learned to recognize the sound of Saint Peter's bells, how to bask in the warmth of the Roman sun, to treasure the caress of her summer breezes, the taste and smell of her food. I learned, with my first Latin history studies, that the *Antichi Romani*, the ancient Romans, called themselves *civis*, which, without any other qualification, meant automatically "citizen of Rome." All the rest, all the people living in but not born in Rome, and all the people annexed to Rome, had to pay their dues, merit the honor to be called *civis Romanus*, and be proud to be able to say: *civis Romanus sum* . . . My father was one; I would like to earn that honor.

I did my studies and married in Rome. My future American wife, Margaret, was a radio journalist, the youngest woman to head the radio station for the Marshall Plan in Rome. At that time, my engineering studies led me to scientific photography and cinematography that shortly turned into a passion for documentary films. To support that budding career I moonlighted as sound engineer for the Marshall Plan's radio station. I ended up marrying Margaret, my boss. As was then chivalrously proper, I quit my job before marrying her. Margaret, her semidiplomatic position being noncompatible, then, with marrying a foreigner, was fired. I had to dedicate all my efforts to my career as a cinematographer, which, as luck wanted, coincided with one of the periodical financial ups and downs of the Italian movie industry. This one was not just a down, it was a deep crevasse. So the launching of my documentary-maker career (with enormous youthful presumption I was my own writer, director, and cinematographer) coincided with the launching of my family, a fact hardly compatible with being paid in IOUs. There is a silver lining: the situation left us with plenty of free time, enough to visit my in-laws in Connecticut. During one of their social gatherings, I met the director of Boston's educational radio station. The station, in a year, was going to leap into television: they needed to set up a film department. Would I care to consult with them about it?

I left Rome when I was twenty-six. A wife, a child: I thought myself mature enough to make the decision to leave my city. It is for professional reasons, I told myself, it will be temporary. It was traumatic. It did not take me long to realize how much I was attached to Rome, how much I would miss it. Boston accepted me: the six-month consultancy stretched into a six-year employment, then more years as a freelancer. I filmed all around the world, but returned to base: Boston.

The temporary absence stretched to almost half a century, but I always missed Rome's air. I missed Rome's water; I missed its light, its stones, its food. And every year, as in a pilgrimage, I came back to Rome. Boston had been good to me, but most of a year's profit was spent on a visit to Rome. Three at the beginning, we grew to be six: we called it a vacation, but it was, and it looked like, a pilgrimage.

And on those occasions, even if briefly, I let all my senses be saturated again with Rome, rejoicing at whatever good had happened in my absence, taking personal offense at the bad. And feeling somewhat left out, as if they should have asked my consent. They should have asked, at least, my opinion.

When my father died, I kept roaming Rome with him, with the sound of his voice. I walked the Rome of the First Empire, of the First Republic; the Rome of the Dark Ages, of the barbarians' plunders; the Rome of the Popes and of the King; the Rome of the Fascist pseudo-empire and of the New Republic . . . and saw what They, each one and all of them, did to Rome. They made her grow, They shrunk her, They made her holy, They desecrated her, They made her beautiful and ugly again. But They could not destroy her: Rome, the Eternal.

Then I realized that all I knew of Rome was her skin, what can be seen and found in a thousand guidebooks. That there is another Rome, a Rome made of people, of feelings, of memories. That somewhere there is someone, minor perhaps, who makes her what she is. If a tree falls in Rome . . . who is there to hear it, who plants a new one? I imagine, hidden somewhere, a huge clockwork that somehow makes Rome work. There are a thousand spinning gears, a thousand engineers manning the levers, oiling the works. No matter how many rods Time or History or Politics ram through her gears, the machinery keeps going. . . .

I have come back for a longer visit to see, or attempt to see, my Rome anew. Half a century is a long enough time to allow me to see it, as it were, with new eyes. And listen with new ears.

A rediscovery of my city from a five-foot ten-inch height, my street level.

Eternal Rome, like eternity itself, is made up of moments. My book — my notebook — about her people, about her face, about her workings, just like a set of snapshots, would cover just one moment. Perhaps some old memory will offer a peek at the moment before, perhaps offer a guess at the next one.

Coming to Rome

Ecco i pellegrini

O VER ELBA THE captain informs us that this famous island not only was Napoleon's place of exile, but also marks
the beginning of our descent toward — (he pauses here for a
second: you can almost hear a subliminal blaring of trumpets in
his voice) — Rome! The engines cut down to a whisper and in
the clear autumn air Tuscany slowly rises up to us. Along the
coastline the Via Aurelia, one of the old consular roads, is clearly
visible: a white ribbon leading — like all roads — to Rome. We
pass over brown Etruscan earth, Tarquinia and Cerveteri; then
the port of Civitavecchia and after that — about fifty miles from
landing — the scattering of farms and country houses slowly
grows into a congestion of tall buildings and then the whole landscape, from the coast to the faraway Alban hills, is almost an uninterrupted urban assemblage. Below us the Tiber snakes south, like
us, and here and there sends blinking reflections of sunshine,
semaphoring a welcome. Now the core of the old city appears:
unmistakable Saint Peter's dome, the Colosseum, the forums. . . .
Soon the brick-colored central maze turns again into the uniform
spread of cement cubes. It is a big city. In a moment the runway is

under our wing and the captain puts the big Alitalia craft down with the lightness of a feather. From the back of the cabin comes a roaring applause: one wonders if it is — in the Italian way — the loud appreciation for a good performance or in gratitude for the end of an uneventful trip. Welcome to Rome.

With a minor hitch: taxis and limos to town are on strike. A hiccup strike, we are informed. There is an hourly timetable for the strikes to start or to stop, but nobody knows exactly its schedule. And nobody seems terribly exercised about it. But then, cheer up: public transportation is supplied by the *metropolitana* train line that will take passengers to the central Stazione Termini. And indeed the sleek trains whisk you elegantly and effortlessly to the center of town and to another minor hitch: buses and trolley cars are (hiccup) on strike but taxis are (hiccup) working. There is a long line to elbow through to get one, an exercise for the practiced, the young, or the luggage-free.

Fate, in the shape of a neatly attired man, takes me by the hand: he knows I need a ride, he has a car. Right up front he tells me that he is not licensed for the job, a pirate cab. But it will take me there; he sees my apprehension and "It will cost you less," he reassures me, "and will get you there faster." The reason, he says, is that to make up for the strike losses a licensed cab — assuming I can get one — will take me all over Rome and charge me for it. . . . A reasonable argument, rationally presented, but I am still suspicious. He ignores my hesitation and asks, "By the way, where are we going . . . ?" and before I can answer, takes charge and piles my luggage into the trunk. I am too tired, or too curious, or both, to fight the situation. I just let it happen, and sit, by invitation, in the passenger seat, beside him. I am going near the Basilica of San Paolo, or, as we reckon together, stretching it a little, almost halfway back to the airport. "Isn't life funny?" he comments, seeing more humor in the situation than I do. "Now you should settle on the fare," he tells me, trying to teach me the ropes of a meterless cab, "and I think that forty thousand lire will take you there. What do you think?" I fall for the game, and say twenty; we settle on thirty. "A good buy. If things go right it will take a half hour; a thousand a minute, that's cheap!" He is cheerful about it all, and his jolliness is somewhat contagious. He introduces himself: "My name is Piero." Deeming that first names are enough, I tell him mine and we shake hands on that. He assumes the race-driver position (all Romans are race drivers manqué), slouching back on the seat, arms stretched out to the wheel, and we are under way. He makes his way out of the huge piazza fronting the station, weaving around stalled (hiccup) buses and clusters of people. I realize now that the piazza is crowded end to end with people gathered in groups. And they do not look Italian. To my query, "*Povera Roma mia!*" Piero answers, "Poor Rome of mine! If you did not know, you would think you were in Manila . . . or Addis Ababa." During the last decade or so there has been a great influx of *extra-comunitari*, immigrants — legal and not — from outside the European Community area. They congregate here to share news with their compatriots, for mutual assistance, for a picnic, for exchanging goods. In their national garb, Filipinos, Ethiopians, Sudanese, Vietnamese, Cambodians, have staked out their own place on the square. "It's a circus!" is Piero's comment. "Nice people, most of them do the work, the low-paying work, that Romans don't want to do anymore. But there are a lot of shady dealings going on. I think the police allow this circus so they can keep an eye on them, instead of having to chase them all over town!" Piero, the good-natured Macchiavelli. "*Pellegrini, ah!*" is his comment. Pilgrim, in the Roman dialect, from the *peregrinus* of Cicero's language, refers to anybody coming from outside Rome. In the past, pilgrims flocked to Rome in processions to ask for grace and benedictions at the various basilicas. They were barefoot and wore penitential cassocks of burlap, they were not too clean and quite worn out from their long travels, and, moreover, brought no wealth to the city; Romans considered them quite a nuisance and looked down on them with some superiority and some derision. The term has remained, in today's strict dialect, to include not only whoever looks different or strange, but also all foreigners. *"Povera Roma!* Taken over by *pellegrini!"* Piero comments sadly, then looks at me and "No offense!" he adds. I reassure him that none is taken: I am almost a Roman. But I could very well be a *pellegrino;* I've been away a long time.

"Where?"

"Boston," I tell him.

"Small world! I have a nephew, my wife's side, in Boston! He is a *capoccione,* an egghead. Studies at meat."

I figure that he means M.I.T. He swerves around a one-way sign stuck on a temporary post, turns on Via Cavour, circles Piazza Vittorio . . . he is really taking the shortcut!

"Now you see Calcutta!" Piero indicates with his chin all the Asian goods and food stores in the area. Piazza Vittorio is one of the large squares in Rome. A sizable rectangle, six by four city blocks, it has a central park and gardens, flanked by the porticos of palazzi that go back, like the square itself, to the beginning of the Roman middle class, somewhere about the 1800s, when the new bourgeoisie attempted to ape the aristocracy. Almost since its inception Piazza Vittorio has been, during the morning hours, the site of one of the largest open markets, a Roman's favorite. All the freshest fruit and produce from the orchards and gardens surrounding the city could be found here, along with quality meat, fish still wet from the sea, and household goods handmade by artisans. Now it has deteriorated, it is Piero's feeling, into a hodgepodge of foreign goods. The air carries the aroma of exotic Indian spices, Asian dried meats, and foods that, only a short time ago, Romans did not even know existed. Piero makes a show of smelling the air, and not with approval. I know he is a Roman: when it comes to foreign things, especially foods, Romans are superchauvinists.

"Calcutta! *La Cina!"* Piero gestures, explaining, with a mixed sense of geography, that the area is full of Chinese warehouses and shops, that the whole place has been taken over by a large community of Chinese. "Calcutta," he insists, "they even have their own mayor!" He thinks for a moment, then continues: "Or perhaps their boss. They are very rich, they stick together in gangs, like the Mafia. You'd think our own wasn't already enough!"

Piero guns the cab as if to leave the area as fast as he can, but we hit a bottleneck at Porta San Giovanni. There are cars lined up as far as the eye can see, enough honking and yelling to split the ears. Piero throws his hands in the air and shrugs. I am surprised at his calm resignation. He tells me that by now he has learned to take it easy and, all told, driving is still better than being a *ragioniere*, an accountant. That is what he was; then he took early retirement and, to do something, he started ferrying people around. "You meet more people than in an office," he says, "and you see a lot of Rome, too." The traffic starts moving again. The stoppage had been provoked by three buses disgorging a load of nuns at the Basilica of San Giovanni in Laterano. "*Pellegrini! More pellegrini!*" Piero chuckles amiably. Then, "You won't believe it," he says, "the other day I drove two Buddhist monks around. Nice guys, I can still smell the incense."

I ask him if he was surprised to see saffron-clad bonzes in Rome.

"Surprised? Nothing surprises us anymore. We have seen them all. Everybody comes and goes. We have seen Turks, and English, and Spanish, and Americans . . . princes and kings, soldiers and generals, on horses and on elephants, some were friends, some were not. We have even seen a Polish pope. So, what else is new?"

I ask him if he is ever curious to see all these people *a casa loro*, in their own habitat, if he ever travels.

"No," he says, "why should I go? I figure that if all the world comes to Rome it must be special, must have something better than where they come from. I am here already!"

Nice philosophy, I tell him.

"Look," he tells me, "I see all the people around me running around, trying to go up, going places, trying to make money and more money. In Rome everybody is a millionaire today. Look around: there are more Mercedes here than in Berlin! I am sixty-five, and I am happy where I am and what I am. I like my life, I wouldn't change a thing. I really like it!" He pauses, and then adds: "Actually, there is one thing that bugs me, but really bugs me." He looks at me, waiting for my expression to say, "What is it?"

"I have it so good, why will I have to die?" he says. I have no answer for him, but then we have arrived. By my watch it has taken twenty-seven minutes, traffic jam included. I want to leave him a tip, but he refuses.

"It was a pleasure. And if you need to go around, give me a call. I will show you Rome, like to a *pellegrino!*" I tell him that after this short trip with him, I'm already back to being a Roman, feeling at home. He hands me a card: it says simply PIERO, with his home telephone number and the number of his *telefonino*, his cellular phone, underneath. Then he waves: "*Ciao, romano!*"

And a romano I am going to be again for at least six months. I have secured a sublet apartment in Vicolo del Cedro, in Trastevere. I will return with Gwen, my wife. Actually, she is my second wife. Margaret, my first, and I had met Gwen at a mutual friend's house in Cambridge and, as I remember it, the two ladies got involved in an exchange about their experiences of living in Rome for an extended period, bringing up children there. Four on our side; one, raised single-handedly, on hers. When Margaret passed away, as fate wanted, Gwen and I got together to share companionship and a common background. It was neither compassion or filling a void. Certain losses and certain voids cannot be soothed or filled. It was just a second beginning, free and unencumbered, for both of us.

Rome, beware, here we come again!

Being a Roman

Semo romani

$\mathcal{B}$EING A ROMAN is a complex thing: it is not only a matter of genealogy, it is a lifestyle, a particular way of feeling and seeing and reacting to the world.

But then, a Roman from which Rome? Ancient Roman maps marked the unknown, hence savage, lands outside their dominion *Hic sunt Leonis*, from here on, there are only wild beasts. In more recent times, only the inhabitants of the Rome contained within the old Aurelian Walls could be called real Romans. When the city expanded past the walls, like floodwaters spilling over a dam, that huge area could be marked *Hic sunt Romani*. But for a real Roman, any inhabitant of these new lands is a spurious Roman.

Through the ages Rome has followed the accordion syndrome, expanding from one citizen — Romulus — to 1,500,000 under Emperor Trajan, then deflating to barely 50,000 in 1527, after the sack of the Vandals and other assorted catastrophes (fire, flood, black plague); up again by the mid-1800s to 160,000; and to almost 250,000 at the beginning of 1910. The ups and downs followed political and economic developments, depending on whether people had to flee or be imported. A great number of artisans, stonemasons, and laborers enabled the building boom of the Renaissance. Later, northern government employees (bureaucrats who could read and write) arrived when the seat of government moved from Turin. The population shrank some during World War II, when people fled to escape famine and danger. Even during maximum expansion, ignoring the few gaps here and there, Rome had stopped at not much farther than the Aurelian Walls, but with the end of the war the accordion's bellow blew up and Rome expanded uncontrolled, as in an explosion, reaching almost to the Alban Hills in the east, to the sea in the west, and to Ostia in the south. Much of the construction was *abusiva*, illegal, and without any urban planning; once a new quarter was in place, it was left to city hall to face the fait accompli and to worry about supplying adequate roads, utilities, and sewage.

Today the population of Rome is above three million (an unofficial number, some say underestimated). The number of real Romans fluctuates around thirty-five thousand or fewer. But if you ask someone from Testaccio, or Trastevere, or Ghetto, or Borgo, anyone from the old *quartieri*, they will tell you that today in Rome there really are, at best, a few hundred real Romans. And like their vernacular parlance, they will lament, they are on the way to extinction. Because, they will explain, to be a real Roman you not only have to be born within the walls, but also be a seventh-generation Roman, by way of father and mother. If you go searching for them, it is more likely that you will find these real Romans in the Ghetto or among the *popolino*, the lower class, than among the old aristocracy. Some may be a bit uncouth, perhaps, but genuine red blood runs in their veins. The noble families, the ones that have palazzi and squares and streets named after them, have been marrying other nobles, or other rich people from other cities if not other countries altogether, and their rarefied blue blood will not be, according to the rule, considered Roman by a Roman. This is another of the many Roman paradoxes, because since the Middle Ages the nobles and the rich families were the ones that gave a face and a shape to the city. The *popolino* just built it, brick over brick, with the sweat of their brow.

The character of a Roman is not a simple one; from past events, a historical psychoanalyst could interpret the reasons for this complexity. The very founding of Rome, or at least the legend of it, could be the starting point. Here are the facts, as I remember them from the history lessons of my elementary school days: during the eighth century B.C. Amulius usurps the throne of his brother Numitor, king of Alba Longa, a city up the river from the future Rome. To terminate Numitor's dynasty, Amulius relegates Numitor's daughter Rhea Silvia, his only heir, to the vestal virgins' cloistered temple: there she could not produce any issue. But the god Mars has his way with Rhea and in due time the twins Romulus and Remus are born. Amulius finds them out and gets rid of them by setting them afloat down the Tiber in a basket. They land in the bushes of the riverbank, where they are rescued and nursed by a she-wolf. Believed to be sons of a sacred *lupa*, Romulus and Remus are subsequently adopted by a couple of shepherds; once grown up, the twins find out their true origins, go and slay Greatuncle Amulius, and reestablish Grandpa Numitor to the throne. Then they set out to start a town of their own along the Tiber; Romulus digs a furrow with a plow to mark the perimeter of the new town and pompously declares that whoever is in is in (and a citizen), and whoever is out is out (and an enemy). Remus, with poor comedic timing, jumps the furrow and Romulus, in a fit of anger, slays him. He names the city Roma, after himself, on April 21, 753 B.C., official birthday of Rome, and populates it with outlaws and shepherds. Not foreseeing much growth in a town of men only, Romulus encourages his men to set out and get some women. They throw a party in a nearby town in the Sabina hills; at the end of fun and games they leave the inebriated Sabini men behind and take the Sabine women to Rome. The event achieves its purpose (by the way, the Italian translation from the Latin *ratto delle Sabine*, the "abduction" of the Sabines, is less violent than the English version, the "rape" of) and the history of Rome is under way.

From these events our historical analyst could unearth a few traits of the Roman character: he is of innate nobility (the bit about Mars and a princess); has a propensity for adventure and survival (floating down the river in a basket); has a taste for hearty foods (wolf's milk); has a strong sense of law and justice (killing the usurper and restoring the usurped); has a short fuse (the Remus affair); and has a rough, he-man, appealing way with the ladies (the Sabine girls episode — could this be the origin of Latin lover?). With a slight trick of philology, considering that in Latin *lupa*, in addition to "she-wolf," also meant "whore" (from which comes *lupanar*, brothel), it could be added that for a Roman being called "son of a wolf" could imply being an S.O.B.

Searching for a real Roman, I found a paradox of my own: I had one in front of my eyes for the best part of my life and did not know it. I have known Marisa Papi since we went to the same elementary school. She was the only girl — I well remember — whose pigtails I could not pull with impunity: her kicks to my shins were lethal. Perhaps, but neither of us is sure, I later courted her. It must have been at that age when one experiments with the art of courting and being courted, a time when one is not particularly interested in a pedigree.

Today, about my age, she is not beautiful, but a close-cropped snow-white mop of hair makes her very attractive, a quality reinforced by her cheerful, up-front personality. Single all her life — it seems that a long, unfortunate, unresolved engagement swore her off subsequent serious ties — she dedicated her full interest to a career in the pharmaceutical industry. She is a good cook, too, and she is serving us and a few old friends a real *Roman* dinner: tripe, oxtails, artichokes. Gwen and Marisa, just acquainted, find themselves reciprocally simpatico and quickly become friends. Gwen compliments her on her cooking.

"I wouldn't be here to serve dinner," says Marisa, "if it wasn't for him."

"Him" is me, and Marisa explains that in our youth, shortly after World War II, we went with our customary group of friends for a picnic and a swim at Lake Albano, on the hills outside Rome. One of the girls, not much of a swimmer, found herself in trouble and another girl, not a better swimmer than the first, went to her rescue. The first grabbed the second and they were both going under when Marisa, in a communal ostentation of courage, joined the first two. Now there was a tight bundle of three heading for the deep. Which fortunately was not that deep, perhaps twelve feet: I dove under and, with my feet solidly on the bottom, grabbed their kicking feet and pushed them up, enough to keep their mouths above water. They yelled, help came, and the day was saved. The glory went to the visible surface rescuers, but only Marisa recognized me as the savior, gave me her gratitude and — to this day — the title of invisible, submersed hero.

I feign modesty for my feat, but exact another *carciofo alla romana* as a belated prize.

And finally I ask her if she is a *real* Roman.

"One of the very few," she answers. Her father's family can be traced back to the twelfth century. They were farmers from Campagnano, a village near Rome; they produced olive oil, which they brought to the city, and eventually they became oil merchants in Rome. The trade vanished but the Papi family continued to reside in Rome for nine centuries. As for her mother's side, the Battarellis, Marisa sheepishly has to admit that it can be traced back only to the seventeenth century. A Battarelli, an expert stonemasons' foreman from Genoa, was called to work in the building of the Rome of the Popes, and remained.

"I feel very proud of this fact," adds Marisa. "I feel as if my blood has contributed something to make my Rome what it is today."

Marisa, then, can easily claim the seven generations required for being a real Roman. I ask her what it means to be one and she tells me that in addition to the number of generations that makes a Roman a real Roman, one has to feel a sense of reciprocal possessiveness: owning and at the same time being owned by the city. Being a Roman is like an incurable disease, she says, you live and die with it. Like being in love with a very old lover and being able not only to ignore the ravages of age but actually to appreciate them. It's an undying love affair.

We move to the terrace of her penthouse. It looks over Via Nomentana, the old consular way, flanked by tall, old pine trees. It all looks like a Roman postcard.

"I am living this Rome of mine," she tells me, gesturing to the view, "this old Rome; I feel as if I am part of it, like a cell is part of an organism."

She cannot understand how some people born and living in Rome are totally unaware of a city that for centuries has been the teacher of culture, of art, of history.

"These jerks are like automatons." She is vehement now. "They walk around without having the least idea of what this city is."

I tell her that I have met those kinds of people: for them Rome is the shops of Via Condotti or of Via Frattina; for them the city is only the chaotic traffic or everything else they have to complain about.

"*Roma* is *Roma*," Marisa tells me. And then in a low, confidential tone: "I feel it in my blood, in my cells, it is like my DNA a heredity thing, like white hair. Do you understand?"

I do. Marisa has had that mane of white hair since she was very young; the way she explains certain things also reveals that she is a biologist. Her relationship with Rome becomes almost a biological affair.

"Now this new, huge Rome," she continues, "is populated by accidental Romans. People — or the sons of people — who have come to Rome from the country like flies to honey, only to take and not to give."

It is intriguing to talk of accidental Romans, people who just happened to be born in Rome; we speculate on the subject, and we agree that if during the night Rome changed into, let's say, Milan or Turin, in the morning these people would wake up and not see the difference, or not care: the important thing for them would be that the soccer teams of Roma or Lazio are still there to cheer or to boo. They remind me, I tell her, of those big historical movies — *Spartacus* or *Ben Hur* — a zillion Romans milling around, clamoring in the circus. These accidental Romans are like those movie extras, not a single *romano* among them. We smile at the notion of a Rome populated by temporary Romans, Romans for a few bucks a day.

I wish I could go back in time and court Marisa seriously; I kiss her on the cheeks, anyway. As properly as it behooves a couple of septuagenarians.

There is a strong belief that the character of the modern Roman is shaped more by the events of the Rome of the Popes — a Rome that was at the same time provincial, parochial and cosmopolitan, sordid and fabulous — than by the Rome that came before that. It is the Rome that emerged from the Dark Ages, recovered from the sacks of the Vandals, comings and goings of Arabs, Huns, Goths, and Visigoths. In the fifteenth and sixteenth centuries, it joined the Renaissance and became the Rome of the Popes. The popes successfully established the temporal power of the papacy, making Rome a treasure chest into which they, their families, their relatives, and their friends dipped freely and deeply. But at the same time they enriched and beautified the city by patronizing arts and letters and giving work for quite an extended period to generations of unsurpassed artisans and an outstanding lineup of architects, painters, and sculptors — Bramante, Fontana, Michelangelo, Raphael, Bernini, and Borromini are just the tip of the iceberg. They resurrected the cult of antiquity; the columns, the statues, the ruins of Imperial Rome were reevaluated and romanticized. (But, also, bricks and columns and marble were stripped from many ancient buildings and monuments to build and embellish the new ones, so much so that — as the saying goes — "Romans did more damage to Rome than the barbarians.")

With all its seemingly civilized grandeur, the citizens of the Rome of the Popes were very class conscious. In descending order: the dominant clergy; the aristocracy (in two flavors: the

Black, directly related to the Vatican prelates, and the nonrelated White), including the big landowners, bankers, and merchants; the military and police corps (the *sbirri*, the much-hated enforcers, the cops); and then the rest, the absolute majority, the *popolino*, the lowest class. The upper classes did not mix with the lower, only in some rare case when someone from the upper classes fell for a *bella popolana*; the union was seldom made official, and the resulting issue was generally destined for the priesthood. (*La borghesia*, the middle-class bourgeoisie, was still decades away.) So the *popolino* was pummeled and harassed by laws, edicts, and precepts from both clerical and secular authorities, persecuted by the *sbirri*, their raison d'être being that of satisfying for meager pay the needs of the privileged; the *popolino* was servant and witness to the excesses of the upper classes. Their reaction to their situation was purely Roman: they did not break but bent with the prevailing wind, taking their revenge by making an art of humorously sarcastic, cutting criticism of all authorities. They did so in vernacular song, verse, and prose, with a smart-ass reaction to all laws. While in more Nordic, Saxon countries the laws are considered orders to be zealously obeyed, for a Roman they are no more than the opening of negotiations, a challenge best explained by the saying: *fatta la legge, scoperto l'inganno* — you make a law, we find the loophole. It is an attitude that doesn't make one a friend of the *sbirri*. Politically quarrelsome, argumentative, quick with a knife, a Roman knows his way to jail. At the entrance of the ancient *Regina Coeli*, Queen of Heaven, jail in Trastevere, there is one last step before the door that leads inside: a Roman is not a real Roman, an old song goes, if he hasn't "climbed the step." It is a bit of braggadocio, but then a real Roman is a braggart. The lyrics to the semiofficial Roman anthem, its motif used by Respighi himself in his *Feste Romane* symphony, begin with *lassatece passa', semo romani!* — make way, we are Romans! — and it sounds like the unsheathing of a dagger, a passport to anywhere. Prodigious artists and artisans, Romans also harbor the gene of creative loafing; they are virtuosi of *dolce far niente*, enjoying the day doing nothing, with plenty of free time to create mischief. They develop a strong sense of group, of gregariousness, and are generous to a fault. Conscious that one day they, too, may depend on the generosity of others, they share whatever they have. They love convivial life and make the most of the few resources they possess. In that spirit, a simple loaf of bread and a few olives can make a meal; add an orange, a few more friends, and a glass of Frascati (or two), and it's a banquet. Throw in a guitar and a song and it's a feast. *La Festa de Noantri*, a feast just for ourselves, is a centuries-old affair of song, dance, eating, and drinking, an annual, week-long party that the Romans throw for themselves to celebrate themselves. And also for *Mamma Roma*. She is always at the party, the belle of the ball.

Experts tell me that a flaw in a precious stone, a hairline fissure in a mosaic's tile, deflects the light in a particular way and makes it, if not more valuable, definitely more interesting. If this theory is true, then there must be some mythical flaw that makes Rome more interesting and — in jest borrowing freely from Dante's *Divine Comedy* — turns her simultaneously into Hell, Purgatory, and Paradise. The borders of the three dominions in Rome are sometimes fuzzy, and the "divine" is apparent only if closely associated with "comedy." In other words, it is essential that you take Roman life, sometimes chaotic, sometime lazy, with a sense of balance and of humor, appreciate the paradox at every turn. It is an art — innate in a Roman, essential to any foreigner who wants to survive — to roll with the punches. Otherwise, forget the "Paradise" and make it "Hell." Rome, now achingly beautiful, now infuriatingly coarse, is seldom "Purgatory," seldom gray.

In coming back to Rome, I am again impressed by the Romans' love for sound — augmented, if that's possible, by modern technology. They love it inordinately, in all its manifestations. Only one of these manifestations is a great love for making music; but whoever does not have the talent for music vents his love for sound through a motorized means of conveyance and makes himself heard, as loud as he can. Unfortunately these frustrated music makers are the very great nonsilent majority. Rome resonates with the earsplitting sounds of cars, motorcycles, scooters or *motorini*, motorized bikes, driven with much sound and lots of fury by old and young alike, who, at any hour of day (and even more unfortunately, of night), attack the silence of the venerable streets and make the old walls and stones reverberate. But cars, motorcycles, scooters, and motorbikes are not the unique expressions of sound: a conversation among friends, a customer's appraisal of merchandise, a merchant barking his wares, the cheering or booing of a play, a mother's compliment or reproach to a child, a political assembly of two, a lovers' quarrel, any sort of vocal communication, public or private, will be interpreted by a visiting alien, for its decibel level, as a violent altercation edging on murder.

I have a theory about this need Romans have for the many manifestations of sound. It goes with self-affirmation and recognition, with the need not only to be seen but also to be heard.

Rome, both before and after the heady days of the empire, has been subjected to predatory attacks, ending in domination, subjugation, and slavery (read: hunger and deprivation). The sense of self-preservation is apparent: defensive walls, dating from before the birth of Christ to more recent times, are everywhere. The various and variously aged perimeter walls of Rome were built with boxcar-sized stones and hard bricks in an age when pointed sticks and rocks were the main offensive weapons; many yards thick and many miles long, today these walls could easily withstand an artillery attack. Whoever built them had to be mightily scared of the bad wolf outside, and made sure that no huffing and puffing would ever blow his walls down. This ancestral fear of strangers, albeit justified, must have left a dent on the Roman soul that exhibits itself in the necessity to create noise, a trick widely used in all of nature, apt to make an enemy think that one is bigger, stronger, and scarier than one actually is. Isn't that the purpose of the lion's roar, of the war drums and horns? The heredity of this defensive/offensive trait is evident today in the everyday loudness of a Roman's voice. The megaphone was not invented in Rome: no need for it.

Modern technology has opened a new frontier for self-expression in sound: the *telefonino*, the cellular phone. It is as commonplace as shoes and just as evident an accoutrement for any Roman with the faculty of speech, and it is used constantly and loudly with absolute oblivion of personal privacy. Or of that of others. It would appear to an alien visitor that Romans, constantly cupping one ear with a *telefonino*, are victims of a vast epidemic of earache. In the street, alone, in company, on public transportation, in church, theater, movie house, museum, driving a car, riding a scooter or a bike, in a restaurant, in a public rest room, in any possible public place, the *telefonino* is used with abandon. It commands a well-studied choreography of emphasizing gestures with the free hand, as if batting the message through the ether, a stagey walking back and forth on the pavement, a pirouette or two if standing, a raising of the voice interrupted by brief, very brief, intimate phrases; but, most important of all, the monologue has to be clearly heard by all within the radius of a city block. It is quite common to see a twosome in a bar, in a restaurant, or even promenading together, one speaking for an incredibly long time on the *telefonino*, absolutely oblivious of the other; or, just as common, to see a group of four sitting at a restaurant table with at least three speaking on their personal phones. The amazing thing is that the left-outs do not seem to be annoyed. Or, I suspect, the batteries of their own *'fonino* have been exhausted and the thing is sitting dead in their pockets.

Just as amazing is the fact that the lengthy conversations, as heard by a reluctant, forced eavesdropper, are about nothing: what you had, or you are going to have, for dinner, how it was or is going to be cooked, and the color of your sister-in-law's shoes. Others, in the fashion of reporters, broadcast their movements to other members of the family at regular intervals. I — and a planeload of other people — have heard a mature man call his mother to announce that he had just landed and would call her back as soon as he had retrieved his luggage.

Which perhaps goes to prove the Romans' reliance on the strength and safety of the pack, the absolute dedication to the group, beginning with the smallest unit: the family. This trait has determined in great part the history not only of Rome but of the whole of Italy: the individual's loyalty goes first to the "family" as group and to its father/leader figure, be it prince, lord, duke, pope, *duce*, or *capo*. It is the kind of trait that has given birth to that most Roman phenomenon of nepotism (from the Latin *nepos, nepotis*: nephew) — take care of your own first. Emperors donated kingdoms to their "nephews," legitimate or not; popes made cardinals of their teenaged and bastard sons; people in power gave key positions to their cronies; and so on. And on.

In Rome, since the day Emperor Caligula gave his horse a seat in the Roman Senate, you are not "who you are" but "who you know." During an altercation you will frequently hear *"Lei non sa chi sono io!"* —You don't know who I am! Meaning: "I am not an anonymous, worthless nobody like you . . . I have important connections that, at my asking, will obliterate you!"

"Who you know" will get you a government job, let you pass an exam, obtain a good seat at the opera, get you at the head of a queue, let you have more solicitous care at a hospital, take your important documents to the bureaucratic finish line. . . . Naturally, the *raccomandato*, the recommended one, is honor bound, as soon as he is in a position to do so, to recommend someone else, and so on and on. The circle is never closed, the pack is safe. The recommendation habit is so entrenched in the Roman psyche that, frequently, people suggesting — or simply giving directions to — a restaurant, a pharmacy, a shoe store, or whatever, will automatically add a *"Vada a nome mio"* — Go and mention my name, tell them I've sent you. It will make no difference at all, but both giver and receiver of the advice will feel better for it.

Italy, originally a crazy quilt of geopolitical entities, has been one single united nation only since 1870. Rome is its capital,

hence a Roman should be an Italian first. But he is so only nomi-
nally: in reality he is a Roman first. He becomes an Italian first
only in the case of great national victories or national gains, such
as when the Italian soccer team wins the World Cup. When a
Roman becomes an Italian first, he will drape himself in the national colors and boast of and bask in reflected national pride and
glory. But in the case of a great national loss, such as when the
Italian team loses the World Cup, he will divest his Italian cloak
and become a Roman again, labeling the losing "Italian" players
for what they are: foreigners and traitors who let Rome down.

Love of sound, love of family, love of Rome all combine in
Rome into a series of big and small performances acted in the
public square, in the marketplace, on the playing fields, in the
evening promenade . . . wherever there is an audience, even of
one. For those who can appreciate the daily *commedia dell'arte*,
life in Rome will be more enjoyable, more interesting. Not sur-
prisingly, Romans have developed an underlying love for spec-
tacle and theatricality. In Rome, life is indeed a stage. Which
explains why, besides the Roman Circus and the Grand Opera,
Romans love a parade. A parade is the best chance to make noise
in a group and, above all, wear a costume, be it secular or religious. While watching a parade, one accompanied by a marching
band or by a chorus of sung litanies, it would be hard to decide
where religion and theater part. Hardly a day goes by in Rome
that a renovated building, a new movie theater, supermarket, or
section of road, or any public space is not *inaugurato*, officially
opened, by a parade of some civilian authority in tricolor sash, accompanied by a bishop, a few high-uniformed carabinieri in
plumed hats, and a little court of praise-takers who — with band
music and flags — cut the inaugural ribbon. Even if it is a pretty
common ceremony, a cheering crowd will always be present.

Romans love to dress. Most follow fashions fastidiously,
dressing up, as it were, for the daily stage. It is my theory that this
love of dressing up is not only a derivation of the love for theater,
but a genetic need for a visible sign of status, a uniform. An official

uniform, that is. This is the ambition especially of the great mass of the anonymous plebs, the generational underdogs. For centuries at the bottom of the power pyramid, once in an official uniform, be it of policeman, postman, meter reader, trolley-car conductor or whatever, a Roman is in command and his decisions are final and without appeal. (Sometimes just an official-looking hat is sufficient: self-appointed street parking attendants, by virtue of their cap, lord it over powerless drivers.) Similarly, the counter in any public office becomes a metaphorical uniform: a postal worker, a bank clerk, a department-store cashier, a railroad ticket agent . . . each is on the right side of the counter, while "You-the-Public" are on the wrong one. You are completely under the employee's thumb (in this confrontation, he is brutally taking revenge on you for all his many superiors' thumbs bearing down on him), and the quantity and quality of attention he will give you is directly proportional to his mood, humor, and, finally, whim. The only thing to do is to accept this reality and be as ingratiating as possible, or to guess — with luck — his favorite soccer team and declare yourself its loyal fan. The "You don't know who I am!" gambit does not work here. Everybody knows: you are the one on the wrong side of the counter. Nonetheless, if you foolishly try to assert your rights and stand up to the uniform, and your futile attempt is done with style and flourish, you will receive applause by all present. You just performed the beau geste, and Romans love the beau geste. Roman history is full of theatrical gestures, which, frequently, are much more important than the historical situation that inspired them. In the fifth century B.C. the Roman soldier Muzzio Scevola, having botched the assassination of Porsenna, the enemy's king, punished himself for the failure by putting his right hand over a brazier's flames, and incinerating it. "That will teach me!" he declared, "next time, my left hand will not fail me!" Standing ovation from his captors and applause from the undamaged king. "*Alea jacta est!*" —The die is cast! — grandiosely proclaimed Julius Caesar, as he crossed the Rubicon, followed by his cheering troops. On his way to Rome,

Caesar had to cross several mighty rivers, but the Rubicon — a mere dry brook that can be easily leapt across — remains in history. The simple soldier Enrico Toti, who had lost a leg in a World War I battle, demanded to be and was sent back, missing leg and all, to the front line. Here, having run out of ammunition, he threw his crutch at the charging enemy. . . . It is the beau geste, not the captain's incitations, that rallies the troops to repel the enemy.

It is the theatrical gesture, by now in the genes, that makes for Roman style. Style is everywhere, so much so that it is natural and effortless. A modest stall in a humble market will display its few goods, apples or oranges, colors or textures, as if they were rich, sophisticated jewelry. Walk with friendly steps, not with the invader's thumping footfalls, and you will be greeted in style and with style. There is style in the unembroidered Roman food and wine, style in the simplicity of its taste. Style is in the architecture everywhere, in the towering basilicas and great palaces, as much as in the little parish churches. Style and beauty are everywhere, in a Roman dawn as in a Roman sunset. Style and beauty. Even if, yes, sometimes they are overpowered by noise.

(The one who understood perfectly these traits of the Roman character — actually they must be extrapolated to all of Italy — was Mussolini, who during his two decades in charge of things put everybody — children, adolescents, and grown-ups, male and female — in Fascist uniforms, gave them flags and banners to wave during interminable, colorful parades, and instructed them to sing — or yell — all together, as loudly as they could. We all did that; I did it myself from when I was in elementary school to almost the end of high school. Even those opposed had to do it, and I have the strong suspicion that even they secretly liked dressing up for the buffoonery.)

It would be unfair of me not to count among the real Romans those people who consciously chose to be citizens of Rome. If not real Romans, then definitely honorary Romans. They are the ones who, children no more, came to Rome for any number of reasons, but then, bewitched by the city, remained for the rest of their lives, and profit or glory was seldom part of the allure. I definitely elect my father an honorary Roman. He came to Rome from a cold northern city, Modena, to study at the *Accademia delle Belle Arti*, fell in love with a *romana* and with her city, and remained faithful to both for the rest of his life. And for the rest of his life he could not shed his northern accent, fulfilling the cliché image the Romans have of northerners: tall and elegant, with more gentlemanly manners, more couth than the local hoi polloi. An architect, he could tell the story of every single stone in the city till I thought there was no more for him to know. But he kept discovering more and more till the day he died. I was still a child, in the mid-1930s, when I realized what he felt for Rome. During a Sunday *passeggiata* in the forums he bent down to pick up some trash and put it in his pocket to dispose of later (an absolutely unheard-of gesture in Rome then as much as now). My mother, the Roman, with unveiled sarcasm asked him, the Professor, if by any chance he had been elected street cleaner. "I have seen you sweep your house," he answered her, "so how's that different from keeping your city clean?"

He was one of the few, then, who referred to the modern, imposing Via della Conciliazione as a murderous wound to old Rome. The Via della Conciliazione was a gift from Mussolini's Italian state to the pope's Vatican state, a memento of the signing of the "conciliation" pact between the two states; building the avenue leading from Castel Sant'Angelo to Saint Peter's Basilica involved tearing down a large swath of the old Rione Borgo. My father's objection to it, besides political, was aesthetic: one of the great architectural sleights of hand had been lost. In the old days, he explained to me, one would walk through the labyrinth of the alleys of old Borgo and then suddenly be faced by, as he called it, the "visual explosion" of the immense square, the embrace of the Bernini colonnade and, as if set on a stage, Saint Peter's Basilica. Today there is no more surprise: one can see the huge edifice from a half a kilometer away and not be overwhelmed by its sudden appearance. He felt the same way about the opening of Via dell'Impero (now Via dei Fori Imperiali): the huge avenue connects the Colosseum with Piazza Venezia and required the demolition of many old buildings. My father felt this demolition as a slash on his very body, not only on general principle but even more so because he had resided in a garret there during his student years. His attachment to the old *quartiere* was evident every time the subject came up: his voice took the same reverent tone as when he spoke of some old friend from his student years, now disappeared.

The history of Rome is full of non-Roman Romans. In 690 B.C., Numa Pompilio, first king of Rome, was not a Roman at all. The same goes for Emperor Constantine (fourth century A.D.) and for the hundreds of popes — heads of the Sacred Roman Catholic Church, bishops of Rome: only a handful were born Romans. Being Roman was thrust upon them; they had little choice. But today there is in Rome a sizable colony of foreigners who, arriving for an infinity of different reasons, decided to stay. A month became a year, a year a decade, a decade a lifetime. They elected Rome to be their city, and now they are more Roman than most Romans.

One of them is Helen Pope, Australian by birth, Roman by choice. She is a very attractive woman (the kind that in Rome still attracts politically incorrect whistles), and her long blond hair and blue eyes betray her as a non-native. But as soon as she speaks you know she is a *civis romana*. "When I was eleven or twelve," she says, "I started studying Latin in a small town in Australia. When I opened my first Latin book there was a picture of Italy and in it was a description of ancient Rome. Suddenly I realized that there was much more world than Ballaratt." She pronounces *Ballaratt* with the cadence of *Podunk*, the sound of a door slamming and its bolt being drawn.

"I got interested in the ancient Romans' culture and it sounded so sophisticated — and that was so novel in Australia — that from then on I wanted to go where the ancient Romans were."

Helen waited fifteen years to get here, but from her first day she knew the wait had been worth it and that she had made the right choice. What clinched it was her first sight of the Campidoglio, which she describes as one of the greatest spaces in the world. Looking down on the forums she says, "I was totally knocked out by the beauty, by the physical beauty, the man-made beauty, by the sense that human beings had been there for so long and had created such wonderful things for human beings still to enjoy today."

Then Rome became not just what she expected it to be, just ancient Rome, but a more complex Rome; she discovered the human texture of the city. "Things I had never imagined, like sitting down in a piazza and drinking coffee and having the realization that that is not incidental to one's life. Taking the time to sit down and observe, and just talk and enjoy watching people and understand that that is also part of the Roman culture."

Helen has been living in that culture for the last twenty-seven years. She teaches Latin, Greek, and art history at Rome's Saint Stephen's American School. I ask her if Rome, the Romans, have reciprocated her wholehearted embrace.

"No, never. And they never will."

"Why?"

"Because I am too foreign. For many years I worried about being so much an outsider, then finally I came to accept it, to come to terms with it. The Romans are very family oriented. I admire that, but it makes it very unusual for Romans to take you into their own personal space. I am here because, in the end, I am less of an outsider here than I am in Australia."

If not an outsider, I ask Helen if she considers herself a Roman. "No!" she answers firmly but smiling, "Romans are very extroverted, they talk a lot, and I don't."

Roman or not, she has to face what both Romans and foreigners call the "trauma" of everyday living in Rome: the shops, the post office, the legal documents, the long disorderly queues, the works that suddenly cease to work. . . .

"It's the dues you have to pay," she says, as if contemplating a barter. "But it's much improved," she adds. And then: "It's still got a hell of a long way to go, but it's improved."

One of the improvements is the streamlining of the bureaucracy — obtaining documents and permits, such as the *permesso di soggiorno*, the residence permit.

"The last time I went to get my *permesso* extended at the main police office, I swore if I had to undergo such a brutalizing experience again, I would leave Italy. There was a long, long line — 'line' is a mode of speaking — there was a huge crowd. Fights broke out. It was so totally brutal, so horrendous, that I swore I would never do it again."

And she never has had to do it again: many offices have been decentralized and one can go to a local registry office, with almost no waiting in line at all. "That's something that's enormously improved. . . ."

Helen stops here for a moment, searching in her mind for other improvements. Slowly she lists them, some with a definite sense of humor, like the elimination of the *certificato di esistenza in vita*, the notarized piece of paper to be presented as proof that you are still alive. It is now possible to obtain all the many other certificates through a computerized system. (It once took weeks to obtain a driver's license, a dog tag, or a fishing license; don't even speak of a passport.) Helen has a good chuckle about that, so removed are electronics from the wax tablets of ancient Rome. Next on her list of improvements is how much cleaner Rome is now, and how much work has been done, not only in the center but also in areas farther out from downtown, to make the city a pleasant environment to be in. She mentions a program that is replacing old trees and increasing the number of new ones: every newborn child in Rome is assigned a tree. As part of the replanting, each child gets a letter from the tree: "Dear So-and-so, I am this kind of tree, and I do this and I do that."

"A terrific initiative," Helen says, "to make the children, as they grow up, have more pride in their city."

For a number of years she rented a top-floor studio apartment; from its terrace she could see the forums on the right, the Colosseum on the left. Recently she bought her own apartment; it is again a penthouse, with a view of the Aventino Hill and most of the roofs and bell towers of Testaccio, one of the very old sections of Rome. I ask Helen if being a homeowner has changed her vision.

"I now belong in a different way than I did before, although even when I was renting I thought of Rome as my home. I never doubted that Rome was my home; however, being a homeowner confirmed it." She feels very proud to be living in Testaccio, a neighborhood, like so many others in Rome, where you go downstairs to your favorite, regular *caffè* for cappuccino and everybody knows you and you know everybody.

Helen travels a lot. Alone or with her students she goes to Greece, Turkey, Iran, Yemen, Egypt — all around the great civilizations' sites, the "musts" for anybody interested in ancient history and art. But, she confesses, she is always happy to return to Rome.

"It's an extremely sensuous city, probably as no other." Helen's face is now radiant, as if lit by an inner flame; her blue eyes are sparkling. "It's the colors and the shapes and the sort of spaces that are here, and the intimacy of the *centro*, and the food, and things like that that bring all the five senses alive. Rome makes you respond in all those ways, it confronts you with all those things. You have to respond to them. Rome is a physical city, a living thing. You cannot be uninvolved. Then it becomes yours."

I am sitting at my desk and all of a sudden the room is bathed in a soft, pink light. I look out the window and the sky is an unreal blue-green darkening into a deeper blue at the horizon; soft, thin-as-brushstroke, vivid pink clouds make lines in the sky. The city underneath reflects the colors, some far windows flashing like mirrors. The light side-strikes bell towers, cupolas, and buildings to create an etched cityscape. It is a different city from what it was an hour, a moment ago. That is Rome, a kaleidoscope. The many bits of colorful glass are arranged to form a sharp pattern, a picture. Twist, and the same bits of glass rearrange themselves to give you a different image. As with the light, with a little personal twist, each of us sees a different Rome.

Helen Pope's Rome is different from Jonathan Turner's. An Australian-Dutchman, he came to Rome fifteen or so years ago, a little bit less than half his lifetime. He is a go-getter, very much involved in the art world, a correspondent/reviewer/critic for international art magazines, a curator of gallery shows for the *avanguardia*, the everything-goes school of art. Jonathan is tall and lanky, his light-colored hair ruffled but not unkempt, his head restless, as if to follow the constant darting of his eyes. He speaks as he moves: disjointedly, freely, constantly amused. I gather he believes in the let-it-happen philosophy of life. It comes naturally to ask him how he got to Rome and, more importantly, why he stayed.

"Probably, like many people, by mistake," he answers. "I came to Rome with the idea of a vacation, or at most a short stay. I never intended to live here permanently, I can assure you of that. But then I made friends, a friend, and I decided to stay longer. I got a job in advertising that lasted about five minutes. I had an impressive portfolio, but was blatantly told that, at my age, I could not possibly have created it. So all my meetings with the advertising people in Rome were unmitigated disasters. Then I realized that I had to get, like everybody in Rome, my own network. The whole concept of friend-politics is stronger in Rome than anywhere else in the world."

Jonathan is slouched in an armchair, his long legs wrapped on one armrest; he resettles himself, swinging the legs to the other side. He does it with the fluid movements of a ballet dancer.

"It wasn't simple. It was difficult to be accepted in Rome; there was fear of an unknown, of someone different. There was arrogance: if it isn't done our way, it can't be the right way. You could feel the constant tension between the old Romans and the new ones, each pulling on the other.

"Rome, of course, is a sponge. It absorbs everything that you have to give, but it doesn't always give back what you think you might deserve. That arrogance I mentioned is, I suppose, one of its characteristics. Rome believes it is entitled to anything you can give it. Anything that you do is accepted as being your dues, your necessary contribution, otherwise what are you here for?"

His legs swing again, his eyes examine a corner of the ceiling for advice.

"You know, Rome might not be so good for the brain, but it is certainly good for all the physical senses. It is certainly hedonistic.

"Everybody comes to Rome. All the major artists, all the film stars, all the singers, whether officially or not, all come through Rome. Many artists, certainly in the visual arts, come for a few days, but then stay and rent a studio for a few months. In my field, it's very unusual for artists not to accept the opportunity to do a show in Rome; even if I tell them that it might not be a huge success, they still want to do it. There's a cachet attached; everyone seems to know that even if the show is an unmitigated disaster, here in Rome it will still be a lovely experience."

In his free-flowing talk, Jonathan shows his mixed feelings about his adopted city. Positive and negative, like the poles of a magnet. It will keep him attached here. Unconsciously, I think, he uses the metaphor of art shows for life in Rome: sometimes it's an unmitigated disaster, but how lovely anyway!

I try to envision, to enjoin "disaster" and "lovely" together. I really cannot, not completely, anyway.

But then, this is Rome, I tell myself.

To talk about the Roman character and not mention *furbo* and *fesso* would be a great disservice. *Furbo* can be translated as "crafty," but more accurately as "smart-ass." *Fesso* is the opposite — "dumb idiot" or "stupid fool." By Roman definition, if you are not or do not act as a *furbo* then automatically and unequivocally you are a *fesso*. And the greatest *furbo* is the one who can make more *fessi* with one single blow. The playing field for this jousting is life itself, and in Rome it is actively pursued at all times of day, in every situation of social intercourse.

I hope to explain the *fesso* and *furbo* terms with a short, one-act play.

IL FURBO E IL FESSO

Dramatis Personae:

A MIDDLE AGED LADY (but she could be a young man, or an old man, a young lady, a child . . .).

A MIDDLE AGED MAN (but he could be, see above).

A number of PEOPLE.

The scene is the checkout counter of a supermarket, but with some slight variation it could be a post office, a bank, the reception desk of a hospital. Several people are lined up in an orderly queue.

MIDDLE-AGED LADY:

Permesso, permesso! (Excuse me! Excuse me!)

She advances through the line with the overt reason of taking a pack of candies out of a bin that happens to be a few steps closer to the cash register. She picks up the candies, reads the label, acts absorbed. Stays at her advanced place. People mumble, complain softly, shake their heads. In a moment she puts the pack back in its bin, moves a few positions ahead for the overt reason of taking a bag of peanuts out of a bin even closer to the checkout, ahead of MIDDLE-AGED MAN.

MIDDLE-AGED MAN:

Signora! Please, I was here first!

MIDDLE-AGED LADY *(with irony)*:

Whoa! What a fuss we make for a little bag of peanuts!

MIDDLE-AGED MAN:

Lady, peanuts, schmeanuts! You have half the market in your basket!

MIDDLE-AGED LADY:

What's the matter with you? I've got six, perhaps seven items . . . You men always exaggerate.

PEOPLE *in the queue protest, some booing. The* LADY, *now at the register, unloads her purchases on the counter. With a theatrical gesture, she throws the bag of peanuts back into its bin.*

MIDDLE-AGED LADY *(with offended superiority)*:

If a little bag of peanuts bothers you so much, there, I don't want it anymore! God, you people have nothing better to think of. With the world the way it is, the millions of people killing each other . . . a few peanuts is all you can think of!

By now she has paid the cashier and is on her way out, smiling, a happy furba *leaving behind a bunch of* fessi. *As she goes to unload her groceries, she finds that someone has double-parked so closely to the left side of her car — as close as she has parked hers to the car on the right — that she cannot open her doors; a third car is parked so close behind she can't even open her trunk.*

MIDDLE-AGED LADY *(yelling, furious)*:

You sonavabitches! What's the matter with you! God-damn Romans, no manners at all. A bunch of bastard sheepherders. Just a bunch of *menefreghisti! (Yelling at everybody in sight)* ME-NE-FRE-GHISTIiiiii!!

(CURTAIN)

Menefreghista is a word that pops up frequently when speaking of a particular, and frequent, Roman behavior; it is an adjective that means "I don't care," but it is actually more complex than that.

"Me ne frego!" is an archaic Roman phrase, resurrected and used in 1922 as a motto by the Fascist *Arditi* commandos, to mean "disregard for danger" and "we will do exactly what we want to do, like it or not." The *Ardito* official image was that of a mean-looking man wearing a black fez with a silver skull and crossbones. To make the *Ardito*'s mood clear, he was generally depicted with a dagger clenched between his teeth. This image pretty much stated the whole Fascist philosophy toward national and foreign policy. Now the verb *fregarsene* (and its derivatives *me ne frego, menefreghista, menfreghismo*) is used to describe the dearth of civic education in a large portion of the Roman population, the lack of concern for anybody but oneself. *Menefreghismo* expresses itself in many large and small things. Driving up one-way streets or double-parking, even (or especially) if that means great inconvenience to everybody else. Disposing of trash where it shouldn't be: "Who cares? What's important is that it's not in my house . . ." Not curbing one's dog, or doing at all times what is easy and convenient for oneself, letting others fend for themselves. It is not a generational attribute: it includes all ages — just like being *furbo*, with which it is closely associated. It also involves politics, where a personal, petty issue is much more important than the larger national scheme.

"Romans are a people who think only of *magna' e beve*, to eat and drink," says Luisa Palombini. She is an optometrist with a small Foto-Ottica shop on central Via Rinascimento, a stone's throw from Piazza Navona; she has been selling eyeglasses, cameras, and film there for forty-one years; her fixed clientele are the residents of the neighborhood and tourists and passersby, like me. I stopped there one day to have my eyeglasses fixed, and before long we got involved in a conversation about Rome. In her late sixties, she has an easy smile and a twinkle in her eyes, and in a minute we were talking as if we were old friends.

"Once they have stuffed their bellies, Romans think only of the *partita*, the soccer game, they do not think of anything concrete. . . . They get all steamed up about the Roma or Lazio teams, but if something important comes up, they simply do not care. *Me ne frego*, that's it."

Now Signora Luisa gets steamed up: "Let me tell you, this block of buildings around here once belonged to the insurance company INA, but during the last year it was sold and bought who knows how many times, first Pirelli, then Eumig . . . anyway, when the time came to renew our lease, the new owners sent an inspector here to see what they had bought, and right away doubled the rent. Double! There are twenty or so tenants like me, and I said let's get together, let's reason with them, let's fight it! Everybody said *va be'*, *va be'*, okay, okay — then for their own reasons, without saying a word to me, they sign their new leases. At first they were all crying *Oh Dio, oh Dio!* My God, it's too expensive! What are we (and they meant all of us) going to do? Then quietly-quietly each one on his own made his own deal. *Se ne sono fregati*, they cared only about themselves."

Signora Luisa is a real Roman, her family going back the required seven generations on both sides; she rolls her Rs with the definite, witty, Roman dialect and regrets how things are going in Rome today.

"There are no more Romans," she says, "they are all imported. You can spot them right away by they way they speak; sooner or later they come out with some *frase burina*, some peasant phrase, uncouth. Most of these people do not care about Rome, even the better educated, the well off, they treat the city as their own trash bin, they break all the most basic civic rules. And they are the ones that complain the most, it is a contradiction, it is a paradox." Here Signora Luisa imitates a complaining, crying voice: "Boo-hoo, boo-hoo! It is impossible to live here anymore — they say — this city is too expensive, it's too dirty, it's full of thieves, the schools are crowded — they say. And they are the ones who let their expensive dogs shit on the street!" She pauses a moment, then with conviction: "Sometimes I think my Rome is really going down the drain."

The door of the shop, empty until now, opens and a lady comes in to pick up her glasses, actually two pair. In her fifties, she is quietly elegant, like everybody else walking on the street outside. She tries on her glasses and looks at herself in the mirror: she is pleased. She chats a moment with Signora Luisa about the frames' color; they decide on a new red frame for the reading glasses, so they can be easily found when left someplace around the house. The lady pays with a check, includes me in the usual pleasantries, *buon giorno, buon giorno,* and exits.

"That was Princess Massimo," confides Signora Luisa. "She keeps misplacing her glasses, and I keep selling her new ones. They are standard frames, thirty, forty thousand lire; nobody spends money on frames anymore. Once you could count on two-hundred-thousand-lire frames, easily. . . ."

I mention how thrilled I am to have come in contact with real aristocracy; the Massimo family is one of the oldest in Rome.

"Well, you know, even them, the *principi,* are in a crisis right now. They own that palazzo, Palazzo Massimo, the one just across the street. Huge apartments, tall ceilings all frescoed . . . I do not think they are renting out any, they use them all for the family. One of the young princesses has married a Carpegna, Prince Carpegna. They have country estates outside Rome; they grow olives and grapes to make oil and wine. They sell them, I think, but, you know, even they have huge expenses, worse than us. Let me tell you, here in Rome when we reach the twentieth of the month, the money has dried up. No one has even one lira left. Not even the princes." Signora Luisa says it without gloating, but with a little sadness, wistfully, as if regretting old times when there was a difference between the pleb and the aristocrat.

I tell her that I do not doubt her words, but as I look around, it doesn't seem to make a difference if it is the beginning or the end of the month, everybody seems so affluent, if not downright rich.

"Ah, yes. A contradiction, *un paradosso.* That's Rome, didn't I tell you?" Then, excitedly, "Not too long ago, two really beautiful young girls bought that fashion shop around the corner, near the bar. You have never seen such elegant clothes, even a nincompoop can see how expensive they must be. But I have never seen anybody in that shop, it's a desert. So one day I asked at the bar, the barman is a friend, How can these beautiful girls make a living? I have never seen anybody shopping there. Luisa, the barman tells me, once in a while someone goes in and drops ten, fifteen million lire for a dress. So, you see, someone still has a lot of money! I wish they could say the same thing about my shop; since they prohibited parking on this street, I'm here all alone all day. Of my old customers only those who can walk here are left. Even tourists do not spend like they did before. Once they came in, bought what they needed, paid, and went. Now they do comparison shopping."

I feel compelled to buy a few rolls of film. "You made my day!" she laughs, and I join her.

I return to Foto-Ottica to pick up my glasses after the suggested two days. The shop is empty; Signora Luisa is reading a magazine in the chair reserved for clients. She welcomes me with her usual smile: "You know," she starts right away, "the same evening of the day you were here, I go home and my key doesn't work well in the lock. I have *a porta blindata*, an armored door like a bank vault. So I don't pay much attention, until the next day my downstairs neighbor asks me, 'Did you hear any noise last evening? Was your apartment all right?' It turns out three other apartments were robbed in the late afternoon, thieves coming down from the roof terrace like monkeys, they got in through the windows. They tried to force my door but didn't make it. *'Mbe'*, didn't I tell you? Thieves all over! *Povera Roma mia*, this poor Rome of mine really stinks."

I pay for my repaired glasses, and I commiserate with her about "her Rome."

"I'm lucky, then. I will escape it for a few days," I tell her. "My wife and I are going to Athens. A week, ten days perhaps."

"What? Athens? Did you say Athens, Greece?" Signora Luisa is indignant, offended. "Why would you want to go to Athens? Leave Rome? *Roma è così bella!*"

Yes, Rome is beautiful. And Signora Luisa confirms, in person, what a paradox it is.

If Paradox were a country, Rome would be its Capital, with a capital C.

To be Roman is a complex thing. It is a mixture of genes, ethnicity, history, and environmental learning. To be a Roman is a process — perhaps a profession — with an early start.

"If I could be born again, I would like to live my life as a Roman baby." This wishful statement comes from a casual acquaintance, an American, at the baptism ceremony for an actual Roman baby. It was prompted undoubtedly by the sumptuous reception, by the mountain of flowers and the pile of gifts brought for the occasion by the parents' relatives, remote relatives, friends and friends of friends, by the father's business associates — superiors and inferiors. The actual religious ceremony had taken place at the nearby church, attended only by the baby's parents and grandparents and performed and dismissed in three minutes. The reception took place in the rented rooms of a small country castle, which also supplied a director/ceremonial hostess, caterers, and liveried, white-gloved servers to pour the champagne. The two-month-old baby boy was enthroned in a corner of the room and accepted the procession of admirers with obvious indifference, unconscious that his career as Roman baby was just beginning. Born not into royalty but into the reasonably comfortable middle class, he should have had an inkling of things to come by the unbridled behavior of the other seven or eight children present at the reception. Aged five to nine, siblings, cousins, or casual guests, they noisily chased each other around the room, under the beautifully clothed, artistically decorated, groaning tables, two-handedly stuffed their mouths with pastries and candies, and overall behaved like *scatenati*, out-of-control unchained devils, under the benevolent, even admiring, gaze of the grown-ups. Behavior that in any other part of the world would have provoked thoughts of infanticide here elicited smiling exclamations of "*che carini!*" — aren't they cute!

My American acquaintance and I marveled at the children's unchallenged conduct and at the expensive stage set up for the initiation of the new baby boy. In conversing with *Grandpapà* we were told that this kind of reception, in various degrees of excess, is expected from persons of any social level — from believers and agnostics alike. People, especially of the young generations, keep remarking that this kind of tradition is anachronistic, something of the past, with absolutely no religious meaning, an unnecessary and empty showing off. But then rich or poor they cannot — or are not allowed to — give it up. (Less affluent families save for many months to have a suitable ceremony.) It would be an unforgivable, even arrogant, social faux pas. Worse, they could be considered cheapskates, misers who didn't care about the newcomer's entry into the family and into the world at large. The baptism is a must-do, an unavoidable event with a definite touch of pagan superstition, a good omen for the baby's future. Also the beginning, we remarked, for what is considered by foreigners a lavishly pampered childhood.

Little do they know: being a Roman baby comes with a lot of prerogatives, but also with a lot of set, definite and strict rules. The *che carini* at the reception were all little fashion plates, immaculately dressed from head to toe, display windows for the taste, stylishness, and affluence of their parents. Any marring, however minor, of their finery — a spot, a smudge, a crinkle — will result in punishment from the adoring mammas. At the exit door of the reception hall, one cannot fail to notice the little dears being administered a few glancing slaps around the head: "That will teach you" — the common admonishment — "to take care of your clothes."

Roman parks are a child-play paradise: there are little fountains and ponds to splash in, paths replete with pebbles to load onto expensive toy trucks, trees to climb and pigeons to chase. But if any of these activities should result in even a bit of spoiling of the play clothes, there is hell to pay. Children in parks with dirty play clothes (which, most of the time, gives them away as liberated, happy foreigners' children) are pariahs to be avoided, deemed — by the mothers, nurses, and baby-sitters of the clean ones — to be carrying the contagious play-dirt virus, the mark of future non-Romans.

Well should I know: as a boy I had to dress as a white-suited sailor to be proudly, lovingly paraded with my similarly attired older brother at the inevitable Sunday-afternoon promenade. Culmination of the exercise was *the* ice-cream cone, purchased at the Gelateria Fassi, *Il Regno del Gelato*, the Kingdom of Ice Cream, reputedly the best in all of Italy — and therefore in the whole world. I inevitably dribbled some of the precious stuff on my pristine uniform, which provoked the much-feared punishment of three weeks' exclusion from the Kingdom. Even worse, I had to watch my brother's perfect performance, sadistically done for my benefit — his tongue lasciviously sculpting the enormous cone held at regulation arm's length and not a drip wasted. Seething inside, to show my indifference, *tralla-lah! tralla-lah!*, I skipped and jumped on the sidewalk and ran, as fate would have it, smack into an ice-cream-licking, white-suited, innocent kid, and made a mess of us both. My parents declared me an unredeemable, world-class white-suit spoiler and rewarded me accordingly. I developed a revulsion for anything gooey and dreamed of running away to join a pirate's crew, where a white suit's cleanliness was not important.

Parental doting (along with the special outfits come special toys, special food, special vacations, special education) is coupled with rigid laws — many made ad hoc — that a child must obey and performances he must accomplish. This situation of loving largesse and unmitigated laissez-faire countered by a regime of law and swift justice wreaks havoc with a child's nervous system. When the breaking point is reached, the child is allowed *i cinque minuti*, a five-minute tantrum. It follows a standard choreography: you stomp your feet on the pavement (preferably the dirtiest spot), following a pattern of ever-smaller circles, disrobing an outer item per circle, stomping on it at the next pass, and so on. The goal is to fall to the ground at the center of the spiral, screaming and kicking and as naked and dirty as possible. With experience the *cinque minuti* can be performed in half the time; five minutes is the maximum allowed. Then law and immediate justice take over, and the cycle of smothering love and stiff repression can begin again. (My *cinque minuti* were registered on film; in the family library, it is the most popular reel.)

The physical development of the Roman child is closely followed. Not only is the child's well-being important in and of itself, it is also a matter of pride for the whole family. Competitions among mothers are constant affairs: who eats the most, who poops most regularly, who walks first, who speaks the most complex words, who has — or hasn't — the most exotic malady, requiring the most expensive cure.

The early education of a Roman child follows, in general, the same comparison pattern, the superachievers separated from the black sheep with little middle ground. The distinction is made early, on tenuous assumptions, and sometimes it takes years for a child to realize that he has been cast into the wrong category. This horrible pedagogical mistake was brought to light by a discerning Roman educator, Maria Montessori. She suggested that the strict, authoritarian teaching methods of the public or Catholic schools be avoided, along with school uniforms, and that the child be allowed to develop and learn at his own speed.

She also suggested that mothers should not subject their children to the warping and humiliating practice of comparison. While the Montessori educational system is followed all over the world, in Rome her suggestion about comparison is not. Mothers will still take two children, line them up against a wall (execution-style), and compare their heights, widths, weights, and general appearance. It is no consolation for the shortest, thinnest, fattest, or ugliest to be told, "Do not cry, dear, Mamma still loves you."

The mystery is that mother-love is reciprocated tenfold. In sons it develops into *mammismo*, a strong, long umbilical cord that symbiotically unites Mamma and baby boy till death do them part.

A grown man still relies on the advice of his mother and, until she is unable to provide it, on her practical help. Baby boy lives with his mamma as long as he can, and if he should marry, either brings his spouse home or finds new quarters as close to Mamma as possible. A recent poll conducted by ISTAT, the Italian Institute of Sociological Statistics, found that 70 percent of unmarried men reach the age of thirty still living at home, and that 43 percent of the married ones live within a half mile or so of the maternal nest. When a close acquaintance of ours divorced in his thirties, he moved back with his mamma so she could do his cooking and ironing. In his early fifties and a university professor, he remarried, honeymooned in the United States, and then brought his laundry back to Rome for his mother to wash. Laundry must have a mythical origin that escapes me: my own nephew, chief financial officer of a large, multinational firm, when transferred to Milan, returned to Rome every week with his dirty laundry for my well-to-do sister to wash and iron. Which she did gladly. I still find more than a bit paradoxical the widespread Roman culture of *machismo/mammismo*.

Franco Censi, who runs a matrimonial service in Rome, advises prospective wives to scrutinize not only their prospective husbands, but their prospective mothers-in-law as well. Because, he tells them, "You are going to marry them, too."

But then the sons are very attentive to their mothers and take care of their needs in their old age, keeping in touch with them at least twice daily, giving and receiving advice, letting Mamma feel she is still at the helm, as indeed she is; the umbilical cord is unbroken. Modern technology makes their task easy: I estimate that 90 percent of Italian men talking on cellular phones are on the line with Mamma.

One day, in a particularly good mood, I tried to prove my theory to Gwen. On a very crowded pedestrian-only downtown street, at midday, I cupped my hand to my ear as if holding a minuscule *telefonino*. "Mamma, please!" I said in a very loud voice. "Please, please, Mamma!" I executed the essential theatrical gestures, then yelled, "Yes, yes, Mamma. I did not forget my medicine . . ." And then, with desperation, even more loudly: "Is it possible, Mamma, that I have four grown-up children of my own and four grandchildren and you are still checking on me?"

Nobody thought the performance abnormal enough to turn around or even notice me. *Mammismo* is still alive and well in Rome, eternal, it seems, as the city itself.

In the second century B.C., the Roman matron Cornelia, daughter of Scipio Africanus Major, wife of Titus Sempronius Gracchus, dedicated her life to the upbringing of her two boys. When an ostentatious patrician lady flaunted her jewelry, Cornelia pointed to her two sons, saying: *"These* are my jewels!"

The phrase made history, and Roman *mammismo* was under way.

III

Managing Rome

Piove, governo ladro!

ROME IS THE capital of Italy, the seat of the Italian government. In addition to the president, the Senate, and the
Chamber of Deputies, there are many *ministeri* (departments)
and about twice as many *enti statali*, semiprivate organizations
that perform work under the supervision and subvention of the
government; each *ministero* and each *ente* is composed of
umpteen *divisioni*. There are also twenty *regioni* offices, each representing one of the semiautonomous regions of Italy, that are
part-embassy, part-lobby to the central government.

The *Presidenza* is located in the Palazzo Quirinale, a huge Renaissance building that sits on top of one of the original Seven
Hills of Rome and from which it takes its name. During the
monarchy it was the ceremonial residence of the king; it is now the
residence, with the same pomp, of the president of the republic. It
overlooks the Senate and the Chamber of Deputies, which are
housed below it, in the center of town, in old historical palazzi.
Many ministries are more frequently called by the name of the
palazzo they occupy than by the function that they perform:
"Palazzo Chigi," instead of the office of the "Presidente del Con-

siglio dei Ministri" (the premier); "Viminale," instead of the "Department of the Interior"; "Palazzo Madama" for the Senate; "Montecitorio" for the Chamber of Deputies. With the swelling bureaucracy and the increasing traffic congestion, many ministries have been moved to newer, in theory less chaotic, parts of town, such as the Foro Italico (the complex of former sport academies and stadiums once called "Foro Mussolini") where resides the Farnesina, the Ministry of Foreign Affairs, or to the EUR, the Esposizione Universale Romana, one of Rome's modern suburbs. The *ministeri* stand quite apart from each other, geographically as well as administratively, and create around themselves, in classic symbiosis, pockets of economic activity: coffee bars, newsstands, restaurants, *trattorie, tavole calde* (cafeterias), bookstores, or any store — including supermarkets — apt to satisfy the multitude of employees' needs before, after, and especially during working hours. All of the *ministeri*, and many of the *enti*, have their own health clubs with gyms, swimming pools, bocce and tennis courts. Several clubs are along the banks of the Tiber, in which case rowing is available — and other athletic or intellectual activities, such as bridge tournaments and — rumor has it — gambling.

If you count the persons working directly for the government as well as those who work for its ancillary services, the state is by far Rome's largest employer. This fact provokes a sort of love/hate relationship with the remaining non-government-employed population, who tend to make the *governo* the culprit for everything that doesn't work as it should, economically, administratively, or, by extension, in any other sector of life — including meteorology. This attitude goes back to the strict (*tyrannical* could be a more appropriate adjective), temporal administration of the pontifical state, and is reflected in that common Roman saying, *Piove, governo ladro!* (It's raining — thieving government!)

The feeling is amply shared by all other Italian cities and towns, which consider Rome a spoiled family member living in whoring luxury at their expense, wasting their hard-earned money on extravagant clothes and bonbons. And they complain and protest a lot: hardly a day goes by that large delegations from one part of Italy or the other do not organize a noisy demonstration at the Quirinale, or in front of a targeted *ministero*, or in any public place most suited to paralyze the city for a few hours. At the risk of sounding cynical, these demonstrative protests seldom achieve any results; the only immediate and real advantage goes to the local bars, restaurants, and *trattorie* where, having put away flags, banners, and placards, the demonstrators go to soothe their inflamed vocal chords with a few glasses of Frascati. And a dish of Roman pasta.

An incongruity — a real paradox — in this antigovernment attitude is that the greatest aspiration of most Romans (Italians in general, for that matter) is to secure *il posto*, to become an *impiegato statale* — a government employee. So much so that when a dozen positions become available and are publicly posted, several thousand applicants show up for the *concorso* exam. A flourishing publishing industry keeps job seekers informed through newspaper-sized pamphlets that list job openings, how many are available where, what prerequisites there are, and the dates of the *concorsi*. A substitute for the application process, the *concorso* is an obligatory exam one must take to procure a government job. Jobs range from cleaning and maintenance — the lowest echelon, at the base of the employment pyramid — up to *capo-ufficio*, office head or chief inspector. The very top is reserved exclusively for political patronage. A Solomonic decision is made in order to parcel out the few *posti* among the scores of people who pass the exams with the same top grades. It is a process that takes a long time, sometimes upward of a year, so that many people do many *concorsi* one after the other, hoping to land a *posto* among the different kinds of jobs available. They become professional *concorsi* takers. Sadly, the exams are almost always pro forma since, unofficially, the essential requisite (frequently purchased) is to be a *raccomandato*, one recommended by important people or by people who know people with the influence.

Preference is also given to the applicant who has (or had) a relative working for the government — and it is not unusual to have generations of the same family working for the same *ministero*.

I can attest to this: my maternal grandfather, Nicola, obtained a job in 1905 at the Ministry of Foreign Affairs as, I believe, office boy at the Department of Protocol; his son Vittorio, my uncle, served as cryptographer in several Italian embassies around the world; Nicola's nephew, my mother's cousin Eugenio, was cultural attaché at the Italian embassy in Berlin; another of Nicola's grandchildren, my first cousin Nando, was protocol officer at several Italian embassies. The one who really got the plum was Nicola's second son, Giuseppe, who became provisions officer for the entire ministry. That gave him access to all kinds of vendors (and them to him) who supplied all sorts of necessities — pens, pencils, and stationery — as well as such ceremonial essentials as gold ashtrays and Turkish carpets. An apartment came with the job. It was on the top floor of the Fountain of Trevi building; its row of windows looked down on the famous landmark. I must confess that, being Uncle Giuseppe's favorite nephew, I was the best-supplied kid in school with, among other things, a Gucci satchel, leather-bound notebooks, and golden fountain pen/pencil sets. (I was the envy not only of my fellow students, but also of my teachers; the fact that all of the items were engraved with the de rigueur Fascist insignia stopped any undue comments. I wish, now, that I had been a student worthy of all that loot.)

Today this form of nepotism, of having two or more people of the same family working in the same *ministero* or *ente*, is frowned upon and is in the process of being abolished through attrition. Almost. A new system, called *la slitta* (the sled or the slide, either way something slippery), is in operation. At Radio Audizioni Italiane (RAI), the overbloated, overly inefficient state radio and television system, an employee close to retirement can pass his job to a relative if he is willing to give up his severance pay.

An element that does not seem essential for obtaining any particular *posto* is, remarkably, competence.

A government job has many advantages. One is that, in general, it is a sinecure, quite suitable to the lackadaisical Roman character, with the added incentive of the *orario continuo*, the uninterrupted work hours, from 8 A.M. to 2 P.M. (but for discretional — wink, wink — coffee breaks). It leaves one with a free afternoon to dedicate to other activities, including doing the *straordinario*, returning to the office in the afternoon for overtime work at overtime pay, simply for doing what could have been done during regular hours.

Another basic attraction is that once a *statale*, forever a *statale*. Short of committing an abhorrent act, a *statale* cannot lose his or her job. (Only by murdering the head of state, or even, perhaps, your superior, will you get fired.) Incompetence, loafing on the job, stealing, and sexual indiscretions are insufficient reasons for dismissal.

The *statale*'s career is programmed from inception and, regardless of aptitude, ability, or proficiency, unalterable. It follows a predetermined path of automatic promotions every so many years, so that, for example, an employee of the *Ministero della Marina* — Ministry of the Navy — could end his administrative career with the equivalent grade of admiral, without having ever left his desk or set foot on a boat. At worst, one's career could be slowed down, at times of promotion, by a poor job assessment from one's boss, but that would be extremely rare. Being a *statale* means being very attentive to any desire of a direct superior, or, if this goes against personal principles, becoming invisible to him (or to everybody: it has been known for employees to show up only for payday). An unforgivable error is to overachieve, or in any way overshadow a superior, which generally translates into doing one day's workload in less than one week. When confronted by a complaining public, this glacier-speed work rule is justified (from day two of becoming a government employee) by the *statale*'s vocal resentment: *"Per quello che mi pagano, faccio pure troppo!"* — For what I'm paid, I am already doing too much! Which, quite frankly, does not take into consideration the *tredicesima*, the thirteenth (and sometimes fourteenth and fifteenth) monthly paycheck. Begun many years ago as an exceptional, once-in-a-lifetime bonus, it is now an established part of the yearly salary. Moreover, an *impiegato* enjoys ample — especially by U.S. standards — vacation time, at least four weeks a year to begin with, increasing quite rapidly to five and six. At the end of his career a pension is waiting for him equal to at least 80 percent of his last paycheck. A recent acquaintance told me, under promise of anonymity (I do not know why, since his situation is quite common and well known), that with a few smart administrative moves and the complicity of one or two bureaucrats (a last-minute promotion, accounting for age, sickness, dependents, sick dependents, and so forth) he is earning more in retirement than he ever did when working.

There is a definite code of etiquette for a *statale*: the higher-ups must be impeccably dressed and treat a *dipendente* — a subordinate — with a certain paternalistic, baronial attitude and address him with the *tu* (second person singular and familiar) form of the verb, and be respectfully addressed back with the *Lei*, the formal third person, and so on down in descending sartorial splendor and respect. The hierarchic order must be respected down to the make of car one owns, the expensiveness and fashion of vacation spots, and so on.

At the bottom of the food chain is the *usciere* — a position between doorman, janitor, and manservant. He should be attired in a reasonably shabby uniform, be able to satisfy (reasonable) requests from all superiors — seeing to their espresso and cappuccino needs is an essential part of the job. Just as the dishwasher in a restaurant can make the operation work or stop cold in its tracks, so can the *usciere* in an office. He is the only one who knows at all times what's going on, who's where doing what — in or out, that is — and, for an outsider in need of an office's offices, he is the one who can, seemingly at whim, advance or stall one's progress. He is the Cerberus guarding the doors of Hell, or at least of the employee one needs to see.

Hence the *usciere* is the first in line when bureaucratic wheels need grease. His starts with the *stretta di mano* — the handshake: the closed palm of the shaker hides some banknotes transferred to the palm of the shakee, in a theoretically surreptitious fashion. The amount so transacted will reveal to the *usciere* how much one has at heart the business — so to speak — at hand, and he will adjust accordingly the speed of one's progress through the ministerial labyrinth. Independent of the kind and size of the business — building a bridge, expediting a pension payment, petitioning for a scholarship — one will finally be admitted to see the *incaricato*, the person in charge of the *pratica*, the folder or dossier containing all the information and all the signed and stamped documents for the necessary completion of the matter in question. Here, too, the performance follows a fixed ritual: half hidden by a three-foot-tall stack of *pratiche* on his desk, the *incaricato*, while talking on the phone, will (perhaps) acknowledge one's presence with a nod. When one is finally allowed to identify oneself with name and code number of his *pratica*, the *incaricato* will stand up, join his hands as if in prayer, and, slowly shaking them in the direction of the tower of dossiers while nodding his head, signify the enormity of the task required. He will follow that up with a sigh while opening his arms, with the double meaning: "È come cerca' Maria pe' Roma" — It's like searching for a Mary in Rome, a needle in a haystack — and also "Per quello che mi pagano." With a short but elaborate maneuver, the *pratica* in question will be located close to the bottom of the stack and the *incaricato* will declare that, even with all his good intentions, the *pratica* will have to wait its turn. With a brief leafing of the documents in the *pratica*, the *incaricato* will add that even when that moment comes, the *pratica* will be stalled for the lack of *the* crucial document. The *incaricato* now opens his arms and nods disconsolately, to signify that his heart is all out for the petitioner, but there is nothing he can do.

Now the ball is in the supplicant's court. He can put on a heartrending scene describing all the misery, unhappiness, and hardships caused to himself and all his extended family by the nonconclusion of the *pratica*, but the most direct and timesaving action is to tap one's wristwatch and declare that, given the hour, it is propitious to have a *caffè*. The two will proceed to the neighborhood bar, and there the petitioner will nonchalantly produce an envelope and give it to the *incaricato*, who will nonchalantly pocket it. The whole exercise is called the *bustarella*, the passing of the "little envelope" containing an amount of money commensurate, again, with the value one gives to the *pratica*. The *incaricato* will return to his office, the crucial document will be found among the zillion other documents, and the *pratica* will move to the top of the pile (or closer to it, depending on the weight of the *bustarella*).

I should mention that most of the *pratiche* on the desk of an *incaricato* are props, old dead files or *pratiche* of people by now long dead.

Expressing my dismay about this bureaucratic procedure to Emilio Cristofori, a smart and successful merchant (now semiretired) in the import-export business, he replied that Italy's economy — particularly the private one — is flourishing especially, if not only, because of the *bustarella*. He went on to explain that if any or all government business were to be conducted by the book, business in Italy would move with the speed of molasses in winter. He explained this with a personal example: one morning, he found he had to clear some foreign merchandise through customs. With the help of the *bustarella* his shipment was released by nightfall; if it had had to go strictly by the rules and regulations (which probably, he said, have been on the books since 1870), his merchandise would have been sitting in a warehouse for months, and probably outdated by the time it was cleared. Besides, he added, by now the *bustarella* is so ingrained in the Roman soul, so capillary in its social structure, that it would take many generations to eradicate it. He put a date on its birth: the sixteenth century, when the Roman popes were selling indulgences and opening the doors of Heaven for the offering of a *bustarella*. But I think it could be traced even before that, back to the times of the Caesars when every important man had his *clientes*, people who garnered his favors through the offering of gifts.

With the European Union becoming a working reality, the Roman bureaucracy is attempting to streamline itself to get in step with the other countries' way of doing administrative business — even if, in fairness, other European countries are, to various degrees, in the same boat as Italy. A few years ago, an attempt was made to reduce the rolls of the *impiegati statali* by removing some of them from established *ministeri*. They were simply moved to a newly created one: the *Ministero per la Ristrutturazione* — the Ministry for the Restructuring of the Bureaucracy. The total number of employees did not diminish, but was actually augmented a little due to the addition of the necessary ancillary positions.

Some streamlining was obtained by establishing an early retirement plan, offering a bonus and full pension to *impiegati* who voluntarily quit working before official retirement age. It freed them to find work in the private sector, or to join the ranks of other *pensionati* in street demonstrations clamoring for a better, more adequate *pensione* for today's high cost of living.

The truly amazing thing is that during the last fifty years of Italian history, Rome has seen almost sixty governments at the helm of the new republic. And all seemingly without any changes — for better or for worse — to the welfare of the hoi polloi. The swollen, entrenched (envious outsiders also say mostly incompetent) bureaucracy has held the fort while the politicians bickered, and, even with all the ponderous grinding of the machinery, the management of daily life has kept running as usual.

Actually, the standard of living has been getting better and better, while the populace's grumbling and complaining about the government is getting proportionally worse.

It all reminds me of an old Genoese practice: it was the rule, it is said, for sailors who signed on to Genoa's sailing ships to be offered two different pay scales: one was for working with *mugugno* (freedom to grumble), and the other — a much higher pay scale — without *mugugno*. It seems that the great majority of sailors opted for the lesser pay.

Oh, well. *Piove, governo ladro!*

But then, when the sky seems dark with flood-promising black clouds, a crack of blue sky appears. Two Italian cities have been testing two revolutionary processes. One of these, started in 1993 in Bologna, is called *Progetto Qualità*, Project Quality. Its goal is to achieve maximum efficiency in all sectors of city administration and to deliver to its citizens the best and smoothest services with the least effort. City hall, then, becomes a merchant/vendor of good urban life to its citizen/client. The citizens themselves will annually evaluate the positive steps achieved by awarding points to city hall: so many for transportation, so many for public-health services, so many for schools, and so on. The point tally tells how much improvement has been achieved and how much is left to go (one thousand is the goal, the equivalent, I suppose, of living in Paradise).

This shooting for quality goes along with another goal that is extremely innovative for the Italian bureaucracy: quality in public personnel competence. Quantity of personnel has to go, and with it the political patronage and nepotism that so often result in the employment of the inept.

The other project is taking place in Siena and is called *le Chiavi della Città*, the keys of the city. The major element of this project is "the card," which is bound to revolutionize the relationship between city administration and citizenry. Similar to a plastic bank card, it contains, electronically imbedded, a citizen's personal data: birth certificate, family status, wedding date and spouse's name, children's birthdays, vaccinations, and, once and forever, all of the zillion documents once needed to navigate through the bureaucratic system. It seems as if *Chiavi della Città* has already reduced by 75 to 80 percent the number of certificates previously granted by the Siena administration. The card also works as a credit card with which to pay city taxes, fines, bus fare, museum entrance, parking, and so forth. This electronic ID card, once it has finished its testing stage, should be adopted by law by all of the Italian city administrations, including Rome's, by 2005.

It is the kind of project that makes room for a lot of interesting conjecture: one life, one card, to be surrendered at the Pearly Gates. The saints and sinners will be electronically evaluated, sorted, and assigned their places.

When it comes to Rome, something really difficult to imagine is the fate of the many thousands of people who, one hand holding an inkpad, the other poised to strike with a stamp, will be out of work, victims of Bologna's and Siena's projects. The government would have, indeed, stolen their way of making a living, and they will have reason to mutter: *Piove, governo ladro!* And either find another umbrella or get wet.

It is, all told, a scary Orwellian speculation. But, being cynical, Rome's resiliency is eternal. It will not be affected, not right away, by the law. Being Rome — *fatta la legge, scoperto l'inganno!* — it will find a way around it and obtain a two- or three-year postponement. It has happened before: laws were passed and deadlines established, for example, to control the earsplitting noise of motor scooters; delayed by two years and then two more, by now the law is totally forgotten and ignored. The same goes for laws against polluting, vandalism, illegal driving and parking in zones forbidden to traffic, and many other rules of law, including the mundane one for curbing dogs. Since the law was passed, the Roman canine population has exploded and the precious dogs all seem to enjoy a prodigious digestive regularity, conspicuously displayed in the middle of pedestrian-only streets. The day will come . . . for the moment, though, I do not look up at the Roman monuments: I watch the pavement and my step, until the dog law kicks in. In a couple of years. Maybe.

Once in a while the populace, via the press, complains loudly about this or that more or less criminal bending of the law. Newspapers come out with banner headlines, pages of photographs prove the misdeeds, fingers point to those allegedly responsible for the situation. Those in authority then order an increase in the ranks of the police on the street and make a great display of catching the culprits. For a few days, anyway, until things quiet down and go back as they were before.

But then Rome would not be Rome if a paradoxical element did not creep in: the massive presence of *le forze dell'ordine*. Namely, they are the carabinieri (a police force that is part of the army), the *polizia* (national police, independent of and frequently in rivalry with the carabinieri), and the *polizia municipale* (the city police, independent from the other two). There are also several other police corps, such as the *guardia di finanza*, also part of the army, which chases financial culprits and smugglers; the *polizia stradale*, which polices traffic on state roads and highways; the *polizia ferroviaria*, which guards the railroads; and a few others, all with specific duties. On street corners, on squares, in front of banks, ministries, the synagogue, near the residences of senators and other important political people, in front of embassies, there are always available a few *forze dell'ordine*, frequently, and for unexplained reasons, of assorted flavors, all on the alert and cuddling submachine guns. The amazing thing is that in plain view of all these police all sorts of minor or major wrongdoing may take place without any interference from any of them. Justification: the particular misdeed did not fall within the particular area of competence of the *forze dell'ordine* present at the moment. It is then up to the good citizens to dial 113 for the carabinieri, or 112 for the *polizia*, who will dispatch — blaring sirens and flashing lights — the appropriate contingent to the spot.

But that, no doubt, could simply be my cynical opinion, and real efforts are being made to ameliorate the general situation; things, indeed, are getting, or will get, better.

The image of a thieving government suggests a large, deprived society begging for handouts from the relatively few political fat cats and their cronies. It is an image that does not jell, in my eyes, with what I see all around me in Rome. Yes, there are beggars, but fewer than before, and mostly young Gypsy children roaming in bunches and Gypsy women holding infants at their breasts, stretching their hands for alms. Pitiful images that, by contrast, underline the appearance of affluence and wealth all around me: the shop windows are replete with goods, the stores crowded. Bookstores are cavernous and brimming with books and videocassettes; people line up at the cashiers. Shoes, clothes, furs, furniture, records, and discs, it is the whole cornucopia of goods spilling on the streets. Many of the simple mom-and-pop food stores have been replaced by *gastronomie*, shops dedicated to gastronomy that guarantee a trip to Dante's gluttons' circle in Hell just by peeking in their windows. The number of restaurants has multiplied fivefold — and so have the bills — and they are always full. People reflect the same affluence, their elegance dictated by the latest fashion's fads, which seem to change monthly and be followed punctiliously, especially among young people. They wear the same obligatory and expensive style, almost a uniform, until the next fashion wave. I can see a multitude of parents shelling out allowances for the little dears' clothes and shoes — and motor scooters and cellular phones — just to keep them abreast of their peers. I took a sweeping tour of the huge, jam-packed quarters outlying the city's center, and the scene is the same: same fashions, same abundance of goods, same glitter, only, if possible, more crowded. Cars, mopeds, and motorcycles seem to outnumber the city's population. It has to be deduced that each family member has his or her own conveyance, often with an extra, expensive one for prestige, the Jag or the Alfa, to be used on special occasions. At any moment of any day, the parked cars — single-, double-, and triple-parked — line all the city's sidewalks, all the streets and alleys, all the squares, every available foot of space. The same number of cars, or more, circulate wildly and uninterruptedly in the same chock-full streets, alleys, and squares, perhaps all in search of a parking space. We have frequently asked friends and acquaintances to join us for lunch or dinner, to be told: "Sorry, can't come; can't afford to lose our parking spot."

Beggars, then? I must admit that among all this in-your-face wealth, I am the one who feels out of step, a bit deprived.

It is difficult to reconcile what I see with what I hear about the precarious national economy. If there is anybody who can alleviate my curiosity about the matter, it is my childhood friend, adolescent mentor, and, later, hero: Luciano Barca. Several years my senior, oldest of seven children (one of his sisters was my first puppy love), Luciano went to the prestigious Italian Naval Academy — assuming right away, in my eyes, a stature worthy of Christopher Columbus, even if, in actuality, he is no more than five feet three inches tall. Just past eighty, he is still spry and dresses with quiet elegance; his posture and piercing, steely blue eyes betray a man accustomed to positions of command. He graduated from the Naval Academy as lieutenant; World War II found him second in command of a submarine. When in 1943 Italy declared a separate armistice with the Allies (turning Germany, our previous ally, into our enemy), he refused to see his submarine and crew surrendered to the Germans and successfully mutinied against his commander. Subsequently, on his way to join the British navy in Malta, he had to escape the chasing German torpedo boats and their depth charges. But even though shaken and at the end of his endurance, he made it to Malta, saving his crew from being imprisoned and his boat from being blown up by the Germans. His odyssey was more involved than I am reporting, and includes the fact that the Fascists officially declared that his submarine sank. His family mourned him as lost at sea until the end of the war, when, more than a year later, he returned home.

Back in civilian life, he studied economics and, following his philosophical beliefs, became a Communist. His large family, neighbors and very good friends of my family, displayed a peculiar political structure: half of the family, with Luciano's mother at the lead, were fervent Communists; the other half, following his father, were fervent Christian Democrats.

Later, as economic adviser and planner of national and international matters for the Italian Communist Party, Luciano was elected to the Chamber of Deputies and, subsequently, the Senate. He held that position until the Italian Communist Party dissolved and he retired. I am proud to say that among the plethora of past and present politicians, Luciano has a unanimous reputation of solid intelligence and honesty, one of the few who has not vastly profited by his parliamentary position.

Upon meeting him, I warn him of my abysmal ignorance of finance and economics, and I beg him to speak in a language I can follow. I tell him of the image I have of the Italian economy: that of a great cow with huge and many-nippled udders from which everybody is suckling to satiation. My question: who is feeding the cow?

"Your image of the cow is or, better, *was* quite appropriate," he starts, and I am grateful he accepted the childish image without laughing at me.

"Now the cow is changing, some. What was the cow before? It was created by the state's system of direct administration, financial participation, and subsidy of all sorts of industrial and commercial activities, of many utilities and services. It began with two great public holdings: the ENI (Ente Nazionale Idrocarburi: oil drilling, petroleum distillates, and natural gas) was the udder under the Communists' control; and the IRI (Institute for Industrial Reconstruction: all kinds of heavy industries) was the udder for the *Democrazia Cristiana*."

He silently questions me if I understand, and I nod back a so-far-so-good.

"The one left out was the growing Italian Socialist Party, so a special udder was created for them. Here comes the Industrie Manufatture Italiane (IMI), which includes armament industries and the big food conglomerates. All these companies' profits were meant to go back to the state, but most were administered by state bureaucrats and, in general, they ran in the red. The state paid for the difference. And the milk flowed."

As an example, Luciano tells me of the Alemagna autogrill, the state-managed chain of snack bars and restaurants that operates on the *autostrada*, the state-run system of toll roads. The state covered the restaurants' operating deficits by paying an average of four thousand lire per lunch served.

"Moo . . . the state pays for dessert!" was my comment.

"Exactly! And the cow was fed mostly with paper money. On the financial scene things operated on almost the same level: there was practically no national banking industry, most of it being in the hands of an oligarchy of great families, the same who ran the few but great private, and profitable, industries. Their financial speculations hardly went to feed the cow. On the economic side, to help the export of the real goods produced, the state resorted to the devaluation of the lira, adding to it the export system of dumping. On top of all this we have to consider another udder — actually we should abandon the cow image and pass to one of a sow because of its greater number of nipples — to which is attached our colossal public administration, our entrenched bureaucracy. Producing nothing, its only function is to perpetuate itself. Between stipends and pensions, it sucks an enormous amount of milk. This, in brief, was the paper-fed cow. The public debt was enormous, the inflation around 22 percent."

I beg him to pause a moment: I summarize my notes to see if I've got them right. He laughs and winks: "Plus or minus 5 percent! Not bad," he says.

"Now, due to a series of economic events (such as the oil crisis of the '70s) and of political crises (such as the *Tangentopoli*, the widespread kickback and graft, scandals of the '80s), it became obvious that things had to change. So a great reform was begun to privatize all, or as many as possible, industries and banks, to start reducing and trimming labor costs, to reduce the public administration, to lower unemployment. Moreover, it became essential to put our books in order and in alignment with the requirements of the European Community so that we could join. Many great steps forward have been made: inflation has gone down to European standards and money is available at decent rates, mortgages are down from 19 percent to 8 percent . . . the better the economy, the better the state revenues."

This, I comment, considering the reputation of the Italians as great tax dodgers, must be the equivalent of Satan becoming a monk.

"Yes, tax collecting has always been considered a great joke. But now, thanks to the use of computerized systems, it's getting better. As a matter of fact, in the last ten years we have passed from a negative balance to, net of interests, a positive balance. The transformation has been profound, but it is a huge, slow-going enterprise because it is against ingrained procedures and ways of thinking. So, to answer your question, the pasture is getting a little bigger, the cow is fed more real hay, the flow of free milk is slowly being reduced, things are going much better."

I tell him that he is one of the few people to whom I have spoken who has a positive, even optimistic view of the situation. He reminds me that Italians love to exaggerate, to complain, that complaining is a sort of one-upmanship competition. As a case in point, Luciano tells me that when Wall Street goes down 2 percent, Italian commentators call it a correction; when the Milan stock exchange goes down 1 percent, they call it a nosedive.

I go back to my question, rephrasing it: "Rome. The obvious wealth. How? Is there a separate Roman cow?"

"Rome is in a peculiar situation, in several different ways. The milk sucked by the huge mass of government employees is digested and stays in Rome. There is the large amount of *lavoro nero*, unreported and untaxed work, not only by the great number of illegal immigrants, but also by many employees who end their government work at 2 P.M., and then take a second job. The extended family unit remains under one roof and takes advantage of several incomes. With bond interest at 2.5 percent and savings as low as 1.6 percent — nobody saves anymore. The Roman has turned from a saving to a consumer society; it spends on goods, it spends on travel, it spends on vacations, entertainment, and food. It spends. Spending, *lo shopping*, has become an end in itself. Money comes in, money goes out. It circulates continuously, not creating but spreading around wealth. And that's what you see on the street. There is your cow."

In parting, I thank him for the effort he must have made to express himself in such pedestrian terms. I hope that even so I got it right, and, I tell him, please get rid of the image of the cow as soon as the door closes behind me; the cow is coming with me. He smiles, and we part good friends.

Almost nine months have passed since my visit with Luciano. I am back in Boston and while reading *La Repubblica* — thanks to modern wizardry, the Italian paper is printed daily here in the States — a headline jumps to my attention: *Il miracolo italiano e i profeti di sventura*, The Italian Miracle and the Doomsayers. It says that national and international sources in the know reported, gritting their teeth, that during the millennium's first quarter the Italian GNP increased 1 percentage point, above the average 0.8 percent of the European Community. It all suggests an estimated 3 percent or more increase for the year, way above earlier predictions. Moreover, the industrial production increased 6.5 percent in the last six months, surpassing even Germany's. Other positive facts: export activity has hit a record, and, in the general picture of the economic "miracle," the Italian south (historically always behind the north) was slightly above the national average. In the north, unemployment has disappeared and industrial and commercial firms find it difficult to fill all the available job openings, in spite of the increased migration of workers from the Italian south, Eastern Europe, and Africa. Further data, as reported by the International Organization for Economic Development, put Italy in third position for industrial productivity, after Japan and the United States. All this, the writer (Eugenio Scalfari) comments, should make us rejoice. But, following the Italian habit, we let outsiders — French! Belgians! — tell us, reluctantly, that we are doing something good. For once we should boast about ourselves; instead, with dismay, we already hear the voices of high-positioned people, politically right leaning, asking if the "miracle," which happened during the center-left watch, is really a miracle, and is it going to last? So — the writer says — the doomsayers warn us not to rejoice too fast. . . .

And while I am reading, I clearly hear Luciano's voice.

IV

SPQR

Senatus Populusque Romanus

$\mathcal{A}$ND THEN THERE is SPQR.

Senatus Popolusque Romanus. I was brought up to believe that those initials terrorized, on sight, the enemies of Rome;
the emblazoned, simple statement also forcefully and arrogantly
implied, "You are facing the combined Will and Might of the
Senate and of the People of Rome," and that alone should have
made anybody quake in their boots. But that was then. Now,
having seen the powerful letters displayed on the entrance arch-
ways of the great public palazzi of Rome, I also think of it as an
exorcism, a vade retro, a defense against the *malocchio*, the evil
eye, and the meanness of the enemy outside. It is difficult when I
see SPQR not to think, in vivid flashbacks, of Signorina Chimens. She was my third-grade teacher, not much taller than her
students, roly-poly, and — having gray hair — definitely as antique as history. She loved history, Roman history, and her
unique way of making us understand it and feel it was to engage
us in historical plays, us as actors and extras, she as producer, director, and costume designer. A devoted Fascist (the name of our
school was Scuola Elementare "Italico Sandro Mussolini," he a

kin of Il Duce), it was her wish, as it was *il nostro Duce's* order, to imbue us with the pride of being Romans, heirs of the Roman Empire's glories, made of the stock of heroes and conquerors. She cajoled our parents into constructing (or helping her to construct) togas and cardboard breastplates, helmets and daggers, and so turned us into ancient Roman senators and soldiers. Some of us, anyway, because she divided the class into two groups, protagonists and antagonists: the Romans and the Others. What distinguished the Romans — her best students — was that they carried broom handles with placards emblazoned SPQR. Then she orchestrated, on the school playground, the reenactment of some vivid historical event: the two factions faced each other and the respective leaders would recite — shout was more like it — their scripted historical intentions, and finally the Romans, by the power of their arguments and the strength of *Lex Romana*, would subjugate the enemy. One of our favorites was the battle against the Gauls. Since Gauls translates as *Galli*, or, in common parlance, roosters, we could confront the enemy with strident (and unscripted) *kik-kiri-kii'*, the Roman equivalent of cock-a-doodle-doo. The *Galli* came back at us with loud pig grunts — their interpretation of SPQR being *Sono Porci Questi Romani*, these Romans are pigs.

Another memorable play-event was the successful defense of the Capitoline Hill. The scenario was simple: the Romans (half of our class, the IIIA) are sleeping the "sleep of the just" on top of the Campidoglio. The barbarians (the other half) stealthily attack the unwary. But the *oche capitoline*, a flock of geese resident on the hill (volunteer girls from IIIB — unfortunately *oca*, goose, in vernacular stands for "dumb broad") start squawking at the silent approach of the enemy, wake up the Romans, a great melee ensues among Romans, geese, barbarians, and Signorina Chimens (a powerless referee) — but finally the capitol is safe and history is set. Most of the time these bestiary enactments got out of hand because in the acting fervor we forgot who historically was who and proceeded to settle personal scores; nonetheless, the theatrics made us remember these milestone events, and just as surely caused dear, unforgettable Signorina Chimens to age prematurely.

Today the Campidoglio is clear of geese, and SPQR is the insignia of the *Comune di Roma*, the heart, brain, and command center of the city.

The central offices of the *Comune* are housed in the Campidoglio and frequently are referred to as such, so much so that "Campidoglio" has become synonymous with "city hall." The Capitoline Hill, morally the highest of the Seven Hills of Rome, once the fulcrum of the *Roma Caput Mundi*, is as prestigious an address as you can get, and Piazza del Campidoglio multiplies that prestige with its beauty. It is, unequivocally, one of the most beautiful and architectonically elegant squares of Rome. It should be approached from the great flight of stairs by the side of the Ara Coeli. The twenty-one steps — each more of a landing than a step since, to facilitate access to a horseman, each step was built nine feet deep and a few inches high — are guarded at the top on each side by the enormous statues of the twins Castor and Pollux restraining their horses. On reaching the last step, the square opens in front of you like a theater stage, and well it might be: designed in the sixteenth century by Michelangelo with a trompe l'oeil perspective, it appears larger than it actually is, majestic, and yet as intimate as a three-sided parlor. The backdrop of the stage is the Palazzo del Campidoglio, at dawn and at sunset a glow of ocher, and its wings are the Palazzo dei Conservatori and the Palazzo Nuovo, almost mirror images of each other. The pavement's geometrical design of inlaid marble accentuates the perspective, leading the eye to the Palazzo del Campidoglio's double stairway and to its central landing, astutely conceived and used as a pulpit. It not only makes a speaker the center of attention of the crowd below, but also, thanks to the perfect acoustics, magnifies his voice like a megaphone.

The square is now barren of the original equestrian statue of Marcus Aurelius. Since 1538 it had been the square's centerpiece and pride of all Romans. (Following Michelangelo's suggestion, Pope Paul III ordered the statue transferred from Piazza San Giovanni in Laterano, where it had been standing for centuries.) The gilded bronze, covered with the verdigris of ages, would occasionally reveal a spot of the original gold; *"è come Marc'Aurelio"* described a person ostensibly rough outside, but golden within. Romans also believed that when all the gold was finally exposed, you had better get ready: judgment day was around the corner. Victim of pollution, the statue was removed in 1981 and now is kept protected inside the Palazzo dei Conservatori. A reproduction is sitting in its place, in every aspect similar to the original but for the gold; there is no sign on the pedestal mentioning the switch, so, for all intents, it is still a magnificent statue to look at. And so is the square, even with a faux *cavallo*. From the vantage point of the piazza entrance, one can see on the left of the Campidoglio the lean column supporting the statue of the wolf suckling the infants Romulus and Remus, emblem of Rome, and inscribed SPQR. Way below, on the right, the Roman forums spread their glory, backed in the distance by the Colosseum.

The square is a sight I admire with reverence, slowly, to absorb each harmonious detail. It is best late at night, empty of visitors and of noise. The subdued artificial lighting, or — even better — moonlight itself, gives the square a lunar serenity and, with only the muffled rumble of the sleeping city as a reminder of the daily chaos, a deep feeling of repose. Or, whenever possible, I try to be there in the early dawn: Rome is asleep, the sun barely trims with gold the contours of buildings and columns, light and shadows are soft, almost evanescent; the morning mist wets the marble and gives it an aroma much headier than that of earth after a rain. And when I am lucky, I imagine a bunch of little kids with cardboard daggers chasing each other around the square, oinking, squeaking, *kikkiriki'ing*; Signorina Chimens sits on a marble step, shaking her head, smiling. The smell and the noise of history.

While two thousand years ago SPQR induced terror only in its enemies, in the recent past it did so only in its own citizens. The sheer dread of its bureaucracy and, when required to pursue any administrative matter, of getting lost among its many departments was enough to make Romans pale. Now, I have been told, the official maze is much easier to master.

The whole of Rome is administratively divided into *rioni* and *quartieri*. The *rioni* subdivisions go back to when Rome ceased to be a settlement and turned from village to city to metropolis. The word *rione* is a Roman corruption of the Latin *regione*, region, and it stands to reason that under Emperor Augustus the big city, for administrative purposes, had to be sectioned into regions. There were then fourteen regions/*rioni* (thirteen on the right side of the Tiber, the fourteenth on the left: *Trans Tiberim*, today's Trastevere). In A.D. 272 Emperor Aureliano began building a defensive wall, about twelve miles long (reinforced, elevated, and restored several times through the centuries), and today the *rioni* still fall within *le mura*, the walls.

In 1870 Rome became the capital of the finally united Italy and the walls were not able to contain its enormous expansion: in a couple of decades many new *quartieri* (the term *rione* too staid for something new) were added, an expansion that continued to the beginning of World War II. Immediately following the end of the war the population that in 1870 was 226,000 reached almost two million and new *quartieri* were born to house it.

At the beginning of the third millennium the citizenry is around three million, and it seems that every day a new *quartiere* is added to the list as Rome expands. Many developments at the edge of the expansion were born *abusivi* (built illegally, without plans or permits, and sometimes with dubious construction materials and techniques); with the years, simply by still standing, these new places are recognized as bona fide *quartieri*. Then the *Comune* brings in a water and sewage system adequate to the standard canons, streets are paved, and all other basic services are, somehow, established with the proper SPQR markings and under its jurisdiction. There are now twenty-two *rioni* and thirty-five *quartieri* for a temporary total of fifty-seven, most with their own post office, elementary school, and parish church.

The subdivisions of *rioni* and *quartieri* are again fragmented into twenty *circoscrizioni*, the administrative local offices in charge of all the legal commerce between the citizen, the city, and the state; they are extensions of the central administrative and registry office, the *anagrafe*, the issuer and repository of all the thousands of documents a citizen piles up from birth to death. The *circoscrizione* was the starting point of many round trips made by a document and its accompanying person between the various offices of the *Comune* and of the state. The interminable trips — marked by the rhythm of pounding, official stamps — sometimes ended when the need for a particular document (or the petitioner himself) had ceased to exist. Now, thank God, much of the bureaucratic journey has been shortened by the advent of the *telematica*, the computerized system that has all of a citizen's events and related certification documents, from start to finish, on a screen. A petitioner still has to go to different operators for a particular document, but, once there, the document is spit out by an electronic printer instead of being handwritten. Another fantastic improvement (since the idea of a queue is nonexistent in Rome) is the installation of number-dispensing machines to establish a service sequence, eliminating the elbowing contests once fought to reach a desired window. And so business is done in a few unstressed minutes: the end of an era.

Or so I was told.

Out of curiosity and as a test, I went to the central *anagrafe* to check on my Italian citizenship status. I had a free day, and, in keeping with my long-past experiences, I was prepared to spend most of it in the noisy company of fellow postulants. The *anagrafe* is in the center of old Rome, at the foot of the Capitoline Hill, in sight of the many-faced Arch of Janus, god of war and peace, and just beside the square Temple of Virile Fortune and the round Temple of the Vestal Virgins. The *anagrafe* building is of stolid Fascist architecture, massive and cavernous, slightly smaller than Emperor Nero's Domus Aurea, which is huge. Stifling hot in summer, freezing cold in winter, it was designed to accommodate with no attempts at comfort — stoicism being a Fascist's requisite — the thousands of unfortunate people in need of official certificates. These had to be requested in person and in writing at the hundreds of windows, each designated for a specific purpose, and to be collected after a week or so at the other hundreds of *ritiro documenti*, document retrieval windows. To reach the appropriate window, one found it in the labyrinth of corridors; in the absence of an established queue one had to elbow one's way through the crowds. Tempers grew short and fights were frequent. The windows were manned, in general, by disagreeable employees who filled the requests, sadistically, with painstakingly slow handwriting. Any voice communication was made through a two-inch hole in the plate glass separating employee and petitioner. Speaking and in turn listening via the hole was not only difficult and a source of lengthy misunderstandings but also a psychological reinforcement of the separation between the authority and the plebs.

My trepidation upon entering the building gave way to surprise: the place was uncannily quiet and practically empty, so much so that I feared that one of the frequent strikes of public services was on and I did not know it.

But I was wrong: a few people were around and the place was open for business. Clearly marked signs addressed me to the Relazioni con il Pubblico, the office set up to counsel the public on correct procedures. A machine dispensed a number and when, after only a few minutes, my number came up on an electronic board I was admitted, no fuss, no fight, to the counseling officer. I explained to the young, clean-cut man the reason for my visit, which, I told him, was my first in three decades. He raised his eyebrows in surprise, but most courteously said, "No problem." Then he tapped on his keyboard and in a second or two my name appeared on the computer screen.

"There you are!" the young man exclaimed, almost as amazed as myself. "You appear on the AIRE (the list of Italians residing abroad). You can go directly to the AIRE office on the third floor's left wing and ask there. They will give you the certificate." I thanked him, commenting how pleasantly surprised I was at the speediness of operations and especially — and I underlined that word with a smile — at his courtesy. "People are not as stressed as eight or ten years ago," he smiled back, "on both sides of this desk." I had to agree.

While on my way to the third floor, I could not help but notice the long rows of empty windows, and that at the open ones only one customer was dealing with the employee behind it; a few other people seated on benches were waiting calmly for their number to be flashed on the electronic board above the window. I considered the irony encased in this structure: designed to be progressive and modern, a futuristic showcase for the "masses" of the Fascist Empire, the electronic age has managed to empty the huge building and make it dead and obsolete.

Up at the AIRE office I receive the same courteous reception. Tap, tap, my name appears. Yes, I am told, it shows here that you have Italian citizenship. Go down to the Certificates of Citizenship window, down on the first floor's right wing. Just ask for a certificate and they will give you one. But . . . but . . . wait, wait, wait! The employee is now peering into the computer's screen, taps a few keys, seems distraught. "It shows here," he says, "that you are residing abroad. But, wait: there is no specific address for your residence." It is only a generic P-3.

"You cannot get a certificate with only that," he says. He writes a note on a file card, stamps it, and gives it to me, saying that I should ask my consulate in Boston to certify my residence there on form #CONS-01, then mail or fax it to the address on the card. He will personally receive it, file it, and everything will be okay, then, for the release of my certificate. "No problem!" he says. We shake hands on that, and I am on my way out. Just out of malice or, again, curiosity, I stop at the Certificates of Citizenship window on the first-floor right wing. Tap, tap, my name appears. No residence, no certificate, says the window. You have to have a residence. Go to the Circoscrizione II and ask for a Rome residence certificate. Any address will do: a friend's, a relative's, a rented apartment. Come back with it, and you will have your citizenship certificate.

It is not clear to me how a certificate of temporary residence in Rome can substitute for one of permanent residence in Boston, but I prefer not to delve into it now. He sees my quizzical look and smiles a sheepish smile. He goes into a subtle pantomime, bunching his shoulders, chin pointing to the screen, a quick nodding in disbelief. What he is telling me is, "My friend, as much as I wish to help you, I really can't. It is the computer talking, I am powerless." In nonelectronic times the petitioner would have vented his frustration at him; an argument, violent and escalating, would have developed accusing him and his family, ancestors included, of terrible, sadistic deeds.

Now he can retreat behind the shield of the computer, ostensibly taking your side, blameless and untouchable. He feels your pain.

"Good-bye," I tell him face to face (plate glass and communication hole have been eliminated) "and thank you."

"No problem. *Ciao*."

I leave the *anagrafe* empty-handed, but happy anyway. To arrive at the same result, it took me only a relaxed twenty minutes instead of a full, stressful day as it would have in the past.

Things have changed, indeed.

The SPQR is presided over by an elected *Sindaco*, a mayor, who oversees a large number of *assessori*, delegates, each in charge of a particular sector of urban activity.

He also delegates and supervises the administrative activities of twenty *circoscrizioni* operating in each city section or borough. It is not too risky to say that a large portion of Romans not working for the state government is working for the *Comune*.

The *Sindaco* of Rome has always had an overwhelming job, performed with different ability and results since the coinage of that name, shortly after 1870. Before this, he was called a *governatore*, governor. Pope Pius IX, *il Papa Re*, the pope-king, relinquished his dominion of the city in 1870, which, as reported by lay historians and vernacular poets, was more of a stranglehold than a government. As for previous popes, a designated governor held the reins of the city, and under him were a number of monsignors in charge of the various aspects of city life. Their word was law; actually they made the laws, frequently capriciously and at their pleasure. And they had at their command the much-hated *sbirri*, the gendarmes, to police their laws and have them obeyed. Some of today's Roman citizens wish — when it comes to the city's quality of life — that things, in a way, were still so. They look up wistfully at the three-by-four-foot marble plaques still affixed and very noticeable on the walls of many palazzos of that era, and wish their clear message could hold today:

> BY EXPRESS ORDER OF HIS EXCELLENCY THE MON-SIGNOR PRESIDENT OF THESE STREETS IT IS FOR-BIDDEN TO ALL PERSONS OF ANY SOCIAL POSITION, CONDITION, AND GRADE TO DARE OR EVEN AT-TEMPT TO DARE TO THROW OR MAKE THROWN UNDER ANY PRETEXT ANY KIND OF TRASH, DEBRIS, GARBAGE, STRAW, WEEDS, DEAD ANIMALS, FECES, OR OTHER SIMILAR REFUSE INSIDE THE LIMITS OF THIS QUARTER UNDER THE PENALTY OF TWENTY-FIVE GOLD COINS, A FOURTH OF WHICH IS TO BE GIVEN TO THE ACCUSER WHO WILL BE KEPT SE-CRET, AND TO WHICH PENALTY WILL ANSWER THE FATHERS FOR THEIR SONS, THE PATRONS FOR THEIR SERVANTS, AND ANY INFRACTION MAY BE CHARGED ALSO BY INQUISITION, AS INHERENT TO THE RULE MADE KNOWN THE TWENTY-FIFTH DAY OF SEPTEMBER 1688, WHICH WAS MOREOVER RE-NEWED BY THE NOTARY IN THE TRIBUNAL OF THE JURISDICTION OF SAID STREETS THE TWENTY-SECOND DAY OF JULY ANNO DOMINI 1712.

The only missing items from the not-to-be-discarded list seem to be used kitchen sinks and toilet bowls, today frequently dumped on street corners: they had not been invented. It appears that the edict was aimed at an affluent district's population: people with grade and position who could afford stables to be cleaned and gardens to be weeded, and who had servants employed to do all the dirty work.

In less affluent, working-class districts, the message, chiseled on smaller marble plaques, is shorter and to the point:

BY ORDER OF THE ILLUSTRIOUS MONSIGNOR PRES-
IDENT OF THESE STREETS IT IS FORBIDDEN TO ALL
PERSONS TO THROW AND MAKE THROWN IN THIS
LOCATION ANY SORT OF GARBAGE UNDER PENALTY
OF 10 COINS ABOVE ALL OTHER PENALTIES BY THE
JUDGMENT OF THE ABOVEMENTIONED MONSI-
GNOR AS EXPRESSED IN THE EDICT ON THIS FIF-
TEENTH DAY OF JULY 1764.

Either way, the messages are quite firm, their tone does not admit lapses, and, being writ in marble, they are not subject to changes or accommodations. The only difference, perhaps, is that the affluent people had to pay in gold coins, the poorer in simple coins, on top of "all other penalties," the corporal punishments to be doled out at the whim of the illustrious monsignor. Even if for a Roman any law was — and is — made to be broken, it seemed too much to challenge a monsignor's disposition. Or that of his gorillas.

Quite a difference from today's attitude when on "these streets" all sorts of rules and regulations are broken with impunity under the very nose of the various gendarmes, who, in clutches of two or four, are seldom in a confrontational mood and, it seems, more involved in their private conversations, with or without cell phones. But then, trying to control "any infraction," such as curbing dogs, or stopping the cars and scooters ignoring the ONE-WAY or PEDESTRIAN ONLY traffic signs, would be like facing the running bulls of Pamplona.

Being mayor of Rome is not an easy task. Not only because he has to bring together the Giunta Comunale, the politically mixed assembly of commissioners, but also because, on top of everything else, he is actually the mayor of several different and multilevel cities that need to be coordinated and made to coexist together under one single name.

There is the large and constantly expanding modern Rome, the Rome where three million people live. They have to be housed, fed and watered, transported, kept clean and healthy. And all of this seemingly against their will, the Romans being stubborn and most ungovernable citizens.

There is the Rome of the forums and of the museums and of all the treasures and beauty that is Rome, which has to be preserved and upkept and guarded and made ready and available to all citizens of Rome and of the world.

There is Rome, the center of Catholicism, the Rome of hundreds of churches and basilicas, a holy Rome that has to be acknowledged as same and different, and made to mesh with the secular Rome.

There is Rome, the capital of Italy, seat of government and of its many ministries, permanent and temporary residence of the thousands of deputies and senators, past and present presidents and prime ministers, with all their courts of past and present vices and assistants; the Rome of the foreign embassies and consulates; all to be treated with special VIP pomp and diplomatic respect.

Each of these Romes comes with its own particular subdivisions, fringes, and political tendencies, which, through the lengthy democratic process of vociferous commissions and committees, have to come together and agree to work as one city.

No, it is not easy to be the mayor of Rome.

Moreover, Rome, compared with Paris, London, Vienna, and many other big cities, is almost a parvenu to the roster of cosmo-

politan metropolises and to the problems that such status comports. At the beginning of the 1900s Rome was no more than a
large provincial town; it was just beginning to expand outside the
Aurelian Walls. New *quartieri* were being built to house the employees of the newborn state, the out-of-towners brought in to run
its bureaucracy, while, to house their offices, big, imposing *ministeri* were built in the center of town. Rome's utilities and services
were antiquated, inefficient, and at best insufficient for a city of
almost half a million people.

The first *Sindaco* with a modern view and the experience to
bring Rome up to par with the rest of the big cities was Ernesto
Nathan. Born in London of an Italian mother, he was put to work
at an early age in his well-to-do family's commercial and financial
business, both in England and Italy, and he had the stamina and
the political support to cut through the old system of honorary positions and widespread nepotism to make room for the experts.
Meritocrazia, once almost an epithet, became a coin with definite
value. Having acquired Italian citizenship at age forty-three, he
was elected mayor in 1907 on a platform of sweeping reforms,
most of which he turned into positive results. Of particular help
were his business and entrepreneurial experience, his international knowledge of the needs of a modern city, and, a novelty for
city hall, his adeptness at making pragmatic decisions. He turned
into *servizi municipali* the various semiprivate agencies that supplied and distributed water, gas, light, sanitation, garbage removal, and all the other services necessary for the functioning of a
modern city. He saw to the modernization of the water supply, to
the electrification of the city lights, and to the development of a
more efficient system of public transportation. Of lofty social, if
not socialist, ideas, he pushed to increase the number of elementary and formative schools (at that time the Roman illiteracy level
was estimated at 56 percent) and for education in general and
developed broad public-health services. He put a stop to irrespon-
sible construction and real-estate speculation with the implemen-
tation of solid urban planning, which favored the lower classes,

up until then almost ignored and living in shanties. He made efforts to balance public finances, abolishing graft and inefficient administration. Naturally, being a Jew and a dedicated Free Mason (at one time he was Italian Grand Master), he ran against the grain of the old, established *classe dirigente*, synonymous with conservative aristocracy and the clerical hierarchy. Most of his projects were criticized and ridiculed, but Signor Nathan (*l'inglese*, since he had maintained his foreign accent) and his Giunta gave the first impetus to get Rome — at least in the material, physical realm — out of its provinciality. He was dedicated and honest, and even if all of his plans didn't come to fruition during his five years at the helm, he was a bright meteor between the previous and the following administrations. It surprises me that among all the public statues and monuments of Rome there isn't one — to my knowledge — honoring Signor Nathan.

Two decades later, with the advent of Fascism, things reverted to old times and Rome was governed by fiat. The role of an elected *Sindaco* was replaced by an appointed *governatore*, a mostly honorary and ceremonial charge, and by a court of *vicegovernatori* and *rettori* whose chief duty was to follow the party dictum: bring Rome back to the past glories of the Roman Empire, turn it into a showpiece of power and leadership to merit the names *Urbe* (aping the Latin *urbs-is*) and *Grande Roma*, the gem of the *Nuova Italia*. The handling of these duties was given to party members or sympathizers — *meritocrazia* not in evidence — and Rome became fair game again to fawners and sycophants with easy praise and easier bribes. This was the cynical view on the street, so much so that the first Fascist governor, Filippo Cremonesi, was nicknamed *Pippo Pappa*, Phil the Gobbler-Upper.

Rome, with a population hovering around one million, became replete with public buildings of dismally austere architecture, supposedly recalling the glory of Imperial Rome. Old city quarters were torn down by the *piccone risanatore*, the healing pickax, a metaphor invented to soften the blow of brutal demolition, as lamented by my father, to make room around historical places (below the Campidoglio Hill, the Teatro di Marcello, the Circo Massimo, Ara Pacis, the Pantheon) and to create wide spaces (Via dei Fori Imperiali, Via della Conciliazione, Piazza Venezia, Foro Mussolini) capable of hosting large military parades and "oceanic masses" of applauding people. Appearances were more valuable than substance. Much pride was taken in the "trains running on time" syndrome, the symbol for things working again as they should or, in other words, for exceptional achievements. Undeniably, at the end of World War I things were in disarray and needed fixing. Under the Fascist administration, buses and trolley cars shuttled people around a clean town, clear water flowed from faucets and fountains, garbage was disposed of, most people cooked with gas, telephones worked. When I was growing up, it took me a few years to realize that that was the normal way for things to behave, and not the exalted exception. As if someone were to boast,"Look, I am giving you a perfect car. And — let me hear your applause — it works, too!" The exceptional element, if there was one, was the amount of money that the city administration put in the pockets of people in positions of power and their courts. Even worse, this behavior established a tradition of corruption in public administration. Not that the tradition did not exist before, but now it was the rule and an accepted fact of life. Moreover, for an honest citizen to decry, to complain, or to finger-point was not healthy: the government's medicine was bitter and included being forced to swallow castor oil, manhandled, and bludgeoned during "political indoctrination" sessions.

This state of affairs taught an insidious lesson to the Roman citizenry: brown-nose or bribe to put yourself in a position to grab what you can when you can, and let the others manage on their own. It was the official confirmation of accepted, widespread *menefreghismo*, a reality that was the opposite of the boasted image of a Fascist citizen: honorable, honest, dedicated to the common good, upright, an unselfishly macho, generously brave patriot. In short, a super–Boy Scout in blackshirt.

In the period between the two world wars, the process of urbanization got under way. Rome began to expand, its population surpassing one and a half million. Urban plans were drawn, revised, started, suspended, and started again. New *quartieri* were built (Flaminio, Salario, Savoia, Nomentano, Tiburtino, Parioli) for the middle and upper classes, and many *borgate*, little burgs, for the blue-collar, less affluent classes; they all bulged well outside the Aurelian Walls. The construction of the impressive, monumental buildings of EUR.42 in preparation for Rome's Universal Exposition of 1942, a project planned to bedazzle the world, was begun but left unfinished. Suspended, so that all efforts could be dedicated to the impending war.

In 1943 Rome was declared "Open City," to be respected, in theory, by all warring sides as a world's treasure, a safe oasis in the middle of a ruthless fighting war. In practice it became a starved city, under siege from all sides. It was a period of survival, with city hall doing what it could to keep things afloat; but it was really a *si salvi chi può*, an every-man-for-himself situation. The reins were taken by a *federale di Roma*, a high-ranking Fascist, more a political watchdog than *governatore*. Then, in 1944, the American Fifth Army, breaking out of the beachhead of Anzio and the roadblock of Cassino, marched into Rome. Food reappeared in the liberated city in the form of U.S. Army rations (most welcome, although somewhat exotic for a Roman palate). With the American Occupation Force, Rome acquired a U.S. military governor, the jovial and talkative Colonel Poletti (*Caro Poletti, meno parole e più spaghetti!* — Dear Poletti, fewer words and more spaghetti — was the populace's singsong), who for a brief time tried to bring American efficiency to the city. In exchange, the GIs stationed in Rome acquired — someone said were infected by — a corrupt, lackadaisical attitude. They indulged in Roman food and wine, fell for Roman girls' (and boys') pulchritude, and to pay for all the above sold on the black market any item removable from U.S. Army barracks or supply depots, from Zippo lighters to eight-wheeled trucks.

With the end of the war in 1945, after twenty years of dictatorship, democracy was reestablished, generally interpreted as a free-for-all, no holds barred. Rome reacquired a *Sindaco* and a Giunta Comunale, and with it the multifactioned, multi-political-party structure of the *Comune di Roma* was set; it has lasted to this day. Rome's population doubled overnight with the masses of disinherited, the flotsam of the war that flooded in, and the city expanded *a macchia d'olio*, like an uncontrollable oil slick. The Fifteenth Department of the Giunta Comunale, the one in charge of building permits and inspections, was so bogged down by scandals and corruptions that it was suggested that it hang a FOR SALE. JUST MAKE AN OFFER sign on its door. And the citizenry let it happen, too busy recovering from the war and too involved in catching up on lost time, wrestling day by day with life's chaos and trying to survive it.

Luckily, my family and I did, and now I remember those long-past days with wonder.

Recently I met with Massimo Triglia, an old, dear, lost friend. We talked about those days, when we were both trying to forecast our future, taking the first steps of our budding careers, which, we did not know then, would lead us to two different continents. We sat at a local *trattoria* — is there a better place to meet an old friend in Rome? — and with the help of a carafe of red, we reminisced about the long hours spent together in a sort of therapeutic friendship, soothing our wartime bruises with as much humor as we could muster. And about the circuslike, improbable life in postwar Rome. Among the many events, one came back to us, vivid as an old film — but barely aged. We named it *Tempi Duri*, Hard Times, agreeing that perhaps time had bleached away, a bit, the exact names of protagonists and antagonists, perhaps even of locations, but had left intact the story and its plot.

Peace, as the saying goes, had exploded in Italy. The country was overabundant in rubble and the willingness to put it, and oneself, back together. Massimo was the embodiment of that mood. He had fought his war and had come back to Rome with a reserve of adrenaline and an insatiable hunger for action and life. It seemed his way to devour time and have none left to think of the miseries and horrors he had seen. His father, an old-time, respected journalist, had become the city editor of a new newspaper, a tabloid, then a novelty on the Italian publishing scene. After many years of censorship, when even the obituaries had to be approved by a Fascist censor, the press was now running wild, an imprisoned bird suddenly let out of the cage. Signor Triglia did not approve of this, but work was work, at least until he could go back to serious journalism. He hired his son Massimo (as handsome as a Latin lover movie star, and as unbridled) as a cub reporter — and hoped to rein in some of the wildness in both paper and son.

After so many years of privations, Romans dedicated most of their spare time (out of real need, habit, or fun) to the pursuit of food. The hunting grounds varied from open-air black markets to clandestine cellars to country farms.

Not too far from Rome, nestled in the foothills of the Apennine Mountains, are a number of small villages and farms. It is a rough, tough region, but renowned for its tasty poultry and pigs.

Tarole is one village in the region, and there was a farm a quarter of a mile below it. The village itself boasted nothing exceptional: a church, a square, a few old stone houses clustered at the very top of a rocky hill. The farm also had nothing special: at the bottom of the winding, steep road leading to the village there was a stone farmhouse, a tin-roofed barn, and a fenced-in muddy pen for a few pigs. It was owned by, as Massimo's newspaper described her, a fiftyish, dried-out, sallow-faced widow. She wasn't legally a widow: her soldier-husband had been sent to Russia and was never heard of again. She wore only mourning black. In those hard, dangerous times she had asked her sister-in-law, Carolina, who had also lost her menfolk, to come and live with her. Perhaps one day the men would return, but for now they were officially missing in action, and it was cheaper and safer to join forces.

The ladies were not unique; there were many in the same situation. Entire families had been "dispersed." Even with the war over, it was not unusual for a person to leave home in the morning — "*Ciao*, I will see you at lunch!" — and never be heard of again.

Carolina was younger and poorer than the widow, therefore in a subservient position. She was also stronger and — as Massimo put it in tabloid-speak — peasantly attractive. Like everybody else in the area, they eked out a living by making and selling sausages and pork products, although — their pigs being not terribly well fed — theirs were of inferior quality. And since soap was a rare and valuable item, the ladies collected leftover animal fat and bones, boiled them in a vat of lye and other ingredients, and, with some industry, produced rough, cheap soap.

One day, innocently enough, a local black marketeer came on his usual visit. It was his business, as that of many others like him, to make the rounds of the farms and buy products to sell, at great profit, in Rome. But that day he made a special offer: he proposed he become the exclusive buyer of all the widow's products, including the soap, for a ridiculously low price. He assured her that his deal would protect her pigs' health. There was a bad contagion abroad, he said: the pigs of a nearby, uncooperative farmer had developed a death wish and had committed suicide en masse. To make things worse, he said, the pigs had taken poison, which meant that they were not only dead but also totally useless to their owners.

The widow considered the offer and looked at Carolina, who bumped the visitor on the head with a heavy iron skillet. Carolina was passionate in her impulses and strong. The visitor left this world without a pain. The ladies dug a hole in the pigsty and buried the body.

A tense week passed. Since nobody inquired about the missing man, the ladies began to relax and went back to their usual affairs, making and selling soap and sausages.

The creaky, makeshift buses that connected Tarole with Rome could not possibly make it up to the village and had to stop at the bottom of the steep road, near the widow's farm. The ladies sold mostly to people who, having trudged up to the village and found nothing affordable, stopped at the widow's so as not to waste a trip. Her soap and sausages were not the best, but they were cheap and better than nothing at all. Sometimes, while waiting for a bus to go by, people would go to the widow's and, for a few lire, she or Carolina provided scrambled eggs, or a sausage cooked over the embers, or a glass of the strong local wine. And a chat.

One rainy day, a rubicund, jolly man came in. He ate sausages and eggs and fresh-baked bread and drank a glass of wine. And then another, and, the bus not in sight, another again. The conversation became lively and funny. The jolly man, in the country manner, told bawdy jokes and then made eyes at the peasantly attractive Carolina. Then he drank a toast to her health, then another to her strong bosoms, and another again to her strong thighs. Then he showed her a bankroll and boldly asked her to have a roll in the hay.

The widow, in a fit of resentment — and perhaps of jealousy — hit the jolly man on the head with the iron skillet. She wasn't as strong as Carolina, but strong enough.

Since it was raining, they decided to park the body in the soap vat. And since where he was going he would not need any money and even less an overcoat, they kept both. In a few days all that was left of the jolly man was a gold tooth and a few bars of soap.

During the next four months more than twenty persons went to the widow's farm and never came away. Some of the missing persons' relatives called the police, who were able to track a few of the vanished as far as Tarole, but all traces disappeared at the bus stop. When and if the victims ever got on or off the bus was too much for the overworked police to find out.

The buses of those hard times were not true buses, but any self-propelled, privately owned contraption that could move people or animals or both. Some were ancient trucks, some four-passenger cars whose bodies had been ingeniously sawed up and transformed into trucks, "truckettes" as they were called; others were residuals of war given new life by the adroit cannibalization of other machines; others were three-wheeled motorcycles with some chairs affixed to a platform, and with the penchant, under an unbalanced or restless load, for tipping over. This fleet of makeshift vehicles was the backbone of Roman public transportation, in the city and out of it. All of them carried twice as many passengers as they should have. They had whimsical schedules, itineraries set by changing road conditions and, especially for those operating on interregional routes, by the activity of the numerous highway bandits. The conveyances broke down more frequently than not, leaving passengers — and their heavy bundles — stranded in the middle of nowhere. From there everyone was on his or her own: once you got on a "bus" your tracks were lost to the world.

The police went to the widow's farm to see if, by chance, she recognized any of the missing persons. The widow and Carolina examined the photos and declared that perhaps, yes, but then not for sure, and then again there could be a resemblance . . . they had seen this man . . . no, it was this one . . . the photos were so poor . . . yes, this one had stopped for a glass of water . . . or was it a snack? . . . just before boarding the bus. The ladies tried their best, but were of no help to the police.

The local police came back sometime later. A nasty rumor was spreading that something odd was going on at the widow's. She seemed to be producing more soap and sausages than ever and, moreover, she had been known, of late, to be selling men's clothes. To the investigating carabiniere (the younger half of the Tarole police force) the women explained that the better production was the fruit of their diligent labors and, as for the clothing, the poor women had decided that there was no sense in letting the moths take their men's old clothes. Better to sell them to someone who could use them now, in these hard times, for a few needed lire.

The young carabiniere found the activity sensible, the explanation reasonable: only terrible rumors spread by envious, lazy neighbors. He accepted the peasantly attractive Carolina's small

parcel of sausages and her graceful invitation to come back anytime he wished. She made a point to inform him, with a wink,
that the religious widow never missed benediction at the church.
Every night of the week, rain or shine, between six and eight,
wink, wink . . .

The last person to disappear at Tarole was a fat, boorish city
slicker. He worked at the *anagrafe*, mainly shuffling birth, marriage, and death certificates. And those of *dispersi*, civilians or soldiers missing in action. He had an attractive, ambitious wife and a
deluxe mistress. He could neither stand the wife nor, given his
salary, keep the mistress happy. He devised a ploy that could, at
once, keep him away from home for days on end and afford him
money for the mistress. He borrowed days from his allotted office
vacations and toured Rome's neighboring villages. He carried an
attaché case containing official-looking documents, a list of relatives of *dispersi*, and, since he was given to heavy perspiration, a
flacon of cheap cologne.

He went from address to address and told the missing persons'
relatives that he was in possession of documents that could shed
light on the whereabouts of their loved ones. More definitive information could be obtained, but it required further research, lots
of work, the collaboration of others, the greasing of the palms of
people in high places, all things that involved certain expenses . . .

Lies, but with them he was able to extract from worried,
loving, simple people a goodly amount of lire. To tell the truth
(Massimo and I remembered it well), many were plying his awful
trade: in those hard times they went by the name of hyenas or
jackals.

Destiny brought him to Tarole, and finally to the widow. She disliked him on sight, and as soon as he opened the attaché case full of
official-looking documents and spoke of almost positive information
he had on certain missing people, his fate was determined.

He was disposed of with professional alacrity. With a touch of
improved ingredients, the ladies produced a batch of cologne-
scented toilet soap.

After a couple of weeks, the attractive, ambitious wife of the fat, boorish city slicker went to the Roman police. She hoped they would find him dead or, *flagrante delicto*, with his mistress. Adultery was not a terribly serious crime for a man, but enough to give her reason to separate. Then she would be free to go and live with Massimo, her lean, hungry, and ambitious lover, a struggling newspaper reporter.

The police followed her husband's tracks to Tarole and discovered his heinous preying on the sorrows of others, but lost all trace of him at the bus stop. They investigated at the widow's, and she and Carolina recognized his photo immediately. This was the man in whom they had sensed something terribly evil, to whom they had refused to sell anything, not even an egg, and who had left in a huff for the bus stop. The ladies thought, but could not swear to it, that he got a lift on a passing truck with a Naples license plate. Naples was the capital of forged license plates (among many other things), and the information led the police nowhere. And that is what they reported to the attractive wife of the city slicker.

The next weekend, following an inexplicable impulse, she convinced Massimo to take her to Tarole. Massimo borrowed a motor scooter (my motor scooter, but he had to pay for the gasoline) and indulged her. A morbid desire, perhaps, to see the place where her horrible husband had finally disappeared. They found nothing of interest in Tarole. On their way back to Rome, not to waste the trip, they stopped at the widow's and bought a length of sausages and a bar of toilet soap.

Once at home, the attractive wife took a long, warm bath to recover from the exhausting backseat ride. She used the toilet soap and its scent reminded her, almost palpably, of her husband. She felt uncomfortable and itchy: she never could stand that cheap scent.

Later she made herself a dinner of broccoli and sausages. Halfway through her dinner she got stomach cramps, the same reaction she developed during the rare times she was intimate

with her piggish husband. At first she thought that her imagination was playing tricks on her, then she put two and two together
and vomited. Then she called Massimo, her lean, ambitious
lover, and told him. He went right over to console her and to wrap
in a bag the leftover sausages and the wet toilet soap. The next day
he had them analyzed, went to the police, and with them went to
Tarole.

It was Massimo's first big scoop as an investigative reporter. It
opened up his career, but also cost him his love for sausages.

That same love got the Black Widow, the Soapmaker and
Monster of Tarole — as Massimo named her in the paper — life
in a prison for the criminally insane. Carolina, considered a slave
(and by now a quite pregnant one) to the evil will of the widow,
and for her helpful collaboration with the local police, got a very
mild sentence. Massimo and I came up with the moral of the
story: *La legge è uguale per tutti*, the law is equal for all, but in the
eyes of Roman judges it helps to have a peasantly attractive (even
better if pregnant) appearance. Also, as Massimo cynically wrote
at that time in closing his story: "Not much has changed in the
whole history of Rome: in tough, hard times, nothing goes
wasted."

Not so today, Massimo and I agree. Now, in Rome, hard times —
like those good old hard times — are something that can hardly
be imagined. For the Romans of today tough times are not the
lack of things but, ironically, the overabundance of everything
and its related waste. Too many people, too many new *quartieri*,
too many new *borgate*, too many cars, too many scooters, too
much garbage . . . just too much of too much. But then Romans,
especially the new Romans, are professional complainers, and the
constant complaining frequently makes things feel worse than
they actually are. Everything is thrown in the same bag: the lack
of adequate health care has the same complaint value as the five-
minute wait at the bus stop, the poor public-schooling situation
weighs as much as the not-oven-fresh loaf of bread at the bakery,

the supercongested traffic as waiting for the last fashion to appear in the store, or waiting for a table at a restaurant. Many things do not work today, many things are out of hand, says Massimo. He has continuously resided in Rome since I last saw him, almost half a century ago, and so has seen his beloved Rome be overtaken by people who always want more. He has seen greed inflate the city like a party balloon: too much fun has made the child reckless, he has kept blowing and now the balloon will soon burst. "For years I have tried to warn, to show the real situation and its very predictable results. And with me," he says, "are many others: architects, urban planners, professional people who know. They called us Cassandras."

Most Romans like the big colorful balloon, they want it bigger, do not see the danger. Sooner or later, some party spoiler will show up with a pin and Rome will burst, go back to real hard times with a bang. Everybody, then, will really have something to complain about.

But for the moment, if you listen to the *vox populi*, hard times today can even be something as inconsequential as an unexpected cloudburst.

I found one of the Cassandras among my old friends, an architect. He is part of a group of fourteen friends — boys and girls — who grew up together in a radius of a few city blocks. We went to the same nursery school and the same elementary school; we played in the same neighborhood park; our bleeding shins were taken care of by the mother closest at hand. If there is something exceptional about this group of friends it is that after so many years, so many happenings, they still meet, every Friday, and have dinner together. I should say "we," but I left for other shores, and left my Rome, my neighborhood, my growing-up memories in their care. I join them whenever I am in Rome and I make believe, and they let me, that I never left. We talk, we laugh, we argue, we tease. Uccio Pizzuti married — and divorced — a woman of the group, both of them intelligent enough to cherish our common friendships and still participate, separately, at the dinners. Uccio began his career as an architect. As soon as he graduated he was exceptionally busy, "building Rome." He worked for a company that built entire new *quartieri*, so busy that the getting more work had become the work itself. Quality had no importance, and all this happened with the push of innumerable *bustarelle*. Here compromises arose, compromises with his conscience that he was not willing, or able, to make. So he abandoned pencil and ruler and became a professor at the University of Rome. Appropriate, then, to ask him my question: "Rome, as the saying goes, wasn't built in a day. Is it over yet?"

"No, not yet," is Uccio's anwer. "The 1960s were the beginning of the end of Rome as a manageable city. It was the period of the economic boom. Many people found themselves with a lot of money and wanted new houses; many people became developers and gave them their wish. Many of the developers were no more than *capimastri*, construction foremen, and ended up heads of huge construction firms. They started making over a small *villino*, a one-family cottage, then another and then another. They now had the money to take over an entire neighborhood and 'rede-velop' it. Previously neighborhoods had space, had sidewalks, had trees, were built with the right dimensions, with right-dimensioned houses, right dimensions for living. The 'developers' turned them into anthills, into horrors, destroying what once had a human bal-ance, a texture . . . they destroyed everything. Many shady deals were made with banks, all based on the most abysmal speculation. Look, for example, at what happened on the Via Cassia."

The old, narrow consular road led out of Rome through rows of centuries-old pine trees; in two or three miles the road cut into open, green countryside, pastures, rolling hills. It was very bu-colic. Then the developers started building semideluxe apart-ments and kept going until now a new *quartiere* follows another and another after that, a mess of pseudo-elegant high-rises along a narrow street without sidewalks, and with many other narrow streets pouring into it like rivulets pouring into a swelling river.

"It has become a great urban agglomerate," says Uccio, "with a great number of people and huge problems. Unsolvable problems. The Cassia is the only umbilical cord tying all these people with the city. How do you manage all the traffic that has been created? How do you solve all the other problems? It is an enormous effort, and it's all at the expense of the citizenry. But this is not a unique situation. Take a drive around the outer edge of town and you will encounter one horror after another."

I had seen it: enormous concentrations of cheap skyscrapers built without permits or urban plan, one almost touching the other, and each jumble melting into the next so that now Rome looks absolutely surrounded. It has happened, Uccio explains, thanks to speculators and, even worse, thanks to those who let it happen: public administrations that, one day to the next, transformed a tract of pasture into prime building land. The value of the land skyrocketed and the companies that owned the land, you can be sure, were grateful to those who had made the decision. No plans were made for access and exit roads to all these new places, which has led to infernal bottlenecks on the existing highways and byways. The whole urban structure of the *borgate* is so snarled that it will be incredibly difficult to put it straight. Not only do all the *borgate* depend materially on the city, with all the drainage and waste of efforts that it comports, but they also depend on it socially. These places offer no reason for anybody to be there other than sleep; huge dormitories, they have nothing to offer, no life. Especially for the young, who flock to the magnet of the city's center not only for work but also for entertainment, for the city's amenities. This large mass of people descending daily to its center has provoked a deep change in the social structure of the old city. The established core of Piazza di Spagna, Via Condotti, and Via del Babuino was one of the most elegant, internationally famous areas of boutiques, high-fashion shops, art galleries, renowned cafés and tearooms. Now it has become a wall-to-wall expanse of fast-food eateries and shops selling jeans, T-shirts, and cheap goods. The pace and tone of the new shoppers has created its own name: *Mordi e Fuggi*, bite and run, in the style of wild dogs.

"It is very hard to correct something that was born wrong and let grow wrong." Uccio takes a big breath, a sigh, as if closing a chapter, turning a page. "But now, finally, efforts are being made to turn the new *quartieri*, the new *borgate* into satellite areas, if not independent — that would be impossible — at least interdependent with each other and with the city. Create elements, activities, interests for the locals, to give the communities a certain autonomy, some vitality. The desire to cure the mistakes of the past, a real interest to get to work on it, is there. It is really there."

After a thoughtful pause, as if checking himself: "After all I have said, it will sound like a paradox, but, at least for a few, it has the zeal of a crusade."

Uccio, who up to now has been pretty somber, breaks into one of his brilliant smiles:

"Let me finally answer your question: even at best, it will take more than a day."

~ v ~

Not in a Day

 $\mathcal{I}$ T ALL STARTED — legend claims in 753 B.C. — with a small clan of shepherds, and in the arc of a few centuries, Rome became the mighty Roman Empire, the forge of Western civilization, the giver of laws, the known world. As in a biblical parable, in a few more centuries Rome returned to where it began: at the beginning of the 1800s shepherds led sheep at pasture among the ruins of the temples and the forums. *Sic transit gloria mundi.*

Yet if the power of Rome is gone, its beauty, miraculously, has remained. Rome has been uninterruptedly inhabited for twenty-seven centuries; not many cities can make such a claim. The process of building Rome up has been frequently alternated with tearing it down. The more one digs, the more one finds layers of ruins, each one dating to an older era. Archaeologists and historians can read this layer cake of a city and tell you who built what when and who tore it down, who moved what from here to there, when and why. Books on these finds fill complete libraries. New shelves are continuously added; through the help of new insights and new technologies, facts are revised by new generations of scrutinizers.

All the layers, so to speak, of ground-level constructions are wormed through by miles and miles of covert works that have never seen the light of day, built underground to stay underground: catacombs, drainage tunnels, sublevel aqueducts, subways. In good times or bad, someone has always been around to call Rome home; throughout history the citizens of Rome, no matter how many or how few, should have become accustomed to having their lives disrupted by this beehive of building activity, over and under. But I doubt it: human nature being what it is, and Romans being Roman, it must have provoked always a goodly amount of ongoing complaining.

History repeats itself: since 1995, Rome has been rebuilding itself — actually more of a general preening — a renovation somewhat deeper than simple cosmetics. Rome has not seen such fervor for more than three-quarters of a century, since the Fascists tried to give her an imperial tone. That was done with a series of public works, designed to be severe and imposing, but that turned out to be plain and cold, if not downright unattractive. This time the official trigger for the works was to ready Rome to be a proper host to the millions of pilgrims coming to pay homage to *Sacra Romana Chiesa* (and gain total absolution from their sins) during the *Giubileo 2000*. And coincidentally — after so many years of neglect — to restore much of the city's exterior and its infrastructure in preparation for the new millennium. Like an athlete limbering her muscles, toning them for the long walk ahead.

The official opening of the *Giubileo 2000* and the celebrations for the new millennium were probably the biggest double whammy Rome will see for the next thousand years.

The preparations cost the Romans a considerable amount of discomfort, if not out-and-out hardship: roads were stripped and repaved, water pipes unearthed and reburied, gas lines replaced, many buildings refurbished and monuments scrubbed clean and repainted, trolley lines laid out, new parking lots opened, tunnels and underpasses bored, subways extended. All in all five thousand *cantieri*, work sites, were set up all over town, and there was hardly a Roman (or visitor) who was not affected by them; it was, by general admission, a plague.

Around the end of the sixth century, Rome was struck by a real plague, the black plague; it lasted a few years and brought Rome to her knees. Legend has it that while leading a procession of faithful praying for the end of the scourge, Pope Gregory I saw an angel hovering over Emperor Hadrian's mausoleum. The angel was brandishing a flaming sword, which he slowly put back into its scabbard. The interpretation of the mythical sign was clear: the plague was over. The mausoleum gained two things as a result of the pope's vision: for its top, a big statue of the angel sheathing his sword, and for itself, a new name: Castel Sant'Angelo.

I will never admit to having mythical insights, but, on January 4, 2000, during my good-night look at Rome from my terrace, I saw an angel hovering over the castello, his flashing red sword going back into the scabbard. In truth, since I accompany my good-nights to Rome with alfresco nightcaps, it could be that I credited the flashing lights of a helicopter to the angel, but to me the meaning was the same: the building plague was over. The next day, January 5, Mayor Rutelli announced to the grumbling naysayers that 96 percent of the work had been accomplished; the rest was on its way to completion. The general cheers were dampened a bit by the political opposition's mathematics: that unfinished 4 percent meant that there were two hundred *cantieri* still operating and, naturally, all were under the complainers' windows. Legitimate excuses were offered: some of the delays were due to the frequent unearthing of ruins by pneumatic drills. The laws for the "Protection of the National Historical and Artistic Patrimony" are extremely stringent and, when it comes to Rome, one can hardly dig more than one foot without hitting something that falls under that law. When this happens an inspector has to decide how historically or artistically valuable the find is. It is a long process that can lead either to the removal of the find to a safer place, if possible, or, if not, to the rerouting of the project; it all adds up to big time and big money losses. On the other hand, more than one digger has found himself, like Alice entering the rabbit hole, in a previously unknown, perfectly preserved ancient Roman house, mosaics, frescoes, and all, a real archaeological treasure. Naturally, the logistical excuses did no more than rekindle the acrimony of the complainers: in Rome, you don't have to be an archaeological Einstein to be prepared for such contingencies.

Billions of cobblestones, the uniquely shaped *sampietrini* (here, too, the grumblers complained that they were not real *sampietrini* shaped by Roman hands from the *selce* quarries near Rome, but imported from China or Korea) went to repave miles of *vicoli*, streets, and squares; millions of square feet of plastic sheathing covering hundreds of buildings being worked on, were, like the handkerchief of a magician, pulled off and, voilà, the palazzi, churches, monuments, fountains, towers, domes, and columns revealed their restored and cleansed faces. Even the facade of Saint Peter's Basilica reacquired its original colors, hidden under centuries of grime. In some cases the surprise at seeing the finished renovation was not so astonishing: the plastic tarpaulins covering the work in progress reproduced exactly, by some sort of ingenious electronic or photographic process, the work behind it as it would be at completion. From some distance, the trompe l'oeil was so perfect that it required a double take to discover the deception. Or a little breeze would give it away, making the faux palace undulate in front of one's face, a strange sensation for sober eyes. I wonder, now, how many visitors came to Rome before the unveiling and left convinced that what they had seen was the real thing, in truth nothing more than a fake theatrical setup, a forest of metal scaffolding caging the unfinished city, still in its days of building.

The next wave of visitors, and the next, will see the real thing, and with a certain degree of physical safety. Many areas have been turned into pedestrian-only zones; once swamped by traffic, they are again human spaces, their monuments protected from vibrations and the acid-laden fumes. Banned to cars and scooters, they are magnificent at any time of day: Piazza Navona, the Campidoglio, the forums, Castel Sant'Angelo, the great embrace of Saint Peter's Basilica, the Pantheon, the whole tourist guide's list of sights to be seen. At night soft, diaphanous lighting, masterfully engineered, gives a perennially moonlit quality to marble and brick: it is a memorable experience to walk Rome at night, when the city is at rest and only the sound of your footsteps is there to share the city with you.

It took a while for someone like me, used to the old Rome, to get accustomed to the newly scrubbed city: it seemed as if the cleaning brush had taken some of the somber nobility, the wisdom of age along with the dirt. Sometimes it seemed even garish, an old lady with too much rouge. But then with a deeper look, details have reappeared: the once-dull mosaics of the Basilica of Santa Maria in Trastevere are alive again, reflecting gold to the gold of the sun; natural light and shadow — not the centennial dark stains — bring out the perfectly measured volume of Sant'Andrea della Valle's cupola. As one ascends the twenty-one steps to Piazza del Campidoglio, the equestrian statue of Marcus Aurelius slowly emerges to welcome the visitor to the best-designed, and now clean, space in the world: it is not difficult to think of this space as the once *caput* of the *Caput Mundi*. Escape from the rushing traffic of Corso Vittorio, or of Via Rinascimento, by going through any small, repaved alley and it will lead you to the haven of Piazza Navona: the again-white marble of the three fountains spewing crystal waters into the air is like a shot of oxygen to the lungs; the trills of children playing in the void-of-cars square, a shot of oxygen to the soul. Also free of traffic is the Trevi Fountain, so that visitors can once again pitch their coins into the waters without having to fight their way through onrushing cars, scooters, and taxis.

The creation in the old center of town of so many *isole pedonali*, pedestrian islands, did, naturally, exacerbate the traffic problem where exacerbation was least needed. The width of most of the *centro*'s streets, more alleys than streets (once one subtracts the space taken by illegally parked cars), is barely enough for another car and a pedestrian to pass at the same time. The streets also seem to invite high-powered motorbikes, scooters, and *motorini* to engage in noisy, high-speed, deadly gymkhanas. Then it becomes a battle of wits and agility between the mechanical monsters and the pedestrians, a fast-learned choreography, a mixture of ballet, minuet, precision step dance, and bullfight. The pedestrian has to estimate, from the approaching noise, the size, speed, and determination of the vehicle coming from behind and jump aside between parked cars or inside a doorway at the very last second and resume his walk a fraction of a second after the passage of the charger. The same split-second ability is required of the motor-driven onrusher, who has to judge the gumption, agility, and hearing alertness of the living obstacle. A couple walking together has to synchronize a pas de deux of skips and jumps with hardly an interruption of conversation. Naturally, cars, bikes, and scooters come in strings, so that a walk in town can easily become a cardiovascular exercise. Walking in Rome is, all told, an acquired skill. Or else. The much-vaunted Roman democracy stops on the street. Here only two classes exist: the drivers and the pedestrians. They hate each other on sight, with absolute irrationality, to, if possible, mutual ruin. And reciprocal it is, since the roles change as soon as a driver leaves his car and becomes a pedestrian, and vice versa. A mixture of the two, like a centaur, occurs when a pedestrian rides a public bus; I have personally witnessed a passenger urge the bus driver to run over a jaywalking lady. Not for the "jay" but for the "walking": get the pedestrian!

All systems of the 96 percent–finished Rome came to a crushing test, not unlike the quick, fast jabs of a boxing match: the New Century versus Rome. The starting bell was Saint Peter's Basilica's very own: the Christmas Eve opening of the Holy Door by the pope. The walled-in door is metaphorically pickaxed down by the pontiff every twenty-fifth year — the Holy Year — after which the door is rewalled. This act signifies, "Come to me, ye faithfuls! The door is open!" A crowd three times larger than expected accepted the invitation, filling huge Saint Peter's Square and neighboring areas: Rome groaned, but did not fall. A day or two later forty thousand children arrived from all over the world for a papal blessing: a few logistic hitches arose, like feeding the kids and supplying enough toilets, but that too passed. Following the sacred jabs came the profane wallop: for New Year's Eve three open-air concerts were organized, all in the center of town, each slightly more than half a mile from the other. Pop music played in Saint Peter's Square, hard rock in the almost-as-large Piazza del Popolo, and classical music in the just-as-large Piazza del Quirinale. All performed by top stars, they attracted, between locals and out-of-towners, an estimated million and a half people, exceeding expectations by 250 percent. Each location welcomed the new millennium at midnight with a phantasmagoria of fireworks and a zillion poppings of corks. The process of egress took until six next morning, January 1, 2000, when the massive traffic jam petered out, no police being there to interfere with its natural solution. Miraculously, there were no incidents besides a few minor acts of vandalism and a flattened Mercedes roof (a bunch of people stood on it to gain a better view of a rock star). And only one sizable scare: a few buildings near Piazza del Popolo shook as if hit by an earthquake: glasses fell off tables, chandeliers swung, the works. The civil emergency service, summoned for help, reassured everybody. The violent shaking was provoked by the synchronous jumping-up-and-down of the estimated six hundred thousand people at the rock concert.

By 11 A.M., January 1, 2000, trained squads of city cleaners had swept and washed the city clean of the tons of empty champagne bottles and other refuse, in time for the thirty thousand runners of the international Rome Marathon 2000 to take off from Saint Peter's Square at 12:30 P.M. The sun shone high, a springlike day, and it all went smoothly, although without many people to cheer the passing athletes: Rome was quietly nursing its millennium hangover. Bruised, but standing.

The computer virus that was supposed to anesthetize all the newly installed electronic brains — the much-feared Y2K bug, here called *il baco*, the worm — and which had been predicted to KO Rome, never showed up. All to the chagrin of a few foreign observers (they had singled out Rome as the world's worst-prepared city), who then had to apologize for their dark predictions.

In the next few days the voices of the complainers about all that had not worked as it should have were many and loud, but the general population basically ignored them. It had been a protracted and trying period, but everybody had reasonably clean fun, no damage done, and Rome, the historical *Urbs*, the Eternal City, somehow didn't go to the carpet; she lived to tell the tale.

"We have seen this one, too," Rome, once more, appeared to say with a veiled yawn. "Now, what can we do, what can we build for the next millennium?"

Rioni

 HEN I THINK of Rome, the Rome of my walks, the
 Rome I come in touch with in the course of the day, I
tend to think of its historical eras as so many bins, like the bins one
encounters at a bakery: here the *pagnotte*, here the *rosette*, here the
ciabatte, there the *sfilatini*. They are all breads, they are all different,
and most are nourishing, just like Rome. I go by the forums, or the
catacombs, or the Appian Way, and I put them all into the *Ancientrome* bin; what I put indiscriminately there may span a thousand
years or more. Something younger than *Ancientrome* goes into the
smaller, *Medievalrome* bin, smaller because that Rome, compared
with the others, is more difficult to spot. Then comes the *Papalrome*,
the more than a few centuries of the Rome of the good Popes and
of the bad Popes, of the Renaissance and of the baroque; and so on
to the nineteenth century of *Romaumbertina*, the Rome first capital of Italy; to *Romafascista*, the so-obvious one; and to *Romaoggi*,
the one most similar to all modern cities, the impersonal one
(even if, I must admit, it has many elegant and pleasant spots).

My historian friends cringe at my simplistic compartmental-
izing. They point out that there should be many in-between bins,

since whoever was in charge at any one time tended to repudiate the previous Rome and built a new one on top, frequently achieving something hard to define in era and style, sometimes mongrelizing things, difficult to file. I am well aware of the Roman layering phenomenon: when I have to exemplify it, I think of San Clemente. Not more than a quarter of a mile from the newly restored home of Nero, the Domus Aurea, almost the same distance from the Colosseum, is the unexceptional-looking — by Roman standards — church of Saint Clement. Also unexceptional — for Rome — is that starting far down below street level is a third-century-B.C. Mithraic temple, with a well-preserved, realistic representation of Mithras sacrificing a bull to Apollo. Over this temple are the walls of a second-century-B.C. palace of the republican era. Its brickwork is still intact; a spring still flows freely from a wall and gurgles away through unseen channels underfoot. Built above the republican palazzo are the remains of a first-century-B.C. Imperial Rome house, and above these are the foundations of the third- or fourth-century-A.D. lower church with frescoes of the legend of Saint Clement. This lower church was destroyed in 1084 when Rome was sacked by the Normans. From the lower church finally one goes up (on the way you may glance, through a grate, down into a catacomb) to the upper church. Built in 1108 and embellished with marble taken from the ruined lower church, it is considered the best-preserved medieval basilica in Rome, even if restored, with the addition of a few modern touches, by Pope Clement XI in the eighteenth century. And that's the church one sees from street level, the top layer of a vertical stack of bins. Perhaps I am an impressionable visitor, but I always feel the presence of a single ghost presiding throughout the various strata, as if in a process of reincarnation the death of one layer gave life to the next. The place (actually the places), I feel, have a soul.

One does not need to be a ghost hunter or a spelunker to trace this historical progression: it is also easily encountered in horizontal alignment. A walk in any of the original fourteen *rioni* is like leafing through a book, with pages and chapters coming at you in a random historical sequence. Trastevere is perhaps the richest chapter. The *rione*, because of its position across the Tiber River (today's Tevere), was always intrinsic to and, paradoxically, also separate from the life of the city. United to Rome only by the two short hyphens of the Isola Tiberina's bridges, Ponte Fabricio and Ponte Cestio (much later also by Ponte Sisto and several others), the *rione* developed its own character and identity. Already populous at the time of Emperor Trajan, residence also of an active Jewish community, Trastevere has always been a dynamic section of the city. Between the seventh and the fourteenth centuries, when Rome was a complex of separate, independent enclaves interspersed with pastures and empty fields, Trastevere already had a unity and a life of its own.

It took strength from the Tiber and its fluvial ports, the lifeblood of Rome since its inception. Most of the produce and building materials floated to Rome on river barges and landed in Trastevere. Handling, processing, and manufacturing of these supplies concentrated in Trastevere artisans, smiths, and workmen, all sinews essential for the needs of a city. The strong base of blue-collar workers shaped the Trasteverini into boisterous, proud, and gutsy people; they helped make the *rione* a stronghold of independence during the *Risorgimento*, the fight for the unification of Italy in the mid-1800s, and of the *Resistenza*, the final fight against the Fascists in 1943–44. The physical and social integrity of Trastevere was altered around the turn of the twentieth century with the opening of the wide Ponte Garibaldi, a six-lane bridge. Slightly upriver from the Isola Tiberina, it joined the wide Via Arenula on the left bank (built at the high cost of "rehabilitating/demolishing" part of the Ghetto) with the wide Viale del Re on the right bank (built at the high cost of "rehabilitating/demolishing" part of Trastevere). While the operations amplified enormously the economic, cultural, and social exchanges by uniting the *rione* with the rest of the city, paradoxically the new Viale del Re (now Viale Trastevere) slashed through Trastevere, dividing it into two sections. On the right section rests the fourth-century Basilica of Santa Maria in Trastevere, the first church dedicated to Mary, and the fifth-century church of San Crisogono, rebuilt in the twelfth; also on the right is the nineteenth-century Regina Coeli, the oldest of Roman jails. On the left fall the third-century barracks of the Seventh Cohort of Firemen, built on a first-century house; not too far off is the ninth-century church of Santa Cecilia, reputedly the inventor of the organ, hence patron saint of all musicians. And so on, skipping back and forth through the centuries. The twentieth century appears on the right side with the imposing *Ministero della Pubblica Istruzione*, the Ministry of Education, where all the curriculums for all Italian schools are set; on the opposite side, bridging nineteenth and twentieth centuries, is the *Manifattura Tabacchi del Monopolio*, where young Roman blades waited at the end of the workday for the exit of the comely Roman Carmens, the cigarette makers.

By the mid-1900s Trastevere had come to represent the real Roman ethnicity: its coarse folklore, its vernacular songs, its cuisine attracted the "proper" Romans from across the Tiber. The Roman bourgeoisie came to Trastevere to rub elbows with the blue collars and have dinner, in a kind of gastronomic slumming, at the local *osterie*, eating tripe, oxtails, and spaghetti *alla carrettiera*, "mule-driver style." At the beginning of the twenty-first century the once-edge-of-town Trastevere has become central, and Viale Trastevere has become a major thoroughfare, a never-ending river of traffic to and from downtown and the new outermost *quartieri* of Rome; Trastevere has become an international tourist destination. Its few *osterie* have proliferated and upgraded into an infinite number of *trattorie, ristoranti*, and pubs. Its nightclubs are overcrowded and noisy till dawn, to the great desperation of the few remaining indigenous inhabitants. Blue-collar Trastevere has been gentrified, its old buildings remodeled and modernized, and is now inhabited by the fashionably rich, the expatriate, the long-term tourist. (It is said that today English is the official language of Trastevere.) From the twenty-first-century flowering roof gardens, one can look back at the unbroken continuity of Trastevere's previous centuries, and wonder what's in line for the future.

Time has also brought in a sophisticated, intellectual side: Trastevere now sports, alongside the few remaining artisans' shops, a number of art galleries, bookstores, and cultural centers. One such is Bibli. The bookstore proper — much bigger than one would expect from its unpretentious doorway on little-trafficked Via dei Fienaroli — meanders through several rooms lined with books, opens into a larger hall, and then sidesteps into a small cafeteria/coffeeshop. The aroma of espresso and fresh-baked pastries gives the whole premises a comfortable, homey atmosphere. Bibli is managed by three partners who keep Trastevere intellectually hopping with book presentations, prose and poetry readings, panel and public discussions of literary subjects, and, now and then, classic guitar, jazz, and chamber-music concerts. The place has also — to keep up with the times — Internet stations. Gabriella Maggiullo is one of the three partners; she is in charge of events and, in a very relaxed fashion, of public relations. Elegant and attractive, it is my guess that she is in her late forties; she could easily fit in to a Cambridge or San Francisco bookstore. I ask her if in the last five years — that is how long Bibli has been in operation — she has noticed any changes in the Roman cultural, literary scene.

Over coffee, she tells me that she doesn't think so. New books are published, but there is not much really new. Most of the blockbusters are foreign, in great part American. Recently she has presented a few new Italian books, edited by experienced, attentive publishers: "They are good, pleasant books but definitely not masterpieces. None to dethrone the 1940s, 1950s, and 1960s masters, the Levis, the Moravias, the Silones. . . . But the public is there; if we do something interesting, they respond. They are of all ages, but a great many are young, of all social levels, and that is really beautiful to see in this *rione*." Gabriella jumps the borders of Trastevere to talk about young people in more general, cultural terms; she finds that young people in Rome, today, are not as vacuous as people like to think. They do have a lot of problems, but that's a global situation. It is a particular moment for them: all, or most of the ideologies have fallen; it is a period of transition. A lot of them are lost, unmoored.

"We see them here in Trastevere on Saturday nights," she continues. "They get drunk, they do drugs, they get involved in terrible accidents. But if we can talk to them, one on one, I find that they have a lot of good qualities, and perhaps are even more informed than we were at their age. They have more possibilities to know and to learn than we ever had, they are exposed to a lot of new sources."

"Like Bibli?" I ask.

"Yes, why not?" she answers. "We are in a particular position to feel the pulse of the young and be in tune with it: Bibli has books, it has literature, it has music, it offers space for social contacts, and many young people come and are interested in all these things. They are sincerely interested in all cultural, intellectual fields." A very promising attitude for the future, she thinks. She is encouraged: among the widespread materialism, she believes that in Rome there is a certain intellectual ferment.

In Rome now there are other establishments like Bibli, she acknowledges, but Bibli was the first. I ask her what made her and her partners choose this location.

"Of all the *rioni*," she says, "we chose Trastevere because it is an old historical place, a particular place, loved by young and old, a really Roman place."

I mention to her that while talking about Trastevere with friends, they told me to make sure I visited Bibli.

"I know, talking of Trastevere today it's impossible to ignore Bibli," she says proudly. Then, smiling: "In America you have a lot of bookstores similar to ours, in San Francisco, Boston, New York, Dallas; they have everything, even more than we do, especially money. But one thing they do not have is Rome."

She is preaching to the choir. When we had to choose where to live, it took us no time to decide: Trastevere. Gwen had previously lived in Trastevere for seven, as she puts it, unforgettable years.

For this stay, our apartment is at the end of Vicolo del Cedro, past a maze of *vicoli*, streets not much larger than an arm span, just below the top of the Gianicolo, one of the Seven Hills of ancient Rome. On the fourth floor of an old building (no elevator), the apartment is full of light even on cloudy days: there are no taller buildings to shade us. All the windows offer a partial view of the cityscape, but it is from the terrace above, on the roof, that that view is almost 360 degrees. From the living room, a spiral staircase leads to a large roof terrace and garden: from there, above the Trastevere rooftops, you can see most of Rome. At our back, on the Gianicolo, is the unmistakable silhouette of the statue of Garibaldi; there is a small terrace below it. This terrace is the site of a daily ritual: a few artillery soldiers roll out a field gun and, at the command of a sergeant, exactly at noon, fire a shot. We are so close that our windows rattle; Romans set their watches by the blast.

Past the Gianicolo we can see the top of Saint Peter's dome, and then Monte Mario's observatory, and then, to the right, here comes Castel Sant'Angelo followed by the white bulk of the Palazzo di Giustizia; then the Pincio Terrace, Trinita' dei Monti, and the Campidoglio tower above the forums. Cupolas and bell towers, big and small, pepper the scape. The bell tower of the Basilica of Santa Maria in Trastevere is so close we can see its bells swing when they toll. And toll they do, every single hour on the hour and every fifteen minutes after that. It is a sound one gets accustomed to, incredibly soothing at night, almost a lullaby, the big bell bonging the hours, the small one following, binging the quarters.

The view from the terrace is the reward for having climbed seventy-two steps up from street level. It is part of our daily routine to shop at the open-air market, or at the small groceries and bakeries, to buy the daily newspaper and head back home. We could easily revert to shopping for a week's hoard at the supermarket, but it would not match the pleasure of talking and discussing daily events with the vendors. In addition to the social inter- course, the trips — down the stairs, down the *vicoli* to the square, from there to market and back up the stairs with loaded shopping bags — are our daily physical workouts, cheered on by the smiles and the *buon giorno!* and How're you today? of the artisans, artists, and merchants whose shops line the way. We also like to think of the routine as a drill for our memory: better remember every item on the shopping list, or you go without, or down and up you go again. Our daily journey makes us feel in touch not only with the immediate neighborhood but with the whole city. We feel like a living part of Rome; the cobblestones feel friendly and lead to anywhere in the city. Or the world.

For a long time all roads have led to Rome. For my mother they all led to the Ghetto, the Jewish *rione* in the center of the city. She went there, with me in tow, to shop for her shoes and for the family's fabrics, which went directly from there into the hands of our family tailor. She went to the Ghetto — as she would prosely- tize to relatives and friends — because of the shopping values: ex- cellent goods at great prices. But I knew better: she went there because she had a great time. As soon as she entered a shop, the shopkeepers, by now old friends, would gush with welcome, bring out a chair, and send out for a round of espressos along with a soft drink for me. Before the incredible number of fabrics were brought out for her inspection, news of the weather and of the re- spective families was discussed to exhaustion. Then the commer- cial intercourse could begin: after the interminable choosing of the goods, the interminable bargaining could begin, ending with my mother's obvious rejoicing in the good deal she had struck (she was too ebullient, too extroverted to keep a poker face). The shopkeepers would have a mock fit of desperation, declaring themselves ready for the poorhouse; then with the good-byes and come-agains they would hand me a candy. I came to despise those long, boring sessions and the penetrating smell of the fabrics that stuck to my nostrils for hours. I knew that my mother took me along not for the privilege of my company, but, as she freely admitted to all, to keep an eye on me, to keep me on a leash. She was convinced I was the most mischievous eight-year-old she had ever set eyes upon, someone she could not trust to leave at home with a younger sister and an older brother. She was convinced that my ingenuity for mischief was unlimited; I took that as a challenge and tried to outdo myself. It got us involved in a vicious circle of action and reaction that we were able to break only many years later, when we discovered we had been the best of friends all along. And when she was gone, I began to think of those Ghetto excursions with longing, still able to taste the shopkeepers' candies: jaw-breaking, hard-sugar red balls with a spicy, fragrant coriander center.

The Ghetto is that section of the city that rests in the shadow of the Capitoline Hill, edged at the southern side by the Theater of Marcellus and the Portico d'Ottavia. The old Tiber River fences it on the west; from its chestnut-tree-shaded banks, the massive, solemn synagogue supervises the small enclave of streets, alleys, and little squares — perhaps no more than ten city blocks — that is Rome's Jewish quarter. Within a radius of ten walking minutes are the church of the Ara Coeli, Michelangelo's Piazza del Campidoglio, the forums, the Arch of Titus, the Colosseum, the Vestal Virgins' Temple, the Arch of Janus, the Palatine Hill, the Pantheon . . . all that miraculous wealth of architecture and history that is ancient Rome. But they all are mere shadows of past history, preserved in lifeless stone and marble. In contrast, the humble bricks of the Ghetto are alive, like the Ghetto itself, witnesses of the oldest Jewish community in the Western world, living uninterruptedly within and with Rome since before the age of Christ.

The story of the Roman Ghetto was told to me by Signor

Luciano Tas — journalist, essayist, and writer of *Gli Ebrei di Roma* (The Jews of Rome) and *Storia degli Ebrei Italiani* (The History of the Italian Jews). We met at the editorial offices of *Shalom,* a monthly magazine of national and international Jewish affairs, located on the Isola Tiberina almost directly across from the synagogue. The minuscule island is in the middle of the Tiber; crammed onto it are two huge buildings: one is the Catholic Fatebenefratelli Hospital, and the other, opposite, is the Jewish Infirmary and Clinic, attached to the church of Saint Bartholomew. Proof, if it were needed, of the old coexistence of Jews and Christians in Rome.

Signor Tas has a very expressive face. He uses it as a visual aid to his exposition, to underline or emphasize a passage; his diction is fast and his voice clear, resonating in the spartan environment of the office.

"The documented signs of the existence of a Jewish community in Rome go as far back as 159 B.C.," he says. "It was undoubtedly part of a diplomatic mission. The community grew, in size and importance, in 144 and 138 B.C. when additional missions were sent to sign pacts of allegiance and friendship between the kingdom of Judea and Rome. The resident Jews were fully accepted by Rome, free to practice their religious beliefs without interference; with time, many Jews assumed positions of prominence in the life of the city. As a matter of fact, compared to other ethnic groups, they enjoyed preferential treatment: when Rome engaged in the Palestinian wars, many of the Jewish prisoners brought to Rome as slaves were allowed to be ransomed by the Jewish community and given their freedom. Others, with impeccable rationale and more than a little guile "here Signor Tas chuckles, his eyes smiling, as if witnessing some childish mischief," convinced their captors that a freed, grateful Jew would be much more productive and valuable than an enslaved, morose Jew."

Signor Tas's office windows look on Trastevere, which is where — he gestures with his hand — the early Jewish settlement was located; it grew to about ten or twelve thousand souls, it is believed, and expanded across the river to where today's Ghetto is, more or less. Even though considered Roman citizens, the community kept to itself. However, with time some of the old Jewish habits and rites took on Roman colorings, and vice versa, in a kind of ongoing osmosis. Signor Tas mentions, as an example, the relaxation of the Jewish rule that decreed that the roasted Pascal lamb had to be consumed exclusively within the confines of the temple. Hardly a coincidence, he says, that *abbacchio al forno*, roast baby lamb, has become one of the classic Roman dishes.

The lives of Rome and of the Jewish community parallel each other through the ups and downs, the good times and the bad times of history, even during the growth of the Roman church's political power. In the eleventh and twelfth centuries many Roman Jews had positions of importance at the papal court, especially as doctors and financial counselors. By the end of the thirteenth century the mood began to change, and some anti-Jewish laws were issued. They were disregarded for a long time with what Signor Tas calls "a curious attitude. The laws were frequently considered by the Jewish populace no more than suggestions, an attitude that still remains as a Roman trait."

A truly black era for the community began with the obsessive quest of the Inquisition to convert the world to Christianity. Roman Jews, living within the shell of Rome itself, were somewhat more protected than those living outside. They suffered humiliation, insults, and heavy taxes, but were spared persecution, torture, and death by fire. Finally in 1553, Cardinal Paolo Carafa ordered all Jewish sacred books burned and then, in 1555, when elected Pope Paolo IV, decided to cage the Roman Jews in their 'ghetto. (Rome was divided into *borghi* — burgs. A small, diminutive *borgo* is a *borghetto*, which contracted becomes *ghetto*. This, possibly, is the origin of the word.) Paolo IV had tall walls erected around that small section of the city, and its few gates were shut and locked at sunset: all Roman Jews were to remain inside until dawn. They were allowed only the most menial labor, such as rag pickers and junk collectors. The restriction lasted three hundred years, the range, strictness, and enforcement of the rules varying with the whims and humors of the ruling pope. Ironically, the purpose of the Ghetto's instigator was to preserve the community as it was, to show future generations what living in error meant, a kind of visual, explicit documentation. In fact the tight, ungilded cage protected the Roman Jewish community from the pogroms, peregrinations, and homelessness to which all other European Jews were subjected. With the waning of the temporal power of the pope, the Ghetto walls came tumbling down in 1848: the Roman Jews were Romans again, alive and on the same spot where their ancestors had been living for eighty consecutive generations. No other Jew can make that claim. Or, for that matter — says Signor Tas — no other Roman.

The walls came down, but the name remained Ghetto. There is no denigration attached to it: it is just another one of today's *rioni*.

Via Portico d'Ottavia runs parallel to and two blocks in from the Tiber. It is the backbone of the Ghetto to which the ribs of small streets and alleys are attached. The style of the buildings that line it is that of proper mid-nineteenth-century Rome. Some facades are embedded with parts of Roman ruins, while others carry a fascia of old stones carved with Latin inscriptions; many protect from view the hodgepodge addition of rooms, landings, half floors, and roofs that sprouted through the years as the need for space grew. One building, on Via Sant'Angelo in Pescheria, grew around an old Roman column, which still goes straight through someone's bedroom.

Classic palazzi of Roman noble families look on the Ghetto and give their name to colorful little squares: Piazza Lovatelli, Piazza Campitelli, Piazza Cenci. The prettiest of them all, Piazza Mattei, encloses one of the most elegant fountains in Rome: the diminutive (compared to other Roman fountains) Fontana delle Tartarughe. Four slim adolescents, their backs to the center post, lift four tortoises to the upper bowl of the fountain. Their dancing steps are so harmonious that the whole fountain seems to spin slowly around like a carousel. The legend attached to it is as whimsical as the fountain itself: it seems that a duke in the Mattei family, an avid gambler, lost more than he could afford at the gaming table. The news reached the father of his fiancée, who immediately rescinded the engagement — and its huge dowry. The duke, to show to his ex-fiancée and ex-future-father-in-law that his wealth and spending ability were still intact, commissioned Taddeo Landini to cast the bronze fountain on short order (a fortnight, says the legend, but that seems excessive boasting). The fountain was positioned so that it could to be seen from one of Palazzo Mattei's windows. Father and daughter were invited to the palace and casually brought to that particular window: the shutters were thrown open and, voilà, there was the fountain. "For you, my dear!" said the duke. Father and daughter were duly impressed; the duke's gamble worked and he gained a wife and a dowry. Rome (legend true or false) gained a splendid fountain.

But now the integrity of the *rione* that survived persecutions, wars, famine, and plague is beginning to break under the attack of the new affluence. Its central location and historical appeal make its real estate coveted and extremely expensive. Either due to attrition or because the money offered is too good to pass up, the old families' apartments are vacated, sold, and "renovated" — gutted and turned into deluxe modern dwellings for the super-rich. Fortunately, the law for the protection of the National Artistic Patrimony has been able to save the facades and shells of the palazzi, saving the look of the Ghetto.

Thankfully, the commercial character of the *rione* has not been impaired. The Ghetto is still the place where enlightened shoppers go, both for bargains and for quality.

"We have been in business for seven generations," says Bruno Limentani, dapper, smiling, and direct. "We began as rag pickers, empty bottle and demijohn collectors." It takes a strong imagination to connect him even remotely with rags, and it strikes me how many Roman Jews count time in terms of past generations; years are quoted in numbers only if you want to be picky.

"Today we carry the whole line of tablewares, all the top names: St. Louis, Richard-Ginori, Rosenthal, Stuart, Waterford for crystal . . ." Ditta Leone Limentani, Bruno's company, is located just across the Portico d'Ottavia from the ruins that give the street its name, and occupies the entire basement of a palazzo the size of a city block. Ten thousand square feet of narrow corridors and rooms are lined floor to ceiling with goods, ranging from classic to the most modern designs: china, silver, crystal, and the whole gamut of kitchen tools, implements, and gadgets. A stroll through the store is a dream come true for anybody, professional or amateur, who has ever used a stove or set a table.

"On that black day of October 16, 1943, Fascists and Nazis bulled through our china shop and destroyed anything they could not steal. . . . My father and grandfather were among the very few able to flee when the Nazis sealed off the Ghetto and dragged everybody away. Not many returned . . ."

The Limentani store — a veritable phoenix, like the rest of the Ghetto — was reborn at the end of the war.

The whole historical experience has made the Roman Jews an incredibly resilient race, Bruno remarks; being forced to survive for more than three centuries living by their wits, bartering, recycling, and trading, has made of the Roman Jews a class of particularly adept, clever, and successful merchants. So successful that most Jewish shops and commercial activities have expanded from the Ghetto and taken over nearby areas; their visibility is so high that many Romans, erroneously, think the Ghetto is bigger than it actually is. Without a break in continuity, one passes from the Ghetto to the neighboring *rione* of Regola without realizing it. Its narrow streets are overparked with cars but alive with shops: from foods to raw wool, old silver to antique furniture, fabrics to shoes, fish to meats, old books to clothes . . . there are few things one cannot find there. A frequent banner across a shop window is: PREZZI ALL'INGROSSO! Yes, we can get it for you wholesale!

Many of these narrow, busy streets open up onto Campo de' Fiori, the oldest and most colorful Roman open-air market: from

7 A.M. to 1 P.M. it is crowded with stalls and carts hawking any-thing that, raw or cooked, seasonal or not, is fit to enrich a table. The still-life displays are works of art, and they have inspired many artists. And cooks. Even if, as one vendor says with a touch of sadness, "the number of stalls is diminishing every year." Times have changed: people do not spend much time shopping or cooking. The old generations would go from *banco* to *banchetto*, from stall to stall, shopping half the morning for the right thing, and cooking it during the other half. Now they are disappearing and the young people do not cook so much anymore; they shop at the supermarket or eat out. Also, a lot of foreigners have moved into this area, and they do not seem to care so much for food, for the special things.

Roberto and Mirella's family has been operating one of these stalls for four generations. When I stop by to chat they are just set-ting up for the day their display of vegetables, greens, and fruits. Roberto is making a construction of artichokes, and my ques-tioning doesn't interrupt his careful building. "I am making my own pyramid!" he jokes; his family name is Faraoni (pharaohs). While he builds, Signora Mirella cleans and prepares artichokes: she shucks a few leaves, then, vegetable in the left hand, sharp paring knife in the right, as fast as a lathe she turns the artichokes into yellow-green rosebuds. She wets them with lemon juice, and in fifteen seconds a *carciofo* is ready to be sold, ready to cook it any way you want.

I ask Signor Roberto why the Ghetto has adopted the artichoke as its own. "All of Rome has, not just the Jews." He goes on to say that the artichoke grows as easily as a weed: "Once, they tell me, they grew in the Forum's ruins and thrived, with little or no care, in any free inch of ground." True or not, Roberto brings up the theme of cheap, good, and available. He proceeds to tell me the *carciofo è buono e bello:* in the artichoke, goodness and beauty go hand in hand. "Look at it!" He holds an artichoke at arm's length, revolving it slowly. "If nature had not invented it, I'm sure Leonardo da Vinci would have!"

Once the stalls are removed and the street cleaners have swept
and hosed down the square, Campo de' Fiori continues to change
faces as the day goes on. First are the children: free from school,
they take over and flitter around the square in innocent games of
pickup soccer and, like the swallows darting overhead, fill the air
with their trills. Their play is like a cleansing of the past character
of the square: its cheerful name, mistakenly reminiscent of a
flower market, is actually derived from *Campus Florae*, Flora
being Pompeius Magnum's voluptuous lover and the owner/man-
ager — on her donated *Campus* — of a *hospitius*, a hotel or house
of ill repute. At one time or another similar "hotels" were located
around the square, permissible under Italian law. Now they are
gone — the last one in the 1960s, when houses of prostitution
were declared illegal.

As a reminder of another activity, on the center of the square
stands the statue of somber, hooded Giordano Bruno, philoso-
pher, poet, teacher, a man of all-around vivid intellect, but, alas,
also a heretic. For this sin — to give him a taste of Hell on Earth —
on February 17, 1600, he was burned at the stake on this very spot.
A not-unique event on this square: on the same spot — before and
after Bruno — religious, political and other common criminals
were hanged, quartered, or burned. The ceremonies were public
and, just to be orderly and civilized, followed a set ritual. This included the Brotherhood of Saint John the Beheaded (from the
name of the street where the brotherhood resided); friars, monks,
and a chaplain who, in their role as Company of Comforters, spent
the night before the execution in prayer with the condemned,
trying to convince them to repent, to admit to the error of their
ways and thoughts. From a Comforter's diary, witness to Bruno's
execution: ". . . but he remaining so damn obstinate in his intellectual sin and vanities, he was brought to Campo de' Fiori and
here, undressed and tied to a pole, was burned alive, all the time
accompanied by the exhortations of our Brotherhood, singing the
litanies, to mend his ways, to let go of his obstinacy which, finally,

brought an end to his miserable and unhappy life." The tone is matter-of-fact; you can almost read between the lines a "Nothing personal, kid. Sorry, but we told you so . . ."

Once the children leave to do their homework, the marble steps at the base of Giordano's monument are taken over by a committee of nannies who exchange gossip while keeping an eye on their perambulated charges.

In the light of sunset, the pastel colors of Campo de' Fiori seem more vivid and at the same time muted; the mood of the square is now more sedate, more like a large parlor, intimate. The sun barely brushes the houses of different shapes and colors that, set all around, form an almost solid facade, pierced only by the seven small streets that access the square. In the elongated, rectangular shape of Campo (real Romans omit the flowers), the big fountain gurgles at the northern end, the mossy edge of its upper bowl spilling silvery threads of water into the lower one. Fruits and vegetables were refreshed there in the morning; now sparrows and pigeons make it their private pool. The field is taken up by sedate groups of adults — by their age, dress, attitude, they can easily be described as golden-agers on their evening outing — who convene to discuss politics or, more ebulliently, the more serious subject of *calcio*, soccer. The many bars, *trattorie*, and wine shops will offer them the relief of a glass. Come April (earlier in mild weather) these same establishments will set out, around the perimeter of the square, chairs and tables that will fill with tourists for lunch or early dinner. Their subdued chatting and folding of maps will be replaced later — the street lamps now painting the square with light and shadow like a stage setting — by the more boisterous conviviality of the locals; it will last, spring to late autumn, weather permitting, till close to midnight. Then, the square that was the Campo becomes the turf of peripatetic friends who, encouraged by a parting glass of wine and cocooned by the deserted square, discuss in confessional tones deep philosophical, political, religious thoughts — forgotten by morning — followed by interminable good-byes, all worth many walks around the sleepy square.

But it is a short sleep, practically a nap: Irish-style pubs have inserted themselves on the Campo's northern end. Their crowds of young people spill outside and take over the silence, shattering it with noise that reverberates almost till dawn. As the last insomniacs trickle away, the first *banchetto* roll in with the first light of day, ready to set up, rain or shine, for another market day.

Giordano Bruno is there, dark and morose, surveying the scene.

The somber presence of Giordano Bruno, together with the preparation for a new day's activity, brings to my mind another *quartiere*, the *quartiere* Coppedè. Actually, it is a small section of the much larger *quartiere* Salario, which, among all its good or bad attributes, includes the one — definitely special for me — of being the *quartiere* where I was born. Even if only a part of my gauzy memories of middle-school days, the *quartiere* is real and as improbable as its name. Gino Coppedè was the romantic, pre-Disneyesque architect with the so un-Italian name who, around 1910, created a whole enclave, a few city blocks of design and inspiration. At first sight the *quartiere* looks as if it came out of a fairy tale, its appearance and reality removed from that of the rest of the city, and perhaps best seen on a misty day, in a dreamy, gauzy, soft light. Coming from the chaotic traffic and the frenzied commercial activity of Via Tagliamento near Piazza Buenos Aires, you dogleg back on Via Dora and soon pass under a huge arch, a sort of Bridge of Sighs with an enormous wrought-iron chandelier dangling under it. Spanning the two anchor buildings, their walls covered with pseudomythical, pseudoallegorical polychrome murals, the arch is the *quartiere*'s impressive entrance (there are other means of access, but none so studied). Halfway up a corner, a little Madonna shrine sheds a feeble, perennial light in the penumbra, blessing the entering wayfarer. Past the arch, all is quiet and subdued like a stage after a performance or, better yet, during a rehearsal's lunch break; something makes you feel that noise and action have gone on before and will resume again sometime. At the moment the only movement or sound comes from the water of the round, pseudo-baroque fountain of Piazza Mincio (a square that is really square), around which all the streets of the *quartiere* seem to flow. I wonder if it is coincidental that the streets are all named for Italian rivers.

Having absorbed the first impression, a visitor will start noticing the hybridization of architectural styles; pseudo-Renaissance, pseudo-Byzantine, pseudo-Romanesque with a pinch of baroque thrown in. The complex is full of details: a gargoyle here, a frieze there, a classic Greek swirl of acanthus, an outside brick stairway climbing to a vaulted entrance, a turret, a scary lion mask above a portal, above another a huge spider — venomous, I always thought. Monsters and dragons, it must have taken a lifetime worth of imagination for Signor Coppedè to figure it all out, and perhaps the same amount of time for a visitor to discover it all.

When I was very young, I always approached the *quartiere* Coppedè with a mixture of curiosity and some apprehension. My familiarity with it was the result of a choice I had to make almost every school morning: I could spend my daily allowance for transportation on a trolley-car ticket, or walk the two and a half miles to school. I chose to walk; the trolley took my money only in the most severe weather. At about one-quarter of the way to school I had to pass through the Coppedè, each time discovering a new feature, a new twisty detail. That was fun; the apprehension came from the fact that I was walking in a world foreign to mine, a world in which I imagined existed very rich, ethereal people. People who had their milk delivered to their doorsteps (I could see that), people whose maids — in frilly white aprons and bonnets — were too delicate and haughty to go to the milk store as our maid did. People who would watch my progress from behind heavy maroon drapes, staring pale faces more suspected than seen, their presence revealed, only sometimes, by the flutter of a lacy curtain. I then walked erect, my step purposeful, looking at their windows out of the corner of my eye, my gaze fixed on the incredible opulence of their houses' walls, acting as if I belonged, making as if I were one of them, fooling them. But I knew I couldn't: kids did not belong, I had never heard a young voice there.

My Coppedè passage lasted no more than ten minutes; my return to Earth was marked, just at the edge of the *quartiere*, when I walked by the wrought-iron fence of a *villetta*, a small villa belonging to Beniamino Gigli. It was, then, the closest I ever came to Fame, Gigli being the most famous tenor Italy proudly gave to the world, a national idol and treasure. The *villetta* had its own decorated turret and was surrounded by a garden. A few times I saw a portly gentleman conversing with an obsequious gardener; a few times I thought he smiled at me (I blushed and waved back), but I never heard him singing. Nonetheless, I boasted of the experience, feeling a notch or two above my Gigli-deprived school companions. Added to my morning's experiences (and afternoon's, too, on my way back) was a purely sensual one: a few blocks after Coppedè and Gigli, an all-pervasive heavenly aroma beckoned me to the retail door of Biscotti Gentilini & Co., a cookie factory my personal angel had managed to place halfway to school. There I traded some of my trolley money for a mixed bag of the freshest-baked biscotti — the ones broken in production, naturally — picking them, one by one, from the reject bins. In school I was a happy student, waiting with all my schoolmates for the final bell, anxious to go home. But I had one more reason than the others did.

Recently I took Gwen to see the Coppedè. We walked my old route, and she found it as I had described it. But the monsters are not as scary, their visages softened by time; the frescoes less vivid, grayed by soot, the gardens somewhat unkempt. Many shutters are closed, hiding inside what the portals now say are Foreign Trading Missions or Commercial Companies, Ltd. Like the rest of Rome the streets are lined with parked cars, some — an unsettling sight — with weeds growing under their tires. But we see no people; the garden of Beniamino Gigli's *villetta*, its ornate wrought-iron fence now backed by solid metal sheets, is blocked off from view.

The Biscotti Gentilini & Co. has moved out, taking its aroma and its bins of rejects to some unknown place out of town, but not out of my memory.

Eating in Rome

De ovo romani

A LL COUNTRIES accept the egg as a natural foodstuff and use it without much fuss. Only the Romans, with centuries-old tradition and experience, used it, and still do, with mystical abandon.

The Roman egg has mythical properties: it is Super Egg, a nostrum good for all contingencies at all stages of life.

Of all Roman eggs, *primus inter pares*, the best of the best, is the *ovetto fresco di giornata*, the day-fresh egg. A day-fresh is the one that goes from production to consumption in the same day. It appears on the Roman gastronomic scene with the beginning of life itself. Nursing mothers are put on a diet of day-fresh eggs: it makes for abundant and nutritious milk. Affluent families once farmed out infants, especially sickly boys, to peasant wet nurses: since they were in the country, went the assumption, they had direct access to a supply of day-fresh eggs or, even better, still-warm eggs, eggs so fresh they still retain the chicken's body warmth. And so, freely flows the milk, a nourishment that makes real men out of many Romans.

The day-fresh appears again at the age of the first serious

Roman tantrum. Keepers of uncontrollable little beasts are advised to serve them *un ovetto fresco battuto*. "Beat a very fresh egg in a cup," wrote Pellegrino Artusi (1820–1911), godfather of Italian cookbook writers, in *Science in the Kitchen, and the Art of Eating Well, A Practical Manual for the Family*, "add plenty of sugar, beat it until fluffy and golden. Then put the cup in front of the child: he will devour it, make a mess of his face and be happy again! Alas! If only all food were innocent as this, how many less hysterical persons would walk the earth!!"

When a child reaches school age, the day-fresh becomes the giver of clarity and sharpness of mind. It appears as *uovo da bere*, which, to leave well enough alone, means that the egg is not improved upon: it is drunk *al naturale*, raw. A Roman child does not exist who has not been cajoled by a loving mother to drink a day-fresh. Break the pointed end of the shell, remove a portion of it and, as from a bottle, bend your head back and swallow the egg. Or do your best. Otherwise Mamma will help you with a well-timed whack (at this, my own mother was a real virtuoso) between your shoulder blades. And down it goes. Not too long ago there would be a rush on day-fresh eggs at exam time. Obviously, the eggs could be fresh only if they came from farms close to the city, but unscrupulous vendors were known to import aging, immaculately clean eggs from foreign countries. To fob them off as day-fresh, they smeared them with substances appropriate to family-farm conditions. A high number of failing students in the merchant's neighborhood revealed the fraud, and the impostors, it is said, were thrown into the Tiber together with their useless eggs.

As elsewhere, adolescence in Rome is marred by pimples. The cure is a cosmetic miracle: the egg. Break it, separate the yolk from the white. Mix half a glass of water with the white and beat it foamy. Apply to the face or other pimpled areas. Pimples disappear or, at least, are temporarily obscured by the foam. Mothers also consider the mixture an extremely good palliative for sunburns, better and much cheaper than all the pharmaceutical products available on the market.

The saved yolk, not to be wasted, is transferred to a spoon and, sprinkled with salt, pepper, and a few drops of lemon juice, becomes *uovo all'ostrica*, "egg oyster-style." Eat it as you would an oyster on the half shell. You may even like it, as many Romans do. If not, consolation rests in the newly acquired stamina and muscle tone.

It is during manhood that the Roman egg, in liqueur form, delivers its most important wallop: the promise of immediate, matchless, boundless, heroic virility. It is no secret: Rodolfo Valentino was brought up on VOV. Some inspired medieval alchemist added eggs in their shell to lemon juice, sugar, and alcohol and came up with pure liquid gold. The commercial bottled version, still found in bars and liquor shops, has a Latin motto on the label: *Viresque Acquirit Bibendo*, loosely translated, "Virile strength is just a swallow away." The concoction can be easily made at home: Take a jar, put well-washed, unbroken fresh eggs in it, add lemon juice to cover. Put in a dark place, and in a few days the shells' calcium is dissolved by and into the juice. Shake, add the right measure of sugar and alcohol, and let rest sealed for a week or so. When ready, a thimbleful of the golden potion will transform a Roman into a red-blooded, iron-boned, glistening-toothed, irresistible bullock, and his next *avventura galante* will be a roaring, wall-shaking sex feast. VOV is what Roman orgies are made of.

The ravages attendant to such bouts of virility pose no problem to the Roman male. What's left of him is returned to its pristine form and complexion by *zabaglione*, a creamy concoction of eggs, sugar, and marsala. A parfait glass of *zabaglione* and the dark circles under the eyes disappear, the vision is clear, the shoulders erect, the step bouncy and leading to the next VOV. *Zabaglione*-fed gladiators succumb only to VOV-fed lions. Pity.

And Roman life goes on. The why is one of the mysteries for which medical science has no answer. Following modern theories about extravagant consumption of eggs, Rome should be awash in a sea of cholesterol. Yet statistics say Romans have lower levels of the dreadful stuff, supposedly, than anybody else in the world. But it is inching up: traditionalists do not blame the egg, but point the finger at the greater consumption of butter and steaks and to the Romans' absolute dependence on automotive transportation.

But nowadays, the supremacy of the egg has subsided some: its natural, elegant simplicity — both in content and packaging — has to compete with modern nutritional fads, more appealing to today's market (and advertisers) ready to propel the newest silver bullets. Magic mushrooms, ginkgo nuts, an alphabet of multicolored vitamins, and Viagra itself make the simple egg and valiant vov look, in comparison, quite dull. Pity.

Mystical egg aside, Roman cuisine is a paradox: if the word *cuisine* implies an art of refined ingredients and techniques, Roman cuisine, you will be told, does not exist.

Leaving out the historical inheritance of Apicius (a first-century-A.D. Roman, more glutton than gourmet, author of detailed cookbooks — ". . . take a milk-fed piglet, stuff it with finely cut roasted thrushes and fig-peckers, and with snails taken out of their shells . . ." — who committed suicide when his finances could not keep up with the desires of his stomach), the roots of today's popular cookery go back to the seventeenth century, or thereabouts, when sheep were still at pasture on the Seven Hills, grazing among the ruins of aqueducts and forums. It was a cookery of shepherds and orchard farmers, of simple, poor, and proud men, to whom anything that could be labeled effeminate or mawkish was unacceptable. And the women of Rome, cut from the same cloth, disliked elaborate productions at the stove and focused on affordability, substance, and staying power. So the traditional Roman dishes are based on simple, genuine, local ingredients, most with assertive tastes, cooked without fuss so as to let the main ingredient dominate the dish. The elaborate cuisine, the rare and expensive ingredients, the crystal and silver, were reserved for the tables of cardinals and prelates, princes and nobles, cooked and garnished by foreign, or foreign-trained, *chefs de cuisine* who offered a fashionably French, non-Roman menu.

So here come the hearty Roman soups of pasta and beans — the unforgettable *pasta e ceci*, pasta and chickpeas; the plentiful Roman *abbacchio*, the very young lamb, described by Juvenal, Roman poet of the second century, as "the most tender of the flock, unsullied by grass, more full of milk than of blood . . ."; the gutsy use of cheap and sturdy *frattaglie* (tripe, liver, kidney, heart, and so forth, all the poor cuts "in between" the good cuts — loins, steaks, ribs, and briskets — that went to the rich). The list of traditional Roman ingredients and dishes is not long, but it is memorable: the famous *pajiata*, the intestine of milk-fed veal, served over hearty rigatoni; the *coda alla vaccinara*, oxtail cow-herd-style; the *pisellini novelli*, the youngest of peas, sweet as honey; the *carciofi romaneschi*, the native, meaty Roman artichokes; and then *cicoria*, the bitter, tiny dandelion greens, wild as the wild *rughetta* of the Roman fields, now known the world over as arugula. To balance the sharp, punchy flavor of the *pecorino romano*, sheep cheese, here comes the *fava romanesca*: one bite of cheese accompanied by a few beans, shucked at the table, of the freshest and sweetest fava. And then the gentle *ricotta* cheese, consumed as a table cheese or to make *torta di ricotta*, the exclusively Roman-Jewish cheesecake; and the *giuncata*, the softest, fresh cream cheese left to curdle in *giunchi*, containers of woven reeds, Heaven in a basket.

On the whole it is an unpretentious, straightforward cookery, sharing a particular place equally in a Roman's heart and stomach. It is direct, it hides no surprises: even Gioacchino Belli, the most Roman of Roman vernacular poets, used this gastronomy in his sonnets to underline a particular mood or to make a point, or, simply, for an appropriate rhyme. No Roman will miss the subtlety when he mentions *costolette d'abbacchio a scottadito* (baby lamb cutlets) or *storione in fricando* (sturgeon stew) to sharpen a sarcasm about the food of the clergy and nobles in contrast with *fagioli co' le cotiche* (beans and pork rind) of the *popolino*, the common people of mid-nineteenth-century Rome.

The traditional Roman culinary repertoire takes a milder tone with the advent of the middle class. At times it is rejected altogether by the new bourgeoisie as vulgar, then becomes fashionable again as a form of gastronomic slumming (the peak of fashion was to go to an *osteria* — the humblest of Roman eateries — to be insulted and cursed at with *parolacce*, dirty language, by a mock-rough *oste*, host/owner).

Now traditional cooking is enjoying a serious revival and is accepted as a valid expression of the local palate and culture, even if allowing for one aberration: to the great enjoyment — and milking — of tourists, several establishments still operate with waiters donning the togas of ancient Rome or with accoutrements suitable to the *Roma Papalina*, one to the accompaniment of a lyre, the other of a guitar.

The revival is strong, yet many Roman dishes have been hybridized, either to satisfy the *ex-urbis* tastes of the large non-Roman citizenry or, worse, to please the demands of the extravagant numbers of tourists who think they are being served the local fare. It is not unusual to hear visitors — mostly Americans, I am ashamed to say — complaining that the fettuccine Alfredo has no tomatoes or mushrooms (neither should ever appear!), as found in the real dish they were served in New Jersey; or that the Neapolitan pizza here is terribly bland — no pepperoni! (Which, by the way, is an exclusively American invention.) In the city of paradoxes, we can add an imported one: food is one of the local attractions, yet many visitors are disappointed that it doesn't even come close to the same as served in the good old USA.

One gastronomic expression that still meets with the unconditional approval of Romans and foreigners alike is *pizza bianca* — white pizza or *pizza romana* — which has nothing in common with the pizza known the world over. *Pizza bianca* is a flat bread, baked in a five-foot-long by one-foot-wide slab, slathered with olive oil and sprinkled with coarse salt. Why such a simple culinary concoction should taste so good is a mystery, an unbroken challenge to poets and food writers to describe its qualities. It is a morning food, a snack to be consumed as fresh from the oven as possible, a pick-me-up before a late lunch or, with an appropriate filling, such as prosciutto or fresh figs (or both, in season), lunch itself. Frequently there is a line of people at the bakery waiting for the *pizza bianca* to come out of the oven, and it seems as if every Roman patronizes and recommends a special bakery for the outstanding, unique quality of its pizza. Ask Romans living away from Rome what they miss most about their city, and nine in ten will mention *pizza bianca*. The tenth is probably allergic to wheat or olive oil.

"If you really examine the facts, a real Roman cuisine does not exist." The statement makes me pause for a moment, but Gennaro Boni, co-owner with his wife of Ristorante Piperno since 1963, continues undaunted. "Romans have come and Romans have gone, but the Roman Jews, since the times of Emperor Titus, have stayed put." And I realize that the assertion of the nonexistence of a Roman cuisine is actually a competition among old *rioni* to claim for themselves the inheritance of the real cuisine. Their cuisine is not of Rome, but of Testaccio, of Borgo, of Trastevere, of Monti . . .

My conversation with Signor Boni takes place at his establishment in the Ghetto, at midmorning, at one of the dining room tables readied for lunch. Behind us, on a large pastry board set on a dining table, an aging lady is producing homemade pasta with the speed and efficiency of a small factory. And she might well be: she's been making it for thirty years, forty-five pounds of it every morning . . . the first twenty-five years as a Piperno employee and now, since she has retired, as a freelancer.

"The Roman Jewish gastronomy," says Signor Boni, "besides following the basic Jewish dietary rules, is shaped, like any other cuisine, by the local ingredients and the economy."

The traditional style, he adds, is that of simple food prepared quickly. Perhaps this explains the frequent use of frying: it doesn't take long to heat a skillet of oil and, also, anything fried tastes good. Poor people do not have time to cook complicated food. And here is where the Jewish cuisine meshes with the Roman; it is hard to know where one begins and the other ends. As we know them today, their roots start at the end of the sixteenth, beginning of the seventeenth century. Rome was then a small town, surrounded by vineyards, orchards, and the famous Roman vegetable gardens.

Among the native specialties, Signor Boni mentions the *carciofo*, the artichoke, and the way he says it, the word is all in capital letters and has a proud, mouth-filling resonance. *Carciofi alla Giudia* — artichokes, Jewish-style — is what has made Piperno famous since 1856 or, as Boni says, for almost six generations. The way it appears on the plate, the deep-fried *carciofo alla Giudia* looks like a chrysanthemum sculpted in old gold: the outside leaves crisp as chips, the inside soft and flavorful. There is almost no trace of the frying oil.

The *ristorante* is located in Piazza Cenci, on a small, intimate square where tables are set in good weather, and, along with the famous artichokes, offers a long menu of classic Jewish-Roman (or is it Roman-Jewish?) dishes: fried fillets of *baccalà* (salt cod), *pasta e ceci* (chickpea soup), risotto with artichoke sauce, *abbacchio alla cacciatora* (baby lamb stewed in a vinegar-wine sauce), *abbacchio alla romana* (roasted baby lamb), *stracotto di manzo* (beef stewed in wine), fettuccine with a *stracotto* sauce. . . . It is all elegantly served and presented but, as Signor Boni says, it is basically simple commoner's (read: peasant) fare. But, he doesn't need to add, at not-very-commoner's prices.

In a candid admission, Signor Boni explains that until shortly after World War II, Rome did not have a "restaurant" tradition: only a few establishments could be so defined — most in high-class hotels. The rest were *trattorie* or *osterie*, simple family-run places serving home-style fare; they catered to the immediate neighborhood, to people who gathered there for conviviality, a glass of wine (or two), and serious eating. He gives the same date — it coincides with the new affluence of a reborn economy — for

the Ghetto's becoming a destination for dining out; many establishments, with their reputation spreading from strictly *rionale*,
local, to citywide made the switch from *trattoria* to *ristorante*.

Such a place is Il Pompiere, almost around the corner from
Piperno. Begun as an *osteria* in 1922 in a basic, rustic locale, in
1962 it moved to the vaulted, frescoed rooms on the second floor
of Palazzo Cenci, a building that is part of the Roman historic and
artistic patrimony. *Pompiere* means "fireman," and as Francesco
Monteferri (third generation) explains: "Here in the Ghetto
everybody has a nickname. My grandfather was known for serving
some pretty fiery *pollo alla diavola* — chicken devil's-style — and
those who ate it needed a fireman to hose and cool down their
throats with wine. The name stuck and so has the escutcheon: a
pompiere holding a hose spewing wine."

The Pompiere's menu is two pages long, and again a variation
on the Ghetto repertoire, with fettuccine *coi carciofi* as a house
specialty. I ask what makes it so special. "It's a secret!" he tells me,
and changes the subject to *carne secca*, dried beef rump (prepared
like the nonkosher pork prosciutto), a classic Jewish antipasto.
The only deviation Pompiere makes from Jewish cuisine is *buca-
tini alla matriciana*, a classic Roman pasta dish, in which cured
salt pork is part of the sauce.

Another *osteria* graduated to *ristorante* is Giggetto al Portico
d'Ottavia, by now part of the firmament of the local gastronomy.
It is next door to the Portico d'Ottavia, the landmark that defines
the Ghetto, and, most important to us, it is at a pleasant walking
distance from our present residence. Gwen and I need only to
don our walking shoes to master the old cobblestoned alleys, and
in fifteen minutes we are there.

On our first visit, we asked a passing lady to point us in the direction of the portico, and hence to Giggetto. She answers us with
a question: "Why?" It is a disarming question, but we tell her it's
because we are interested in knowing more about local food. In
less than thirty seconds she has quizzed us to see what we do and
what we don't know about Roman-Jewish food. One question

stumps us: do we know *aliciotti coll'indivia*? She proceeds to tell us the recipe, but halfway through it she is corrected on a procedural point by another passerby. Bettina Sonnino, the first lady's name, assures Letizia Sermoneta, the second, that in her eighty-four years she has prepared many *aliciotti* without any nosy outside help; Letizia replies that she is just as adept . . . and perhaps, at eighty, a bit sharper. Neither lady looks much older than sixty-five. They were born and raised here, they tell us, in the Ghetto. Whatever this *borghetto* has to offer, be it the food, the water, or the wine, it definitely agrees with them.

Claudio Ceccarelli of Giggetto (third generation) tells us that the restaurant has been in the same location for eighty years. To be consistent with its origins as an *osteria*, the entrance room has been left untouched. The *osteria* — Claudio explains — was a place where friends met for a glass of wine, a game of cards, and a few laughs. It had a very limited menu: most customers brought their own food wrapped in waxed paper and bought only the wine. This wine, Claudio adds, came from a friend in the Castelli Romani (the vineyard-laden hills near Rome), and, as a matter of fact, it is the same vineyard that supplies their Frascati today. He reminds us that until a decade or so ago, in all *trattorie*, wine meant house wine.

In Rome, the offering of the wine followed a standard routine: as soon as a customer was seated, the waiter would give him an option: *bianco o rosso?* white or red? and a carafe of the chosen wine would appear with a basket of bread and the menu. The carafe was the official measure, the now classic clear glass bottle with a neck that opens up like a funnel or a trumpet. On its body was the lead seal of the Inspector of Weights and Measures from the Ministry of Commerce, guaranteeing its correct volume. There were three basic sizes: *litro*, the liter, *mezzolitro*, the half liter, and the *quartino*, the one-quarter liter, a generous glass. The measures allowed the customer to communicate with the waiter — at a distance if necessary — in sign language: one finger up for the liter, a short horizontal slash in the air with the hand, palm down, for the half, and barely raising an empty glass for the *quartino*. The measures were filled with a local, simple, honest wine that perfectly accompanied the establishment's fare and also cuddled the warmth of conviviality. A transparently empty carafe was an invitation to gesture the waiter to "do it again." Now a new sort of snobbish appreciation for wine (either fad, hobby, or serious interest) has encouraged the eateries to bring to the table a wine list; the waiter will go through the ritual of uncorking the chosen bottle, allowing the customer to smell the cork, and pouring a sip for a taste. Even the house wine now comes bottled; often the label carries the name of the establishment, explaining that the wine was "especially bottled for us" or "from our own vineyard."

Perhaps I am cynical, but to me the only differences from the old carafe are the fancy label and the higher price. Moreover, a labeled, empty bottle has a certain finality, much like the word *finis* at the end of a book. Fortunately, either as a fashion statement or as a return to reason, many establishments now serve the house wine in the *litro*, *mezzolitro*, and *quartino* carafes. An empty, widemouthed carafe on the table does not say "the end," but "to be continued."

"The menu is much improved," says Claudio. "Since the times of the *osteria*, it has been lengthened and lightened." It does not offer many surprises, and Claudio admits to it. "All the real Roman eateries serve the same traditional dishes . . . only some of us do something better then the others," he adds with a wink. Giggetto's *carciofi alla Giudia* or *alla Romana*, by general consensus, are special, and so are its *filetti di baccalà*.

But the real kingdom of *filetti di baccalà*, as Roman a dish as one would wish to have, is a little *osteria* by the eponymous name. In big letters over the door a sign says: FILETTI DI BACCALÀ. It is located in Piazza dei Librari, a stone's throw from Campo de' Fiori; it has been there for a good sixty years, serving only the *filetti*, to which, recently, they have added a green salad and a local cheese or two. Only house wine is available, red or white, served in carafes. The oblong room, with perhaps ten tables lined against the walls, ends in an open kitchen; its only visible equipment is two huge vats of boiling oil below a humming ventilation hood. Two sizable ladies are working the cauldrons: the fillets of dried salt cod, which had been soaked for two days in running water until plump and unsalty, are dipped in a yeast batter and deep-fried first in one vat, then, when barely golden, passed into the second, kept at a higher temperature. Only when deep golden are they scooped out to drain, put on absorbent paper, and served: crisp outside, moist inside, hardly oily, and hot enough to burn one's fingertips — which are the only table implements used by the connoisseurs and aficionados who crowd the little place. It is a most eclectic clientele, and at any time one can mix with the Roman intelligentsia, the artisan and the artist, the blue collar and the student. People come quite a distance for these cod fillets, and the place is always full.

In all Roman restaurants, large or small, there is not much table turnover. At dinner, once seated, customers are there for the evening. Conversations are lively and loud; the general din escalates as the wine flows, and — as in a progressive reaction — people have to talk louder to be heard, which makes the din even louder and so voices have to be raised again, and so on to the threshold of hearing's pain. A moment of relative vocal rest is generally offered by aging, wandering musicians, whose enthusiastic and loud renditions of traditional Roman songs make the already difficult conversations absolutely impossible. The old adage applies: if you can't beat 'em, join 'em. And many people do, creating an impromptu, mostly out-of-tune, but joyful and happy glee club.

Food is conviviality, food is mood. Roman food is recognizable and friendly. Now it is like a Sousa march — brassy, zesty with a beat that asks to be shared; now sprightly and spicy like a Rossini aria; now soft and intimate, embracing and caressing like a Venetian barcarole. Roman food seldom needs intellectual worries and rationalizations: an atonal John Cage piece leaves Romans cold.

Romans love their food. Food is so ingrained in the Roman psyche that the answer to the friendly greeting "How's it going?" is "A *burro e alici!*" — a buttered piece of bread with an anchovy on top being the equivalent of "Couldn't get any better!" Perhaps it is a throwback to ancient Roman times when *garum,* a sauce made with fermented fish, was used to enrich almost all Roman food.

In Rome, gastronomy is more a way of life than a way of cooking. Food is a serious affair: eating it and talking of it are an important part of the texture of everyday life. Since the remotest of times, Rome has suffered wars, invasions, pillaging, and resulting famines, the harshest of times for the rich and the poor: under those conditions food, the idea of food, escalates to become the most important element of the day. By now, it is in the Roman blood, a genetic affair. All Romans talk of where the good food is to be found, of the cooks who make it better, of how to appreciate the best. They romanticize it. A Roman's talk about food is infused with a certain sensuality, almost like foreplay, or a dance of the veils, where flavors, ingredients, techniques are peeled slowly, each savored, to finally reach denouement. Eating is just the crowning glory.

Anywhere, but especially here in Rome, I love to eavesdrop on the conversations of passersby, of people waiting for buses, or sitting at nearby tables at a restaurant. I know eavesdropping is not a correct, polite exercise, but through what transpires I get the pulse of a place, the mood of its citizens in a more direct way than reading the local paper. In Rome, I can bet on it with assurance, the principal subject of conversation is generally food: it is not unusual even in a restaurant to hear from a large congregation of people, obviously enjoying good company and good food, conversations about food. Not of the food at hand, but mostly of other dishes eaten in other places, exceptionally prepared or cooked differently from what was expected, not as one's aunt used to make. The present dish is seldom discussed.

Just being on one's plate makes it above scrutiny: it is, after all, the reason why the partakers came to this eatery; any criticism would put in doubt their knowledge of food and where to find it at its most pleasing.

Besides the enjoyment of the company of friends, when Romans go out to eat they choose first not the eatery but the food. *Ristorante, trattoria,* or *osteria* become target destinations based on the reputation they have for the preparation of a few — sometimes just one — specialty. Romans, depending on their mood, will decide first if it's going to be fish, meat, or fowl, and then pick the restaurant. Most frequently the choice is guaranteed by, and is a matter of pride to, one individual. The phrase most frequently heard when friends plan to eat out together is: "We shall go there, the only place I know where they make [name a dish] as it should be made."

If mood is important in making a choice, so is the day of the week. It can suggest, if not dictate, what to eat. Food is so important that it has, like the names of saints, its own calendar of special days of the year and even of the week. For the feast day of San Giuseppe you must have *bignè* (the whole *rione* Trionfale will be an open-air frying pan, engulfing most of the city in the aroma of frying oil, producing zillions of crisp, moist, puffed-up sweet-dough spheres); for San Giovanni you must have *lumache* (snails), and for a few days before the date — June 24 — food stores and stalls will display basketfuls of the crawling creatures. In a tradition recently lost, the *rione* San Giovanni was crowded with street cooks who dished from big vats bowls of tiny snails in a spicy, minty sauce.

And then there is *panettone* for Christmas, and *colomba* for Easter . . .

As for linking days of the week with particular dishes, the lineup is just as strict and unchangeable, a tradition that seems to resist the whim of fashion. Restaurants and humble *trattorie* alike still post the traditional menus. The day of the week and its dish are so entwined that if you mention one the other will pop up.

Only a short time ago, Gwen and I boarded a bus at its terminus downtown. Having boarded it ahead of its scheduled departure, we were alone, a welcome few minutes of quiet — buses have to turn off their engines when parked, thank God — enough to review and savor again the glories of the day: the Teatro di Marcello, the Bocca della Verità and Piazza Navona, the view of the forums from the Capitoline Hill at sunset. Our musings were interrupted by a cheerful group, a man and two young ladies who sat, in the empty bus, just behind us. They, too, were commenting on the experiences of the day — actually of the week — and it became obvious that the man had been showing the sights to the two lively out-of-towners.

"So much, and so much fun!" announced one of the young ladies out loud. "I have even forgotten what day it is."

"*Sabato,*" I couldn't resist helping.

"*Trippa!*" added the escort in jest, obviously a Roman. It was established then and there that Saturday and tripe are — as far as Romans are concerned — synonymous. The ice was broken, and for the erudition of the out-of-towners, we engaged (Gwen, at first somewhat embarrassed by my nosing in on the group, joined forces) in a review of the gastronomic calendar.

"Thursday: gnocchi!" started the gentleman. The round-robin continued with Friday, chickpea soup and, also, stewed salt cod; Sunday, fettuccine with giblet sauce; Wednesday . . . The bus had slowly filled and was now under way, and by the time it passed under the old elms of the Lungotevere our little group was involved in settling the various niceties of preparing *trippa alla romana,* which, as everybody knows, requires fresh mint. "But not too much," butted in a portly fellow passenger, "it could be overpowering." Briefly, with passengers getting on and off, the bus had become a cheerful open forum, with some volunteering their opinion ("My mother adds a pinch of thyme, it makes all the difference!), some querying, a grandmotherly woman acting as moderator and referee. By the time we reached our destination at the Basilica of San Paolo we had gone through the entire gastronomic calendar and heard the correct — mostly to be improved — cooking knowledge of each individual. As we alighted, the bus driver, obviously a good listener although till then silent, honored us with: "*Ciao!* And Happy Tripe! And if you want to find a really good one, go to Cesarino a Testaccio."

VIII

Being Healthy in Rome

Parole, parole . . .

I AM A GOOD whistler. It comes naturally, for no reason at
all. In addition to keeping me entertained (I'm not so sure
about others), it is a gauge to my well-being: when I get up in the
morning, after thanking the mirror for once more giving back my
image, I get in the shower and unconsciously whistle. It means I
am fine and everything is fine with my world. I am also a good
winker. The two abilities give me an edge in amusing young girls
— of the infant persuasion: a wink of the left eye, a wink of the
right; the right index finger corkscrews slowly (boro! boro! bizz!)
to her belly button and when it makes contact, my lips squeeze
tight and produce a thin whistle similar to, but more harmonious
than, a toy squeak. Gales of laughter and happiness all around.

Recently, on one of our flights to Rome, I tried my magic on a
little Indian girl, as beautiful as a porcelain doll, huge dark eyes as
shiny as black pearls; she was on her mother's lap, on their first leg
to Delhi. The little girl was anxious and tense, on the verge of
tears, barely under the soothing control of her mother. Gwen —
my boss, assistant, mentor, guardian, protector, and wife — sat between me and them, and I thought it was not only my pleasure

but my duty to relieve the girl's unhappiness: wink, wink, boro, boro, bizz, squeak. The girl broke into inconsolable crying, terrorized. She had seen the left side of my face, which I realized, with much greater terror than the girl's, was unresponsive. The left eye was wide open with the glassy stare of the possessed, the left lip drooped down, the murderous smile of the gargoyle, my prize whistle the limp blowing of a candle.

My medical knowledge, unlike that of most Romans, is at best sketchy, but enough to make me think stroke; and my whistleless-ness was a grim foreboding. I took a pin and pricked my face. Both sides produced blessed "ouches!" — which reassured me only partially, and Gwen even less. Hesitantly, I ordered my limbs, left and right, to move. They did.

Whenever we left the States for Rome, we always told each other we would never set foot again in a Roman hospital, both of us having had difficult, if not terrifying, experiences in the past for ourselves and our children. We vowed that if either of us got sick, we would be on a plane right back to Boston. But here I was, our plane barely landed at Fiumicino, on the phone trying to contact all of the doctors I knew, dearest and established Roman friends. So was my sister, the take-charge Roman, proposing her own doctor-friends, even more influential than mine. Being high-powered medicine men, they were all busy in faraway parts of Rome, available only through the *telefonino*, their cellular phones. The verdict was unanimous: get yourself to a *pronto soccorso*, emergency room, fast.

They all, including my sister, recommended the Ospedale Fatebenefratelli on the Isola Tiberina, within walking distance of where we were staying. The Fatebene, built in 1709, is a Catholic hospital with an excellent reputation, run by monks dedicated, as their name translates, to "Do good, brothers" around the world. The Isola Tiberina, the only island on the Tiber, can be reached from both banks by old pedestrian bridges. The ruins of an ancient Roman bridge foam the waters just past the island, which is practically a single floating building, like a ship at sea. (In the island's center, just across a small square from Fatebene, the Basilica of San Bartolomeo, repository of the body of Saint Bartholomew the Apostle, is attached to the Jewish Hospital.)

At the time of this visit, the beauty of the area is marred by the restoration and beautification works that are preparing Rome for the year 2000: touching up the old lady's makeup. I am observing all this not out of a particular desire to sightsee, but more simply just to see, to test how much of my half-sight is reaching my brain and how it is processed once there. Gwen, my Seeing Eye dog, leads me through the labyrinth of orange plastic netting marking the path through mounds of uprooted cobblestones to the *pronto soccorso*. Now, I had come to think of the *pronto soccorso* as a bloody M.A.S.H. unit, quite dirty and manned by not-too-clean, surly personnel whose first reaction was to reproach you for putting yourself in the position of needing to be there in the first place. These impressions came from those blessedly few, but never-to-be-forgotten moments of need in the past — the childhood and adolescence, with all their prescribed bleeding scrapes and bumps, of my four children were spent in Rome. During the seven years Gwen lived in Rome, she and her son had their share of scary encounters with emergency rooms.

The Fatebenefratelli's entrance is immaculate and freshly painted. The young nurse at the reception desk is attentive and interested: she asks my name, age, residence, and to explain problem as best as I can. She looks at my face and says *"Poverino!"* with sincere concern. Since I'm having a problem with speech, Gwen takes over and asks where we should register, whom and what we should pay. The girl informs us that no matter what citizenship, race, religion, or persuasion, all assistance will be given free, courtesy of the National Health Program. She assures us that a doctor will check me shortly. Gwen admires the comely nurse's earrings, a long stretch of pearls all along the pierced edge of one lobe. My sister arrives accompanied by my brother-in-law, to make sure I am given proper attention and also to make known that her close friend, Doctor Paolo Mascagni (grandson of composer Pietro), albeit not present at the moment, is chief of surgery at this hospital, hence I am due particular care. In Rome, you are who you know. We then embrace and she scolds me for putting myself in a position to have to . . . etc. etc.

Shortly thereafter, I am escorted to an examination room. The earlobe nurse takes my blood pressure, congratulates me, comments on Gwen's fashionable hairdo. A doctor in immaculate scrubs examines me. He doesn't say much but, by his attitude, conveys the message that what ails me is of the common, garden-variety complaint (in all my life, I had never heard of it before): a temporary parietal paralysis of the left side of my face due to a *colpo di freddo*, a blow of cold air. That's his diagnosis, but it must be checked, and the cure prescribed, by a neurologist. We all retreat to the waiting room and a neurologist, not in the hospital now, is summoned by *telefonino*. We are reassured that he will be here as soon as the Roman traffic will permit. Gwen and I, who are pleasantly impressed by the efficiency of today's Roman medical care, at the same time express a good dose of guilt for our old reservations. No mention was made about a medical bill, or of our medical insurance policy, HMO, personal wealth, or residence. Implicitly, the nurse has made us understand we could be from Mars and we would get the same attention.

The neurologist arrives. He is a very professional-looking, middle-aged man in an elegant, perfectly cut tweed jacket; long salt-and-pepper wavy hair, carefully disarranged, brushes his shoulders; he has a serious countenance but a friendly smile. By Gwen's reaction I know she is trying to decide which movie actor he resembles. While we go through the urbane introductions, he is already scrutinizing, examining my face. By the time he gets to the examination proper (probing, pinching, touch-the-tip-of-your-nose, walk-a-straight-line routines) he already has a diagnosis, confirming his colleague's. He talks with Gwen (the caregiver — I, being simply the patient, am left out). "Not serious," he tells her, "but it will take time." Gwen presses him for a prognosis. "It is subjective," he says, "it depends on . . ." "One month? Two months?" she presses him. He gestures noncommittally with his hand: a vague thing. She congratulates him on the good taste of his silk tie, just like the one she gave me. As a colleague to a colleague, "One or two months, sometimes longer," he tells her. He then writes a prescription for a set of pills, to be taken twice a day for a week, at 9:30 A.M. and 3:45 P.M., with plenty of water and an aspirin. He then asks the nurse to make sure I have an appointment to see him again in a week, Monday, at 8.40 A.M. She taps a computer, and "It's done," she says.

Gwen and I both feel we are in good hands, taken care of as professionally, as cleanly, as cordially as if we were in Cambridge, Massachusetts, U.S.A. We recall our preflight vow, but now we are more confident.

We leave the *pronto soccorso* and march en masse — Gwen, my sister, my brother-in-law, and myself — and in sixty-eight steps we are at the corner pharmacy. Carved oak-wood paneling all over, amphoras, crystal chalices filled with colored potions, reassuring camphor smells, two or three customers. Gwen waits her turn (it marks her as a foreigner), offers the prescription to the smiling young white-clad pharmacist. She examines the prescription front and back. Twice, to make sure.

"Signora," she says, holding the prescription with two fingers as if a rare specimen, "we have not filled this kind of prescription in the last three years! That medicine was taken out of our pharmacopoeia at least two years ago."

Gwen and I look at each other silently, the only noise that of our hearts falling to the floor.

"Probably what he meant is Bentelan," suggests a customer in line behind Gwen.

"I could have told you so myself," adds my brother-in-law. My sister confirms. They mention friends and relatives who at one time had the same — or what looked like the same — problem I seem to have. They were all assisted by Bentelan. The pharmacist endorses the choice: Bentelan is what she has been dispensing carloads of for the last three years, but she is adamant: we have to go back and have the prescription revised by the doctor.

Sixty-eight steps back and we are speaking to the pearled-ear-lobe nurse, explaining. She looks at the prescription, gets on the phone (to the *neurologo*, presumably) while writing a new prescription on an official pad: Bentelan it is. Six injections, one a day. Beginning now. Back to the pharmacy, then back to the examination room, where the nurse cheerfully produces a horse-dose syringe with a needle that makes me glad that I am only half-sighted, and just as cheerfully and efficiently spears me in the butt. What about the daily injections after this one, we ask? Oh, the nurse replies, that's easy, you can give them to yourself or your wife can give them to you. Terrified, Gwen admits her ignorance and the girl offers — for a reasonable compensation — her teachings or services at our domicile. Otherwise, she says, you will surely find a neighbor, or your building's janitor, or someone who will gladly do it. Italians hardly ever take their medicines in pill form, but almost always by injection, and it seems that anybody in Rome is capable and authorized to shoot me in the butt.

The nurse reminds us not to miss the follow-up visit with the doctor in six days, 8:40 on the dot. Nonetheless, if we should miss that rendezvous for any unexpected reason, not to despair: the doctor has a private practice and we could make an appointment there, naturally a fee is charged. . . . The not-too-subtle hint makes us revise our naive opinions about the National Health System.

Six shots of Bentelan — cortisone, basically — go through my system. With me prone on the bed, Gwen (the sadist), after a quick indoctrination from a friend, can wield a syringe with the best of them, painlessly. She asks me if I feel any better but doesn't get the joke when I tell her that no, not yet, but probably the mattress does — the long needle must have gone straight through me and into it.

On the following Monday at 8:40 A.M. we are at the Fatebene-fratelli, building C, fifth floor, neurological outpatient clinic. At the reception desk a lady in a white smock (nurse? secretary? doctor?) is having an animated conversation with another white-

smocked man (nurse? secretary? doctor?) — being Monday, probably about Sunday's soccer game — and they ignore us for a good
five minutes. Finally they part and in a moment or two the lady dis-
covers us, looks at us blankly, her conversational art disappeared.
We tell her of our appointment: she checks a computer screen.

"*Non risulta,*" she says. We insist. She tells us to wait here, she
is going to check. She disappears down the corridor in a room
marked INFIRMARY. We hear several voices engaged in conversation, muffled laughter; we wait at least fifteen minutes, abandoned in admiration of blank walls. Gwen suggests we leave, that
we have been given the runaround. Just then another lady comes
and takes her position behind the counter. In a couple of minutes
she notices us, astounded, as if we had just materialized from
nowhere, and then gruffly tells us that we should not be there at
all: wait in the waiting room, that's what waiting rooms are for. We
join the three other people who are there waiting, resignedly.

It is now 9:45. Gwen is furious at the way we are being treated,
at the system, and, at the moment, mostly at me. She cannot understand my meekness, she tells me, how can I stand it at all. "I'm
curious," I slur to her, "I want to see how it ends. I never leave a
movie before it ends . . ."

"This is a bad movie, a nightmare," she huffs, and suggests that
Bentelan has affected my mind. She storms back to the gruff lady
who now is kindness personified. Sorry, she says, but the doctors'
schedules have been inexplicably altered. The neurologist we
want to see is now in building B, third floor, doing his rounds.

Down five on C, up three on B. We find ourselves in a white,
mirror-clean, absolutely void-of-visible-life ward. Many doors
open on a long corridor, which ends with a shrine to the Holy
Virgin. A young nun appears, seemingly as lost and disoriented as
we are; she suggests, nonetheless, that we "look around." Doctor
Paolo Boccasena, the neurologist, in white smock and identifying tag (associate to the chief neurologist), appears out of
nowhere, recognizes us, and reproaches us for having missed *last*
Friday's appointment. A misunderstanding, apologies all around:

Doctor Boccasena examines me and is pleased with this checkup. A slight downturn is expected in a *paresi*, it's normal. He strongly suggests a set of ten Marconi therapy sessions, ten of facial massage therapy, and at least a half hour a day of facial exercises: tongue in, tongue out, blowing, pursing lips, furrowing of the brow, squeeze the eyes shut, open the eyes wide. He prescribes more injections on a diminishing dosage. Come see him again, right here. Next Friday, 8:40 A.M. In the meantime, as a jaw exercise, I should chew *gomma americana*.

I hate chewing gum; at a *salumeria* I buy myself a piece of raw pork rind. Dogs chew on it; I can, too. At a medical supply store, I buy a black eye patch, which I attempt to wear in an elegant way, reminding us of the old Hathaway shirt ads. Unfortunately, however, the gray wool ski mask pulled over the left side of my face to keep out the *colpi di freddo* tends to diminish any appearance of elegance.

We investigate several physical therapy clinics to make appointments. Yes, they do facial massage therapy, but Marconi therapy has not been administered for at least three years . . . they will check for appointment openings and will call back, right away. No one does.

Our confidence is seriously shaken: so, these are the ways of Rome. Friends, relatives, acquaintances are surprised that we are surprised. This is Rome, you know. Haven't you heard? Have you forgotten?

I will go back to *Dottor* Boccasena, on Friday. I am totally hooked; I want to see the end of this movie. In a position of pretty high responsibility, he seems to be the only one on a track abandoned three years ago. Why? I want to talk to him about that and about the National Health System.

I have also capitulated: at the insistence of Gwen, of sister, of friends and acquaintances, I have made an appointment with a private neurologist at a private clinic. Just in case. Doctor G. Bruno is booked for weeks, but being a friend of good friends he finds an opening just two days from now. Saturday, 9 A.M.

—⌒⌒—

Friday, 8:40 A.M., third floor, building B, *Ambulatorio di Neurologia* ward. Orderlies are shining floors, cleaning up breakfast. No medical staff is visible. We roam around a bit, bump into a young doctor.

"We have an appointment with Doctor Boccasena. Where do we find him?"

"You sure? Did he say here, Friday?"

"Absolutely. Why?"

"On Friday, every Friday, he is on duty at the *pronto soccorso* . . ."

Down B, pass by A, by the registration, through a labyrinth of cubicles and doors, into *pronto soccorso*.

Gwen doesn't talk, but by her looks she is telling me — loudly — I told you so, I could have bet on it . . . Let's quit and go home. I can't. I am totally engrossed, the movie is still rolling . . .

At the end of a corridor, Doctor Boccasena pops out of a door, confabulating with two other doctors, sees us, waves. He gestures that today is a hell of a day, but please wait a minute, he will be with us shortly. And he is. He leads us to a private examining room, welcomes us as old friends. He notices an amelioration; asks if I have followed his instructions. I ask him how come at least two of his recommended medicines and therapies have ceased to be used for years. He smiles an understanding smile:

"Pharmacists, therapists, patients . . . they all decide what's in and what's out. All of a sudden a medicine, a cure, falls out of favor and another becomes fashionable. Someone tells a friend, a friend passes it on, a magazine writes a story . . . Marconi therapy — it worked once, it still works — is out, the magic mushroom is in. Everybody knows it, everybody wants it. Naturally, doctors have to look up to date, and soon even they begin to believe it . . ."

I manage to smile, actually half a smile is the best I can do, and he is pleased that I can keep a sense of humor: "It's good therapy," he says. He recommends I follow up on the massage therapy and writes a prescription for ten sessions of *ionofaresi calcica in territorio del nervo facciale sinistro*, a type of massage for the left facial nerve. "If they object," he adds, "tell them to call me." As an afterthought, he gives us a set of telephone numbers, including the *telefonino*, where we can reach him.

Saturday. The Clinica Paiadeia is on top of a hill, among clusters of ancient pines, in a fancy residential section of Rome just above Ponte Milvio — the oldest extant bridge on the Tiber. The plate-glass doors slide silently; we are in an ultramodern, chrome-and-crystal, shiny-marble-floor environment. It could be Hollywood. An inviting aroma of coffee and fresh-baked pastry emanates from the little coffee bar on the left side of the hall, but we resist the temptation and go straight to the reception desk. Doctor Bruno? Ask for Norina, we are told, right turn, desk at the end of a mirrored corridor. Norina is busy on telephones, desk calendars, papers. "We are here to see Doctor Bruno." "Do you have an appointment?" "Yes, at 9." We all check a wall clock: 8:55 A.M. on the nose. "You sure?" "Yes, I am." Then I ask Gwen: "Are you sure?" She is, and we all agree that an appointment has been set for today, Saturday, 9 A.M., with Doctor Bruno. Norina, a very businesslike, well-dressed, middle-aged lady, tells us to wait in the waiting room. As soon as Doctor Bruno arrives she will call us. Leather armchairs, large picture windows look out on a mixed cyclorama: the Via Flaminia just below, flanked by the Tiber; on the left, in the distance, the tall spires of a minaret; Saint Peter's dome far on the right; on the horizon the Terminillo mountain, capped by snow.

An elegant gentleman is waiting with us. He is perusing two newspapers; opens and folds them, opens them again searching for something he hasn't read yet; he is bored. We look at each other; by the resigned shaking of the head, shrinking of the shoulder, we tell each other here we are, and settle in for the wait.

"*Mutua?*" he finally asks me.

"No, *privato.*"

"*Ah, beh!*" He means I have a possible recourse, leaving; he, belonging to the *mutua*, the Italian state health system, has none: if you lose your turn, you will have to go back to square one.

We both have time; I try my gambit.

"I am visiting from Mars; how would you explain to me the *mutua*, your National Health System?"

His face breaks into a warm smile, gets the jest: "I am an engineer, an environmental engineer," he says, "not a doctor."

"On Mars," I tell him, "we think highly of engineers, rational men. And it is more interesting to hear from a health-taker than a health-giver . . ."

He looks around, at the ceiling, at the marble floor, at his wristwatch, as if to concentrate on how to begin. Then in a harmonious, low, deliberate voice: "Every citizen has the right to free medical attention." He pauses for effect and after a moment: "We have what is called the *tassa sulla salute*, the tax on health. In proportion to one's income, a tax is levied, and that goes to cover the public-health expenses. Whoever does not have sufficient, or any, income does not pay the tax, but receives complete assistance anyway. Doctors have their fixed stipends for their public work, but are also free to have their private practice. Or they can choose one or the other. As for medicines, some are covered totally by the state: you bring the doctor's prescription to a pharmacy and pay only a small portion of the bill, five or six thousand lire, the *ticket*. The pharmacy then has the difference reimbursed by the state. For optional medicines, you have to pay the full amount. The medicines defined as lifesavers, for life-threatening situations, that cost millions and millions of lire per month, are fully covered by the state." Or, he explains, in cases such as his, if a special clinic like this one offers a cure not available in public hospitals, his costs are paid, or partially paid, by the state. I do not ask what ails him; by his looks and elegant attire I would guess he is pretty well off and could do without the *mutua*, but then you never know.

During his talk, the engineer has been touching the fingers of one hand with the other, as if checking out the various parts of his explanation. I comment that it all seems pretty good to me, very

generous and civilized. Attentive to the needs of people, propor-
tionate to their finances. He seems pleased with my opinion, then
starts again his peculiar habit of touching and shaking his fingers
one at a time, as if itemizing:

"All of that, basically, is the way the *mutua* *should* work. But
when one goes to make an appointment for a visit with a doctor,
or for a test, or a special procedure, such as a CAT scan or MRI,
unless it is a special emergency, as in a *pronto soccorso*, he could
easily wait for months. But if he goes to a private clinic and pays,
then he can be taken care of the same day. Why? Because *mutua*
doctors are overbooked. And there is no room at the inn: hospital
beds are all occupied. It is standard procedure to be admitted for
a day or two, sometimes a week, just to have a set of blood tests
done. Or to be admitted overnight for a procedure that takes one
or two hours. It is not infrequent to find patients in gurneys set up
in corridors for their hospital stay. The hospitals are reimbursed
by the state for the length and related charges of a patient's stay.
So administrators do not have much interest in speeding things
up. And neither do doctors working for the *mutua*; they prefer to
detour the more affluent clients, the ones who can pay, to the private clinics where they also practice. There they take so much
per visit. So they do not have much interest in smoothly working
public institutions. If they did, then everybody would go to them.
It is a paradox: they are good doctors, good surgeons, actually
they are very good, excellent. I do not believe that when they operate on a poor patient they are not as good as when they operate
on a rich one. But then, obviously, they prefer to operate for
thirty or forty million lire a pop than do the same thing for almost
nothing, a fixed stipend."

I can see the pitfalls of the system, I tell him. Unfortunate but,
given human nature, I believe it is something that goes on all over
the universe. I hope I am not too naive to also believe that it
cannot be so for every doctor; there must be a lot of dedicated,
honest professionals who give special care to their *mutua* patients,
regardless of the great profits they miss. He agrees:

"Yes, there are good doctors. But there is something terribly wrong with a system that is based on the fact that a doctor has to be a missionary. It should be up to the system to impose certain rules and regulations and not rely on the fact that one is a missionary and has to renounce the profits."

Here the engineer pauses, then brings up some other common complaints about the National Health System. They concern the perceived lack of trained personnel in the public sector, or their availability when they are needed. Or the mystery of why a CAT scanner or an MRI machine, extremely expensive equipment, when bought by a public hospital (somehow the money is always found and allocated) never works as it should, or works only a few hours a day; but when they are in the private clinics they work perfectly well all the time. "Is it because the clinics have better technicians, or assistants, or nurses?" he asks me.

I admit my ignorance, fall for the bait: "I don't know, but I don't think so . . ."

"You are right!" The engineer is now more animated: "The doctors, the technicians, and the nurses are the same ones who work in the mornings at the public hospitals. How is it that in the mornings they are inefficient and in the afternoons they are wizards at the private clinics?"

I answer with what seems to be the explanation for everything in Rome: "It is a paradox!"

I tell him that I have heard it said that it is the public itself that promotes this situation, wrongly perceiving that they get better care in the private clinics. But I think it is an explanation that doesn't hold: the public would be very happy if the *mutua* structures worked well. Everybody knows that the excellent *mutua* doctors and surgeons are exactly the same doctors and surgeons they pay for in a private clinic. Also, I have been told that most public hospitals, for certain operations, are better equipped than the private ones.

"Yes, perhaps that's true. But if one goes to a public hospital for an appointment and says, 'I need care urgently,' and they tell him,

'Okay, come back in a year,' what can he do?" The engineer is querying me, but I give him no answer.

"He goes to a private clinic, that's what. He spends his millions of lire — even if he has to make sacrifices — and the next afternoon he is taken care of. He is not at all happy to have to spend that money, but that's the way it is. He knows that the same surgeon who an hour ago was operating on a long-waiting *mutua* patient will now take care of him in the *clinica*. And spend more time with him, provide a more thorough follow-up until he is well . . . but then, why not? The doctor is going to send him a nice bill for it."

We check our watches; we try to get Norina's attention, but she is too busy on the telephone to notice us.

"We have not yet found a system that works well for everybody, and it is not just a matter of greed, of money. As a matter of fact, in my opinion, in Italy we have too much money. The state tends to make enormous expenditures — in many cases in the context of hospitals and universities. It has spent billions of lire for equipment that is still in its shipping crates. I really do not see a solution. But I think it is all a matter of organization." It is the engineer in him speaking.

There is now an ongoing attempt at reform. Doctors will have to choose between the public and private sectors, and will not be able to work both sides of the fence. It's a debate that's been going on for a while, and comes up regularly during every local, regional, and national election.

"*Parole, parole, un fiume di parole!*" Words, he says, a river of words.

"A bit cynical?" I ask him.

"I am sure you understand: it is only my opinion." Again he checks his watch. "And you would not have heard it if we had not had to wait . . . but it's also my brother's opinion, and my cousin's . . . and, I think, of whomever you wish to ask . . . by the way," he asks with a chuckle, "how do things work on Mars?"

I begin to tell him that in Boston — sorry, Mars — we do not have a comprehensive health system at all, not yet. It is a political affair, you know, *parole, parole, parole* . . . but now Norina appears and, quite curtly, announces that Doctor Bruno has arrived and is waiting for me. I thank Signor Liuzzo, the engineer, for his explanation and say I hope to see him again and continue our talk. "Monologue!" he specifies, smiling. It is now 10:05.

Doctor Bruno is the essence of civility, athletically slim, young looking, and absolutely professional in a perfectly cut gray suit. He barely apologizes for the wait — traffic, everybody understands — and we introduce ourselves. He wants to know who I am, what I do, where I am from. Ah, yes, Boston! He spent a few years at the NIH in Washington, his wife is from New York. He speaks excellent English. Before examining me, he asks for my complete health history, and that of my parents, of my children. How long have I had this problem? Come Thursday, I slur, exactly two weeks. Hum, hum. Then the exam: pinching, pulling, pricking my face; blinding penlight in the left, in the right eye; follow it here, there, up, down. Close eyes, walk a straight line, come back, stand still. Sit there, relax: taps with his rubber mallet every single joint. Bare feet, runs a cold, sharp object on the soles. Ouch! Good, he says. His diagnosis is the same: paresis of the left parietal nerve. Bell's palsy, in English. Not serious, but a long affair. How long? It is a subjective affair. Sometimes three or four months, some patients never recover completely. No, I do not want to scare you, but I don't want to give you false hope either. I feel I should tell you. He then goes into a complete description of the nerve's anatomy — where it comes from, where it goes — of the jaw, of the ear, of the facial muscles operating the lips, the eyelids. The Latins called this case *paresi a frigore,* paralysis due to cold. Now we know that cold has nothing to do with it. It can be a viral infection, a constriction of some capillary vein irritating the nerve. Even stress. It is scary because it looks like a stroke. No, no, no, I do not want to scare you! Anyway, I think that there is no immediate cure, no physical therapy. Just keep doing your ugly-faces exercises, keep scaring children. But one thing he is recommending strongly, not ordering, just recommending, is to have an MRI of my cranium done. Just to see, just to know what could have provoked the event. He is positive that nothing will show up, even if at my age there is a chance that a few little scars will be there, so do not get scared. He has a specialist, the best with the best equipment in town, a dear friend, one he trusts completely (he writes, hands the notepad page to Gwen — I am just the simpleton, the innocent bystander who got hit): call for an appointment, mention my name, he will perform the MRI even this afternoon — no today is Saturday — definitely Monday or Tuesday. He will call me with the results, and I will let you know. Also take this (he writes a prescription on the notepad): it is not a cure; it is what we call brain food, a compound to revitalize the nerves, the muscles. Thirty injections, one a day. Oh, no? No! Well then, you can take the pill version, three at breakfast, three at lunch, for two months. I am reeling under the impact — I count mentally — of 360 pills, but we get up and shake hands. I want to see you in one month, just call Norina. Well, he says, keep the faith, keep your sense of humor. . . .

I have been entertained, in the most thoroughly professional way, for exactly one hour and five minutes. In parting Gwen asks him what his honorarium is. Just stop at Norina's desk, she will tell you. And she'll give you a receipt. For your insurance in the United States.

We do, and she does: 250,000 lire.

We stop at a pharmacy and get the pills. We start with one box, barely enough for one week, at 44,000 lire.

Each pill looks as big as a hamburger, and I take them, gagging, for three days.

It is now exactly twenty-one days since the airplane "event." Against all recommendations, I have refused to get the MRI, stopped seeing doctors, taking pills, wearing the pirate patch over my eye, or wrapping a scarf around my face.

My face is 95 percent normal, whatever that is. In the shower this morning, I whistled. Even if the high notes are somewhat tentative, everything must be 95 percent okay with my world.

On the street, I also whistled and winked at a little girl (not that little, really) and she didn't cry. Actually she smiled back.

I can whistle, I can wink: Rome is the place to be.

Perhaps. Only two days have passed, and all newspapers, radios, and televisions are yelling SCANDALO! A patient has died on his way to a hospital's *pronto soccorso;* the ambulance that carried him had to wait behind six other ambulances that also could not unload their patients. All the hospital beds were full. A list is given of ten major city hospitals that have closed their *pronto soccorso*'s doors until the situation is remedied. The most serious situation is at the Fatebenefratelli Hospital, which, a paper says, is "literally under siege." A banner title in the *Messaggero* shrieks, "Hospitals warn citizens: it is absolutely forbidden to get sick!" Underneath, a photo shows patients in gurneys lined up along hospital corridors.

Lionello Cosentino, *assessore regionale alla sanità,* regional commissioner for public "health" (not to be confused with "sanity"), declares that there is no crisis; in fact there are more hospital beds than needed. It's a matter of organization.

The Honorable Domenico Gramazio, of the Associazione Nazionale (the extreme-right, neo-Fascist party) shows up incognito at the Pertini Hospital, looks at the long line of patients lying in stretchers, and declares, "What confusion! This situation is unacceptable!" He is accompanied by the vice president of the Department of Public Health and by a legal counselor. They summon the hospital director, Doctor Daniela Ghirelli, for an explanation. "What we do not need now," she strikes back, like a snake uncoiling, "is a bunch of busybodies snooping around! We are busy enough!" She calls security guards and has all three thrown out.

Representatives of the extreme-right, right, center-right, center,

center-left, left, and extreme-left parties open an investigation in parliament into the situation of the *pronto soccorsi*, and the hospitals in general. They all agree that heads should roll, changes should be made.

I cannot help but think of Signor Liuzzo: *parole, parole, parole*. . . .

IX

To Die in Rome

Morire a Roma

*J*DO NOT THINK that it is easier to die in Rome than it is to die somewhere else. If anything it is a more familiar thing, something to which any normally sensitive Roman is accustomed. In Rome death, the image of death, the feeling of death is everywhere. It is present in squares, in parks, in gardens, on walls, and above all in churches. I thought about this while walking around the Gianicolo Hill promenade and found myself sharing the magnificent view of Rome — the domes, the bell towers, the ancient buildings of the city — with a hundred or so marble busts of *Garibaldini* heroes (all multidecorated officers: death in Rome has its own hierarchy), most of whom fought and died in or around this spot defending Rome against the French in 1849. Propped on marble pedestals, the perfectly aligned busts form two lines that lead to the center of the large Piazzale del Gianicolo. Smack in its center, the huge equestrian statue of Garibaldi commands the city; around the monument's base a bronze lady, representing Italy, shares with a bronze Victory the privilege of supervising dead or dying soldiers lying about. To make sure the message is not lost, the inscription on the monument's base says: ROMA O MORTE, Rome or Death.

Exactly across town, from the belvedere of the Pincio Terrace, you have the reverse view of the city, a view and a space shared with another two hundred or so marble busts of honorable — and dead — persons. These, too, like the ones on the Gianicolo, are slightly larger than life sized and propped on pedestals of human height; they come face to face with the viewer. The busts are of poets, writers, scientists, astronomers, politicians, soldiers, navigators, doctors (and now that I think of it, only two ladies: Grazia Deledda, the writer, and Catherine of Siena, the saint), all unsmiling, gloomy, and dead.

A walk in the old center of town will be punctuated now and then by some *edicola religiosa*, small altars to religious images, affixed on the walls of rich and poor buildings; most are no bigger than a few puny square feet. Many are ancient and of real artistic value, a perpetual votive light flickering under the image of a Madonna, or of a saint, or of a martyr: in most of them death, present or impending, is the protagonist. The same representations appear in larger scale inside the myriad churches of Rome; saintly figures (represented in frescoes, on canvases, in mosaics, in bas-reliefs, or in full round marble sculptures) are eviscerated, decapitated, pierced by arrows, blinded, crucified, upended, stoned. . . . After a while the grim violence — even if artfully romanticized — becomes commonplace and one doesn't take long to get accustomed to it, and to the idea of death.

For a more realistic contact with death in Rome, a visit to the Cimitero dei Cappuccini is a must. At the very beginning of elegant Via Veneto, the birthplace of *La Dolce Vita*, the very glorification of *Dolce Morte* is inside the church of Santa Maria della Concezione. In the entrance, on the left, a narrow, steep stairway descends to the cellar of the church, where the bones of some four thousand saintly Capuchin friars are assembled to form the most baroque — and morbid — decorations. On corridor walls, vaults, and ceilings of the underground chapels tibias, clavicles, femurs, spinal bones, ribs, all the components of the human skeleton, are put together to form floral decorations and arabesques. Bones form elaborate niches, abodes for a host of mummified friars. Some are propped up, standing, some recline; all are cloaked in their brown cassocks, little friars smiling toothy smiles, their skulls half hidden under the raised hoods. And, the hundred-or-so-foot-long corridor being quite narrow, they are all at arm's reach. In the deadly silence you can easily hear the beating of your heart; you imagine you feel their musty, ghostly breath. On the wall at the corridor's end, as if elegantly scripted by one of the once friars, there is a legend: "You are what I was. I am what you shall be." It makes one ponder.

At the edge of adolescence, as a rite of passage, it was the place to visit with two or three contemporaries. We shared the first long shiver of terror and repulsion by crowding closely to each other, and then, communal courage mustered and back in the light of day, we bragged proudly of having passed the scary test, of having looked death in the face with nary a shiver. The friar-custodian of the place, *il padre guardiano*, stayed at the top of the stairs and kept an eye and an ear open on the goings-on down below and, gifted with a particular sense of macabre humor, he frequently would turn off the already dim light. On subsequent visits, the fifteen-to-twenty-second event (an eternity!) was the expected thrill of the tour. Once a few years older the Cimitero dei Cappuccini was the place to take a young *inamorata:* while holding her trembling hand, the sudden darkness produced squeals — hers — and a groping, supporting embrace — yours. Like touching everlasting Paradise. Dear dead friars: *Mors tua, vita mea.* Sometimes the jocular *padre guardiano*, having read your intentions, left the light on. It felt, then, as if all the little shriveled parchment friars laughed at your failed sinful plan, at your frustration. Death in Rome.

Acquaintance with death starts early for a Roman: barely exists a third-grade child who has not been on a school excursion to visit one — or more — of the many Roman catacombs. Down into the dark, damp shafts of those early Christian burial grounds, grasping for dear life the sweaty hand of a companion in one hand, a shaky candle in the other, the poor child makes his first acquaintance with real skulls and a few dusty bones. "Dust to dust," the sadistic teacher will teach; a grim initiation, one that will leave the poor child pale and without appetite for a week.

But then, even if not in such massive display, every old Roman church has its own supply of sarcophagi and tombs; important churches were used as cemeteries for affluent and important people, while simpler parish churches were for the hoi polloi. Hence it is not unusual, while visiting an old church, to find yourself walking on someone's tomb, a more or less ornate marble slab, its inscription smoothed by time and barely legible. One can get a jolt of surprise — it has happened to me — to find out (in the church of San Pietro in Montorio) that one is walking on Hugh O'Neill, 2nd Earl of Tyrone (1547–1616), peace be to his Irish soul.

For olfactory and hygienic reasons, that custom was abolished at the beginning of the 1800s, and the citizens' remains had to be buried in fields specifically set aside for that purpose. Blessed by the church, the *camposanto*, in order to comply with an ordinance in the Napoleonic laws for the Roman states, had to be somewhat away from the city and walled in. So here comes a paradox: while the display of death in churches, gardens, squares, and catacombs is visible and open to the public, the reality of death in functioning and active cemeteries is not. The world of the dead is concealed from the world of the living by twenty-foot-tall walls and sturdy gates to keep either the living out or the dead in. Mourning is allowed at visiting hours only, the dead — it seems — keeping office hours.

That a cemetery is behind the gloomy wall is signaled by the forest of perennially green, tall, and lean cypress trees within, pointing to the sky like so many exclamation points. "*Sta a fa' terra pe' l'arberi pizzuti*" —he's making loam for the pointed trees — is a Roman metaphor equivalent to "he's pushing up daisies" for saying that someone has died.

The walled-in cemetery is quite different from the Anglo-Saxon custom of the open, gardenlike cemetery, its tombs set in small familiar clusters in a churchyard, or on a rolling green hill, or on a rocky spur above the sea; in any case, the dear deceased are given an open, serene space with a view. Here in Rome even the little Protestant cemetery — il Cimitero Acattolico — conforms to the local rules and is fenced in by the Aurelian Walls, in the shadow of the Pyramid of Gaius Cestius, and closed behind locked iron doors. It dates to the eighteenth century, its tombs lined on graded terraces. Some tombs are simple slabs of gray stone; some elaborate examples of romanticized funeral art with sculpted angels or with serene busts of the deceased. It is as cheerful as a cemetery can be, full of cypress trees, well-tended flowering bushes, and fruit plants. "It might make one in love with death to think that one should be buried in so sweet a place" was Shelley's opinion of the grounds, and that is where his heart is buried (the rest of his body was cremated), brought here by his friend Edward Trelawny, the writer. John Keats's body rests here also, and Goethe's only son, Julius; and so are the remains of many foreigners who made of Rome their beloved, and now perpetual, residence. It is indeed a place to come and meditate, to be alone with your thoughts for a while, leaving the commotion and noise of the city muffled behind the ancient walls. The cemetery does, indeed, imbue one with serenity. I have been there in winter when the light is cutting sharp, shadows are dark, dead leaves blanket the ground, and oranges and lemons on trees spot the gray with points of color; I have been there in spring when the light is soft and blue-pink, shadows are gentle, and the Acattolico is a gardenful of flowers. I have been there in fall, and the visits always made my thoughts tend to life; the "so sweet a place" did not "make me in love with death," and the "be buried" part did not even cross my mind. A beautifully serene place, yes, but not to die for.

Only a few hundred yards from the Protestant cemetery the old Aurelian Wall assumes a noble and protective stature, safeguarding the lines of white headstones of the Commonwealth's 429 young soldiers buried at its feet. This is the Rome British Military Cemetery. Here, too, is serenity, but it is lined with sadness: the souls of these young people must be sharing my feelings. No matter how serene and "sweet a place," being buried here (or, at their age, in any place) is not as romantic as Shelley made it out to be.

The decision to stop burying the dead in churches and parish cemeteries, or in any other place within the city, but to do so only in a prescribed *camposanto* was argued strenuously for religious, logistic, and administrative reasons. The chosen place was the Campo Verano (from the Verani family, who once owned the land), and it took more than a half century for the cemetery to become functional — and for a long time the citizenry resented it. The fact that the cemetery wall wasn't complete and that cows, goats, and sheep could sneak through the gaps to pasture among the tombs spurred the feeling that the *camposanto* (the holy field) wasn't that *santo*, after all, and that the church grounds held a better guarantee for a quieter afterlife. Many were the bodies unburied at night from the Verano and brought back to their parish church. It was only during the second half of the nineteenth century that Il Verano achieved the somber, monumental appearance that it has today. Well-known planners and famous architects went to work to give the cemetery a unified texture, with a grandiose entrance, and avenues, and streets, and monuments, all in all copying for the city of the dead the basic canons of the city of the living. A pamphlet about the cemeteries of Rome by P. Menacci, dated 1865, reads:

> The Campo Verano, which rests grandiosely near the Basilica of San Lorenzo, has nothing in common with the cemeteries of most of the other European cities, which do not follow the Christian mold but that of a voluptuous and romantic paganism that transforms their cemeteries, the very kingdoms of death, into so many gardens of delight made for enjoyment, just like the Esperides and the Elysian gardens of the pagan fable. None of this is in Rome: once you step into the Verano, everything is solemn, everything is sacred,

> everything is venerable; the holy terror of the last day
> on earth, together with the sweet certitude of resurrec-
> tion and the consoling faith of reaching the true home-
> land of Paradise is everywhere, it is always present and
> it moves you in every single fiber of your being.

And, but it is only my opinion, the architecture, like the prose, is replete — in a lugubrious key — with a considerable amount of kitsch. A more recent booklet titled *I Percorsi della Memoria* (Trails of Remembrance), published in 1998 by the *Sovrainten-denza ai Beni Culturali del Comune di Roma*, describes one by one the many and valuable tombs and mausoleums in the Verano that represent Funeral Art.

My parents are buried there. It has been many years (my choice) since I have gone to pay homage to them there. Their crypt is a classic of funeral architecture: climbing ivy spirals up two truncated columns, symbolizing truncated lives; ornate bronze flower urns surround a marble platform; above this is another marble slab that can be moved aside to access the tomb proper, a chamber with space for six more caskets. The slab has not been moved in a long time.

My mother's and father's photo-ceramic pictures — "similitudes" they are called in the bureaucratese of the cemetery — are embedded beside their chiseled names on a vertical, shiny black slab of Carrara marble. Similitudes they are not. From the oval frames, their faces look past me with the stared, unfocused, inane look of passport pictures. The photographs actually make them look even more dead than they deserve, and I much prefer to keep my memory of them, the two most alive people I ever knew, removed and away from this place. Moreover, the Campo Verano, the city of the dead, is becoming more and more similar to the city of the living with overcrowding, neglect, decay, and illegal structures.

Massimiliano De Gese manages a *Pompe e Servizi Funebri*, a funeral home, in Trastevere, a family business. Unlike other Roman funeral homes this one does not have a mournful look or a full-view display of caskets, like home appliances; from its appearance and decor it could be a real-estate office or a public-service agency. I have been walking by the *Pompe* almost every day, and only now I read its unobtrusive name above the storefront door. I cannot resist walking in.

Massimiliano is behind a desk piled with papers; I introduce myself and right away tell him that I am not coming in for business, but only — if he has the time — to have a chat about dying in Rome. He must be no more than thirty, diminutive and athletic. There is a lively twinkle in his eyes and an amused smile on his lips.He has an educated but strong Roman accent; it is easy to converse with him.

"The whole logistics of entombment are in the hands of the *Comune*, City Hall," Massimiliano tells me, "actually, of the *Azienda Municipale Ambiente*, AMA, a company under contract with City Hall, the same company in charge of street cleaning and garbage removal."

A citizen can use their services for free, he tells me, but then he has to go through the whole painful administrative paper shuffle and arrangements on his own.

"We take care of all that. Actually, AMA takes care mostly of the destitute, and it doesn't get much work, not terribly much," he continues, "because its material is second rate. Which is understandable: to make things economical they have to cut corners, somewhere. We, for example, supply mahogany, or walnut, or cherry, all sturdy wood caskets; they go with pine or larch, stuff that doesn't last much. After a few years it's gone. Their hearses are Fiat vans, like delivery wagons, not much to look at, and in this business people care about looks." He turns on his swivel chair and gestures to framed photos on the wall: "We supply Mercedes, even the latest models with four headlights, for those who want to cut a good figure and can pay for it."

Massimiliano talks about his business in a direct way, devoid of the standard metaphors of the trade. I find it a bit disturbing at first, and then, given his relaxed, cheerful attitude, realistic. For him it's just a business; I am sure that he performs it in a direct, dignified, and professional way.

"The *Comune* is in charge of all the bureaucratic rigmarole; it also owns the land and all the communal structures that belong in the cemeteries. The burial grounds, the vaults. And, quite frankly, it takes advantage of the situation. They lease you, let's say, a second-tier vault for five million and some thousand lire, then after thirty years you have to give it back; they take the bones out and put them in little boxes and you have to pay again to have them put in an ossarium. It's the same for an earth entombment: after ten years — the earth eats the remains faster — the remains are removed and a new space becomes available. '*Requiescat in pacem,*' they say, but here with all this shuffling there is neither much resting nor peace."

I ask him if there are any alternatives, any options, aside from going on forever, not dying.

"I wouldn't recommend that," he says with a smile, "I would be out of a job. But yes, there is: cremation. Cremation is free. The *Comune* pays for it. But then you have to buy a *cinerario*, a vault, to put the urns in. So in the end the *Comune* still makes a profit. Cremation is becoming fashionable here, as in other countries. Mostly because there is no more space. They are now building a new cemetery in Tritoria."

Massimiliano now uses a common Roman hand gesture: he touches a finger with the mention of each cemetery available to Romans: "At the Verano there is no more room; at Prima Porta idem; Ostia is full, Fregene, too, and so is Fiumicino. So now they are building this new one, and already they have almost filled all the reservations for the tombs. And, you know, a tomb today costs about the same as an apartment. I do not know how it works in America, but here, today, it's an investment. A tomb costs around 250 million lire."

I agree that, yes, you could get a small apartment with that. But you would save on furnishings. . . . The conversation swings back to the subject of economics.

"Certainly one can save some money and do a funeral oneself, go directly with the *Comune*. You have to get all the certificates and licenses, follow all the bureaucratic *pratiche*, make all the arrangements for the monument, the photographs . . . . They call it *pompe funebri*, but the municipal choice of pomp is quite limited. No style; quite frankly, it's sad, depressing."

Way back, before his time — I remind him — the municipal *funerali* came with choices: first, second and third class. The third class, even if modest, was still very decorous, the second a little better, but the first class was something to stop the traffic: the hearse was a monumental coach of sculpted ebony and crystals, two black-and-gold liveried coachmen in front, two equally liveried footmen in back, all wearing gold-trimmed black three-cornered hats; four shiny black horses, in black-plumed harness, pulled in synchronized steps the huge apparatus, the enormous steel-rimmed wheels rumbling on the cobblestones. A similarly impressive coach, covered with wreaths and flowers, followed, and then came the long, long line of grieving people, mournfully shuffling along after the hearse. Passersby would uncover their heads. "That must have been an important person!" they would whisper (and also scratch their crotches, and make the "horns" sign with their fingers against the *iella*, the bad luck: you never knew, death could be contagious). And sometimes, at the sight of the horses, we children, inspired by some western movie, would tease the coachmen, whisper-yelling from the sidewalk, "Fifth Cavalry! Charge!" and then run away from their long, snapping, red-and-blue-tasseled whips.

Massimiliano, visualizing the scene, agrees that those were the good times.

"But even today people care about funerals" is his comment. "After all, after baptism, graduation, and marriage, the funeral is one of the most important events in our lives. It is your last chance at *bella figura*, to show off. Some people ask why spend so much money for it, but then it's the same reason that people spend extra for a dress by Valentino or Armani instead of buying a cheap one at basement prices. Or go for one casket instead of another: it's like kitchen cabinets, solid wood is better than veneered plywood. People know."

I ask him if Romans, when it comes to funerals, are religious. "Yes, they are. Even if Rome has a lot of foreign, different religions. Buddhists, Muslims, Protestants, they are religious, too. But yes, Romans are religious."

Massimiliano's mentioning of "different" religious beliefs brings up the fact that most Romans consider Roman Catholicism "the" religion. They have been brought up with it; it's a fact of life. All others are — like the *pellegrini* — alien. But they refer to other faiths without malice or intolerance. Still, there are limits. Recently, a large, modern mosque was allowed to be built, but only if its tallest minaret was a few feet lower than Saint Peter's dome.

"Nobody wants to pass up the last rites," he continues. "Out of one hundred, perhaps two or three do not want a religious service. Here, too, we take care of the arrangements and decide the price for the service, which, naturally, can be simple or elaborate."

On this religious subject my mind wanders. I tell Massimiliano that he made me think of my father, in religion an agnostic, in politics a *mangiapreti*, a priest-eater. When he died he left for us children a handwritten will, his moral testament. He told us that he loved us very much, and wanted us, if he was to go first, to take care of and love our mother just as he did; that in all his life he tried to do the right thing, not hurt anybody, follow his conscience; that he did not believe in the presumption of another human being, a priest, to act as God's self-appointed go-between. He, my father, could face his own God, accept His verdict, if there was one to be had. Hence, he preferred not to have a church funeral. But if this would provoke unhappiness in my mother, who was quite religious, then, so as not to upset her, we could go ahead and have a simple, pro forma church service. Which we did. I loved my father very much, and I frequently think of his last-rite decision: it was a generous and altruistic decision; nonetheless the old fox went, with as little fanfare as possible, for the man-made heavenly pass-port. Like insurance: you never know.

"We arrange to have the funeral mass around 9:30 or 10 in the morning. It gives people time to get ready without rushing, espe-cially for the ones who have to face the morning traffic. It also al-lows the corpse to get to the cemetery before 12:30 P.M. Admissions are allowed between 8:30 and 12:30. If the body arrives at 12:31 they will not let it in. They park the casket in a mortuary chamber with all the other latecomers until the next day; then it has to get in line until all the others are buried. Cemetery hours are 8:30 A.M. to 5 P.M., but the burying stops at 12:30!"

I ask him if there is a particular reason for this schedule. "Go figure!" he says. "Perhaps it is a rule from 1557 or something, and nobody got around to changing it; perhaps it's the diggers' unions, who knows?"

I ask him if there is a dying season in Rome, and he gives me the obvious answer: "Death is a year-round customer. But there are peaks in very hot or very cold weather, especially for older people. They just give up, and she comes and takes them away . . . but the yearly average, a few more, a few less, is around eighty to ninety a day. Quite a few more than births."

His company has been in this location for more than thirty years, and I ask him if its activity is focused in Trastevere or, in other words, how does he get his clientele? In America, I tell him, funeral parlors advertise in all media.

"No, we do not advertise. We have another outlet in Monte Sacro, across town, and, as in all other businesses, if you do a good job, people come back. In moments of tragedy, people are con-fused, cannot think straight. Oh, my God, what should I do? Where should I go? So there is always a friend who will tell them to call us, that we treated them well . . . word of mouth, you know."

Massimiliano is curious about the advertising, and I tell him that, yes, in America the funeral industry advertises heavily, in newspapers, on TV, radio. Even through direct mail, and it can get pretty morbid. They ask you to put money down toward your own funeral, your tomb. It's rational, makes sense, perhaps, but it is morbid.

"America," he says, "what a country! I always wanted to go there. Go there to fight . . ."

"There are no wars now," I tell him. He laughs and explains that he is, actually was, a professional *pugile*, a boxer. Flyweight and bantamweight, 112 or 118 pounds, a member of the Italian team for five years.

"We went all over the world; we were a good team." He says wistfully, "I won several tricolor belts, here in Italy, as a professional. I'm telling you, I was dangerous! The American team came here for a championship match and we were going to go there, to America and Canada . . . but I broke a hand and couldn't go. Now I have given up professional fighting, but I still do it for pleasure. And I still want to go to America . . ."

An imposing lady in mourning has entered the shop; it looks like she means business, and Signor De Gese returns to his professional pose. I shake his hand and, thanking him for his time, leave his office.

It is evening now and outside in Piazza San Cosimato a quartet, sponsored by a political party, is playing New Orleans jazz — and they are good. Children are running around, mothers are hurrying home with grocery bags, the hundred eateries of Trastevere are broadcasting their presence with their kitchens' aromas. The sky is clear, a luminous blue, and I repeat to myself Dante's verse: ". . . and so we walked out, again overwhelmed by the sight of the stars."

And for a brief moment I thought that in Rome nobody really dies.

X

Faith in Rome

Mille campanili

*I*F YOU ASK this traveler to name one experience, just one, that can define Rome, that makes it different from other places on this globe, that one-among-the-many identifying lines of its fingerprint, I would have to say the bells. Church bells. Whenever I can, I spiral up the staircase that takes me from the living room of my temporary quarters to the terrace above and sit in wait for noon. As a space traveler who landed on this little flat of bricks and flowers, I enjoy the view of the eternal city sprawled beneath, extending almost to the faraway mountains in the north and to the hills in the east, a large bowl of buildings with the seven ancient hills all there to be counted. A beautiful cityscape; different from Paris or New York or Hong Kong, but otherwise it is just another cityscape among the many. What makes it unique is the stroke of noon. That is when the Gianicolo's cannon fires its salvo and all the church bells of Rome are let loose in any season, in any weather, to celebrate another midday. And every time, just as with the first, one feels elated and engulfed by the sound, a resonating sound with a thousand voices covering all the registers, coming from all points of the compass. It quiets down slowly in a

long coda, the final sound of a bell coming in late, having trav-
eled from far away to reach your ears. I wonder if such a majestic
sound will travel the ether and reach my home base, Mars — or
Boston. With the sound just an echo, one is now attracted by the
other striking element of the cityscape: the hundreds of slim
towers and round domes that punctuate the city like notes on a
musical score. In the immediate vicinity of this terrace I count
eighteen churches, seven chapels, and one basilica. Aided by a
spyglass, I can see also the synagogue's dome and, farther away,
the thin minarets of the mosque. This, indeed, I tell myself, must
be a very religious city.

It is almost impossible, when walking around town, not to feel
the presence of a church — frequently more than one, with two
facing each other and a third one down the street — and almost as
impossible to resist its mystic pull and enter. And every time, Ro-
manesque, gothic, baroque, or rococo, one cannot help but be impressed. In some it is the sheer vastness; in all — big or small —
the richness of the decorations, the value of the art. The obvious
expense, all the material effort applied to a spiritual end; this luxu-
rious demonstration of devotion to a humble deity through worldly
materialism makes one think. The attempt to reconcile the two
creates an uneasy seesaw between rationality and religiosity. This
duality is accentuated during the ceremonies, especially high
mass: the complex liturgy, the pomp of the officiants' vestments,
the heady smell of incense mixed with the choir's ethereal sound,
the opulence of the gold and of the silver, all make for a rich and
fulfilling experience. The jarring contrast comes when, as in the
church of San Carlo ai Catinari, at the edge of the Ghetto, one
sees suspended above the main altar a ten-foot-wide gold medal-
lion, golden rays bursting from it as from a burning sun and, artfully draped across the middle of it, a sash with golden letters.
They spell HUMILITAS. The incongruity between mysticism and
worldliness couldn't be made more evident.

The seesaw continues when one notices the attitude of the
congregation: except for a few concentrating in prayer, a large

portion of those present seems remote and absent, engaged in semiwhispered conversation. Some, mostly men, in a stretched compromise, "attend mass" just outside the church door, indulging in a cigarette. Gwen and I have witnessed an impromptu game of soccer among some teenagers carried on with great glee inside the portico of the church of Santissimi Apostoli. The enthusiastic "score!" yelled by the winning team is answered by a loud, equally clear blasphemy from the losers. Suddenly the church door swings open from inside and a young boy comes to summon the others: "Come! It's communion time!" The players quickly compose themselves as best they can and file back inside the church just in time to receive the blessed sacrament. Gwen is less surprised by the event than I am; having spent many years in the south of Italy, she is accustomed to this familiarity with religion, religion that is accepted as a given, seldom questioned, always exteriorized publicly, loudly, colorfully, mindlessly. Chanted prayers to a saint may readily become beratings if the expected yearly miracle (like the liquefaction of the saint's clotted blood) has not been performed on time. At first, this religious attitude was so astonishing to Gwen's fresh American ears that she associated it with paganism. And even now, she reminds me, few are the private homes — or shops or public offices — that do not display a sacred image. Nonetheless, and in the immediate presence of the icons, blasphemy — a major sin — is a common interjection. Even here in Rome, the world's center of the *Chiesa Cattolica Romana!*

How deeply religious is this city? I decide I will try to find out by asking a clergyman, a priest. Someone, as they say here, *con le mani in pasta*, someone — like a baker kneading the leavened dough — deeply involved in the business. But then another popular saying makes me change plans: *È come domandare all'oste se il vino è buono*, it would be like asking the wine dealer if his wine is good. I will save the priest for last, I promise myself, asking my questions first to people who should know, even if not directly in the business.

I put my query first to Fabio Troncarelli, a professor of *scienze umane*, a field that is a mixture of history, philosophy, and sociology. I met him at the presentation of a new book: *La Chiesa e Giordano Bruno*. It is the philosophical interpretation, through the reading of historical archives, of the Inquisition's trial and burning of the heretic Bruno. The presentation of a new book in Rome consists of a panel of four or five literati who, in the presence of the author, sit on a raised podium in front of an audience and pontificate. In theory, they should discuss the merits of the book, but in actuality they talk at anesthetizing lengths about themselves and their work, generally getting involved in diatribes among themselves, jockeying for a position of superior knowledge. Fabio was the only panelist able to stick to the subject and rein in, with a great deal of tact and humor, the remaining panelists. I liked him and I got to know him. He looks younger than his age (early fifties), and to his credit, in addition to his professional credentials, is the fact that he was born in the heart of Rome, on Via dei Giubbonari, in the immediate vicinity of Campo de' Fiori, in the shadow of Giordano Bruno's statue; he is also a seventh-generation Roman, "one of the few," he says with pride, "still in existence."

We meet at a café for a morning cappuccino and I pop my alien's question: I saw the bell towers, I saw the domes, I heard the prayers and the chants. What is the relationship between Rome and the church, Romans and Catholicism?

He makes himself comfortable, digesting my question, thinking. I promise that I will not interrupt him, a willing listener to an erudite speaker. With his permission, I take advantage of technology and record his voice on a minuscule tape recorder.

"I can talk about the relationship between Romans and my religion, Catholicism, through my personal experience — knowledge, if you wish — and the experiences of the people close to me. I went to religious schools and I was active in parish activities; I, and my friends, used the church as a point of association, a group to which we belonged — a tribe into which we were born.

"In Rome, from my point of view, religion as a spiritual expression is absolutely absent."

My visible surprise at his terse statement stops him for a second, then:

"What I mean is that religion is only an exterior expression, a pose. You see all the churches, you see them all full of people, but the adhesion is purely superficial. To explain: I frequently talk to people who profess themselves to be Roman Catholics but who do not know what it really means. My parents, for example, are going through a mystic phase in their old age; for about ten years they have been all *casa e chiesa*, home and church, but of Christianity they know absolutely nothing, they just go through the routine."

Fabio has a deep voice, and his words come in fluid, fast sequences, as if they had to rush to keep up with his thoughts. He tells me that sitting in a church is not enough to be a Christian. One needs a strong commitment, not only a social one but especially a deep, individually spiritual one. At one point in recent history, the *Democrazia Cristiana* party inherited from the church its social and organizational functions, implying a spiritual commitment by its name. Under the name of Christian Democracy — here Fabio's narration slows down to underline the seriousness of his statement — some of its leaders were the worst kind of people one would want to know. He illustrates this with a fact recently revived in the newspapers. On September 8, 1943, Italy's king declared a separate armistice with the Allies, instantly turning the Germans from allies into enemies. The Italian garrison on the Greek island of Cephalonia — the number of soldiers remains uncertain, somewhere between five thousand and sixty-five hundred — was left, without any warning, to fend for themselves. They refused to surrender, so the Germans massacred the entire Italian garrison in a single day. It was an inhuman slaughter, an absolutely unnecessary and illegal war action. Many years later, sometime in the late 1970s, a group of the Italian soldiers' relatives wanted to bring to trial the German officers responsible for the massacre. Here Fabio comes to the point: Paolo Emilio Taviani, then the Demo-Christian minister of foreign affairs, explained that since the Russians were making a big fuss about Germany's rearmament, and since Germany, like Italy, was a part of NATO, accusing Germany of a war crime at this stage would play into the hands of the godless Russians. Hence he denied the petition as politically inexpedient and diplomatically offensive.

"To think of this explanation as justifiable," Fabio pronounces one word at time as reinforcement, "must be the filthiest thing a Christian can do. It was profoundly immoral not to ask for justice. I've met personally with Mr. Taviani: he attends mass every morning at 7:30, but I assure you that there is absolutely nothing Christian about him."

The anecdote reinforces the point that in Rome religiosity equates with Catholicism, and church with clergy, and clergy with politics. Catholic clergy have taken the authoritarian governing role for a long, long time and Romans, historically accustomed to the authorities' vile behavior, are profoundly anticlerical. Perhaps, Fabio elucidates, the only time the Roman church had a real spiritual role was during the fourth, fifth, and sixth centuries; with the arrival of the barbarians' invasions came the church's great shake-up. After the pontificate of Gregorio Magno, the church lost all of the authentic Christianity it ever had. Since then, Romans have suffered this pseudoreligiosity as an imposition from high above, with the power trickling down to the local parish priests. These priests, vicars of the pope more than of the Lord, kept the faithful under a kind of moral blackmail: displease me and I will open the doors of Hell for you; I'll decide myself if you deserve to receive the sacraments or not.

"Naturally," Fabio says in a softer tone, "I do not mean to say that there aren't any good priests: there are a lot of intelligent, caring priests who do laudable parish work — who assist the poor, work with the community, and participate actively in the education of young people, trying to keep them away from harm. These are priests who behave intelligently and are in tune with today's demands and morality, who do not follow the strict dogmatic, frequently hypocritical, dictates of the church."

As a matter of fact, it is the kind of social work that is very important, especially now, in the new Roman suburbs. Until recently the various political parties were organized to offer these social services for the young and the elderly and served as useful meeting places, complete with recreation facilities. With the great political crisis, however, people lost faith in the parties, and the politically organized clubs disappeared. But the local parish was still there to resume its social functions and, in so doing, brought people back into the church. Even so, there is a big split between church life and religion. Hence, Fabio tells me, it is not hard to explain the paradox of so many anticlericals within a large population of churchgoers. That is not to say, however, that there has not been at times a rapprochement with the church, in the event, for example, of particularly popular priests, or even popes, such as Pope John XXIII in the 1960s. This renewed bond bursts like a flame and ignites like once-wet gunpowder. The feelings are authentic and visceral, starting from the ground up.

"Pope John XXIII was a totally different pope, not a politician like Pius IX or Pius XII, or even John Paul II. He was a generous shepherd with a sincere and devoted love for his flock, not full of resounding, empty words. People were genuinely attached to him. When he said to the faithful: 'Go home and give your children a caress, tell them that it is from their pope,' it was a real Christian caress, there was a feeling of participation; the latent Christianity became more real, more profound. I saw people shedding real tears at his funeral; religion then is more than a social expression, something more than just a belonging to a group. It became like the spirit of Saint Francis, of love and charity for all living things. When this does not exist, which is the case in the majority of papacies, Romans become cynical and detached."

As his talk progresses, Fabio clearly shows his Roman pugnacity, what could be spoken of as getting hot under the collar. I remark that what he is telling me does not seem to conform with the idea of Rome as the theological center of Catholicism, as the seat of the many theological schools and seminaries.

Fabio makes himself comfortable and we both stir our second *cappuccino*.

"First of all, a Roman theology does not exist, it never existed." He says it with assurance, a statement that does not expect refutation.

"Definitely nothing that can be compared with Paris, which produced such theologians as Saint Thomas Aquinas and Albert Magnus. Naturally there have been a lot of important theologians in Rome, but they were guests. They came from outside Rome; they were formed outside Rome. Rome has been the refuge of many religious people who came and flourished and produced great works. The Roman ecclesiastics have not been able to express anything but pure, simple bureaucratic power; they are incapable of producing a single theological idea of their own. Why is this?"

I do not answer his rhetorical question, so he proceeds to say that it is because nothing can be said or written, not a single comma altered, without the approval of a higher church authority. The result is that the only thought that can be produced is a carbon copy of the authority's; there is an inability to express anything new. In Rome there is no religious philosophy, not a single religious, theological thought. And, yes, Rome is the center, the head of Catholicism. It is, I think, a paradox worth thinking about.

"Even in the Roman sainthood, which can be one of the more elevated aspects of the church's mythology, there are none of the great bishops, none of the great exponents of the Curia. I challenge anyone to give me an example of authentic Roman sanctity, authentic pastoral care of the souls, that did not come from the lower ranks."

I dare to propose that perhaps things are going to change: I have heard of the Vatican's motion for the beatification, the first step toward sainthood, of Giovanni Mastai-Ferretti, Pope Pius IX. Fabio corrects me: "Pope, yes. Roman, no. He was *marchigiano*" —a man from the Marches, a region east of Rome and, then, one of the Pontifical States. I apologize for the faux pas. Fabio seems pleased with my mistake. It gives him the chance, I suspect, to get involved in a subject closer to Roman lore than religion. He explains that Pius IX brought to Rome a lot of his compatriots from the Marches, and gave them jobs as tax collectors, hence the popular saying: *È meglio un morto in casa che un marchigiano alla porta!* Better a death in the family than a man from Le Marche knocking at the door!

Pope Pius IX was the longest-reigning pope, thirty-two years, from 1846 to 1878, the last *Papa Re*, pope-king, with temporal powers over a large portion of central Italy. He was totally political, with a strong despotic bent, disliked and feared by the intelligentsia and the *popolino* alike. At the beginning of his papacy he feigned liberal tendencies and people saw the possibility of the Vatican taking a leading moral position in an Italy on the verge of being united. But he soon changed course and showed himself for what he was: a religious fundamentalist. He fought, with the support of Napoleon III, to maintain his temporal power, which he was finally forced to give up in 1870 when Italian troops took Rome by storm.

Fabio counts in short succession — a historical treatise would take more than a few cappuccinos, he says — the main events in Rome under Pius IX: the kidnapping and conversion of Jewish children; the closing again of the Ghetto doors in 1850, after they had been torn down, *vis populi*, in 1848; the proclamation of the doctrine of papal infallibility; the publication of the "Syllabus of Errors," a list of all past papal mistakes to be corrected and recanted, such as the leniency shown toward other religions, especially Judaism; and the mistake of allowing Catholic believers to participate in politics. He was brutal toward anyone who transgressed his or his monsignors' edicts. Under his reign there were hundreds of public executions.

"All told," concludes Fabio, "I would hardly think of Pius IX — Roman or not — as material for beatification, let alone sainthood."

The subject of executions prompts Fabio to remark, parenthetically and with a touch of morbid humor, that not too far from where we are sipping our cappuccino, in Vicolo del Campanile 4, in Trastevere, lived Giambattista Bugatti. Under the name of Mastro Titta, he was the most famous Roman *boia*, executioner, a real virtuoso in the administration of death. He exercised his profession — someone defined him an *artista* — at the service of the Vatican state. No matter how the condemned was to be dispatched (depending on the crime's seriousness, or the judges' humor, by clubbing, garroting, hanging, hanging *and* quartering, beheading) he was a most able and detached professional. A chronicle of 1886, Fabio tells me, describes Mastro Titta as

> short, roly-poly, clean shaven and always very neatly dressed. His assurance on the scaffold, his visible indifference and almost pleasure in his work, served to calm down and soothe the condemned; sometimes he would produce a snuff box, take a pinch of tobacco and, people have testified to it, even offer some to the condemned. . . . As a good Roman Catholic *boia*, Mastro Titta confessed himself and took communion regularly.

Under the tutelage of French experts, he became proficient in the use of the guillotine, chopping off — between February 28, 1810, and December 18, 1813 — fifty-six heads. Including those, his professional services numbered 514. His career ended because of old age and ". . . partially because of a mishap: the severed head of Antonio Ajetti, thief, fell from its impaling post, provoking great consternation among the public." He retired after sixty-eight years of service with a generous pension from the Vatican state.

"All told," concludes Fabio, "another conscientious Roman Catholic bureaucrat."

Throughout his talk, Fabio Troncarelli interjects a sort of disclaimer to assure me that what he is saying is removed from any partisanship or personal feelings; it is all historical observation, proven facts, and, as he says, *a cognizione di causa*, from his studied knowledge of the matter.

I trust him implicitly, and yet, his being so much a Roman, I wonder if he is not genetically inclined to color things with that hard-to-describe Roman hue: part sarcasm, part irony, part detachment, part reality as seen by an imaginative mind.

And also, experience has taught me that one knows where a conversation with a mercurial Roman begins, but seldom where it will lead to.

I happen again on the subject of Roman religiosity and spirituality in a conversation with Piero Benetazzo, who, being a northerner from the Venetian provinces, should be free from that Roman coloring brush. He has been living in Rome for twenty-five years, however, and therefore is dedicated to, and knowledgeable about, the city; he hides his proverbial native wit under a mask of professional seriousness. He has recently switched from print journalism to radio journalism — in the field of foreign affairs — because, he confides, "the required norm in today's Italian newspapers is not to let the facts interfere with a pseudoliterary, prolix style."

It is a crisp, clear morning and we converse while we walk, a peripatetic school of two; from Via della Lungara, where he resides, we amble along the chestnut-tree-lined Lungotevere, the avenue along the bank of the Tiber, heading north toward Castel Sant'Angelo. There is no aim to our walk; it is just a beautiful day — not to be wasted inside, we agree; the traffic is light at this hour, the walking pleasant. He has a resonant, cultivated voice and speaks in short sentences, so as to get to the point as clearly and briefly as possible.

"A few years ago a poll stated that 93 percent of Romans professed to being Catholic," he says. "They were all baptized, and all followed the required sacraments of confirmation, communion, marriage, and, when the time comes, extreme unction."

The poll further stated that a high percentage of the interviewed also believed in ghosts and consulted astrologers and palm readers. Of all Italian cities, it turned out that Rome had the highest number of licensed fortune-tellers.

"About 50 percent of those polled admitted they did not believe in the *aldilà*, the hereafter, at least not as it is proposed by the Catholic church. In one way or another, Roman religiosity showed a strong presence of pagan beliefs. This, plus other polled data, came as a surprise to the public, something that nobody seemed to be aware of. The fact that it was a surprise to them came as a surprise to me. Because all these pagan expressions are not new, not at all. To mention just one, there is a very old 'Cult of the Phantoms'; practically every section of Rome has its own *fantasma*."

I am aware of it, I tell him. Here in Via della Lungara, there is Donna Lucrezia. She was a beautiful Renaissance noblewoman, the lover of cardinals — some say of popes — who one day mysteriously disappeared. Now, once in a while, in the middle of the night, she races in her carriage up and down the Lungara, the steel-clad wheels rumbling over the cobblestones. Once, at the morning market, I heard the old locals say: "Did you hear Donna Lucrezia last night? She really made a racket, didn't she!" She is, they told me, a good phantom; she somehow watches over the neighborhood. Something, I thought, like a guardian angel, pagan-style.

"In Rome there has always been this conflict between Catholicism and paganism," Piero continues, "between the old and the new, a conflict that has never been resolved. There are neither victors nor vanquished. The results of that poll prompted the Vatican, the pope himself, to declare Rome a *terra di missioni*, a land in need of missionaries, as in darkest Africa of old. They sent a thousand or so missionaries — mostly Polish, by the way — to roam the city and proselytize the Romans. A year afterward, I interviewed the missionary in charge of the campaign and asked him what the results were, and he expressed satisfaction with the positive outcome. But I do not believe that he was able to resolve much. You cannot correct in a short time a situation that has existed for thousands of years. And yet, considering all the popular impiety, when they came to bless their homes for Easter, everybody opened their doors and accepted the Polish missionaries."

On this subject, I have to comment to Piero how times have changed: when I was a child, a priest came to bless our house at

Easter: he was fluent in Latin but very tentative in Italian. He was Korean, and at that time nobody — definitely not my mother — had ever seen an obviously non-Italian priest. She made all the welcoming motions and smiled at him, but as soon as the blessing was over and he was out the door, she called the parish house and asked for a real blessing from a real priest, not necessarily Roman, but at least Italian!

Piero smiles at the anecdote, commenting that the traditional high level of *campanilismo*, chauvinism, has sensibly decreased, if not totally disappeared. After all, there was some hesitation when Polish Karol Wojtyla was elected Pope John Paul II, but no revolution. And yet, religion and superstition are intertwined in Rome, he says, and it is not a novel thing.

"I have read somewhere," Piero continues, "that Edward Gibbon was inspired to write his *History of the Decline and Fall of the Roman Empire* by an experience he had during a visit to Rome, presumably around 1760. While visiting the old ruins, he saw some barefoot monks dancing, as if possessed, on the ruins of an old Roman temple. He was so astounded by the sight that he decided to write the history of Rome before it became totally obfuscated. He sensed the attempt of the church of Rome to destroy the pagan memories of old Rome, an attempt subliminally still going on. As a matter of fact (I will find for you the exact quotes, says Piero) the pope himself recently exhorted the faithful not to go and visit the Roman ruins because they would be distracted from the Christian aspects of Rome. This preoccupation of the pope's, publicly expressed, underlines that not-yet-resolved conflict between Catholicism and non-Catholicism, not to call it paganism. The Holy City and the Sensual City, the city of churches and of processions, and the pagan city that bewilders the senses."

This duality was recognized in the literary world as well; people came to Rome to find life, to find themselves. Goethe was fleeing from an old, obsessive lover; Byron and the Romantics came to escape from the constrictions of puritanism, the boredom of the northern fogs. Henry Adams advised people against coming to Rome, using harsh words, calling it a city of sinners, a city where one lets himself go to all wickedness, a city that corrupts. Rome, the pure old whore.

"As I see it, Roman Catholicism never had great peaks of mysticism; it has always been a pragmatic Catholicism; it has always had to adapt itself to the cynical mentality of the Romans. A Catholicism that has always been a prisoner of Rome's old stones. They are a presence that cannot be ignored, they are what makes of Rome the complex city that it is. No victors, no vanquished."

It is close to noon; the traffic has picked up considerably and it is getting a bit difficult to be a peripatetic. Without planning it, we have reached Ponte Sant'Angelo. Flanking the bridge, Bernini's ten marble angels frame against a terse blue sky the austere Sant'Angelo fortress, once Emperor Hadrian's tomb. Saint Peter's Basilica, residence of the Prince of the Church, dominates the scene from the background. The sacred and the profane, the worldly and the spiritual, a visual, and exceptionally beautiful, compendium of Piero's views.

The traffic and the hour — close to lunchtime — allow me just one last question. Rome and the church: who owns what?

Piero has to project his voice to be heard above the noise: "It is a pretty complex situation. Definitely the real estate of the basilicas belongs to the Vatican state, and some of the convents, too. They enjoy extraterritorial rights: as soon as you step inside you are in foreign territory. The subject of Vatican-owned real estate and the city of Rome is a delicate one, perhaps the most complex of the whole relationship. The Vatican is a full-fledged state, a bona fide foreign nation located within Rome; almost every nation of the world has an embassy to the Vatican, with full diplomatic — and economic — privileges. In a quiet, hushed way, it involves a lot of money. And that is alway a magnet for malfeasance. There have been real-estate scandals on the lofty, big-money, international scale. On a day-by-day basis, on the parish-church level, the churches are the property of the Italian state, and the Vatican is officially the guardian and administrator of the real estate. The clergy and attendant personnel are on the church payroll, but with a subsidy from the Italian state. The proportion of the subsidy is determined by the agreement, *Il Concordato*, made in 1929 between church and state. At that time, Fascist Prime Minister Benito Mussolini, looking for acceptance and full support from the Vatican, and therefore international recognition, made great concessions to the Vatican. The Concordato was renewed, somewhat revised and trimmed, in the 1980s by Socialist Prime Minister Bettino Craxi.

"Some churches are under the tutelage of the *Comune*, which is responsible for their maintenance and upkeep, especially for the ones that, for artistic and historical value, fall under the jurisdiction of the *Sovarintendenza ai Beni Culturali*. Following an old tradition, the parishes used to collect from church benefactors a certain fee for each mass officiated; this for-the-souls'-salvation money went toward the upkeep of the church. To keep up with the tradition, the *Comune* now pays the churches a yearly amount commensurate with the number of masses performed."

Piero confirms in my mind his premise that the subject "Rome and Church" is a complex one, one that would take Aristotle himself more than one long walk to explain to his pupils. There is a huge legal body dedicated to the laws regulating the relationship, and many tomes exist about it — constantly revised and updated, and available at the public library.

"Only, at the moment the library is on strike," he adds with a smile.

It takes me a few days to transcribe and sort Fabio's and Piero's information. Then, following up on my initial intention, I stop at the closest parish church to talk with its curate. As I enter the church I ask the sacristan where I can find the parish priest. The ancient, grumpy sacristan asks me why I want to see the priest. Nothing to do with parish business, I reassure him, nothing that would involve more work. In which case, he says, he does not see why I need to disturb the *parroco*. I lie, explaining that all I wish is to know more about this beautiful church, actually basilica, of Santa Maria in Trastevere. He shuffles away, still suspicious, dragging his feet across the church and into the sacristy. After a long time — I thought he had forgotten about me — he comes back with the news that the *parroco* is busy, but I can come back around five in the afternoon. Which I do: the church is dark and deserted. The sacristan is nowhere to be seen, so I make my way into the sacristy, toward the parish office. Old Grumpy intercepts me: feigned or real, he does not recognize me, and I have to go through my explanations again. Again he disappears to come back with the information that the *parroco* is busy; I should come back in the morning, before 6, before first mass. The parish priest's first line of defense doesn't give up easily, but I do. I seat myself in a pew in the darkened church; exquisite golden mosaics reflect the lights of votive candles; three or four people near one of the altars are whispering the litanies. They echo around the church with the sound of a soft breeze. These people remind me of Fabio's parents, here in the church for mystical comfort and sustenance. Perhaps they are ignorant of theological philosophy and devoid of *spiritualità*, just going through a rote performance, but feeling better for it, receiving from the church what they came in for. Praying, hoping — or perhaps assured — that their prayers will be granted from high above.

I think of Fabio's and Piero's rambling assessments, obviously kept on a simple level for my ears, yet dictated by knowledge or intellectual reasoning, looking down on all the mundane aspects of the faithfuls' religion — insinuating, and they are not alone, the presence of paganism and superstition. There is a veiled condemnation of the Romans' religiosity, but I wonder how different this is from any other form of "religious spirituality" around the world.

Almost alone in the huge, cavernous church — for some arcane reason or none at all — I feel wrapped in a cocoon of quiet and serenity, mind and body at ease. Perhaps, I tell myself, this is mysticism.

On my way out, I light a votive candle and place it among the many already flickering in the darkness.

Tomorrow, at noon, I will go up onto the terrace and listen to the call of the Roman church bells. And, who knows, perhaps I will even say a prayer.

XI

Fountains and Pines

G WEN AND I love to take long walks in Rome, in old Rome, that is. We descend from our flat on Vicolo del Cedro and march downhill across the cobblestones of Trastevere. We reach Ponte Sisto over the Tiber and, in the middle of it, we pause for a moment. It is a sight we donate to ourselves twice a day, coming and going. On our left we can see Saint Peter's dome catching the morning sun, peeking over the spans of Ponte Mazzini; a mile to our right, just behind Ponte Garibaldi, the Isola Tiberina splits the rushing river, making it foam like the prow of a ship. In the middle of the newly scrubbed Ponte Sisto, a group of young people — some colorfully scruffy, some simply unwashed — convene most of the day and a good part of the night. Vagrants by choice, Germans by birth, they park their bedrolls, their mongrel dogs and puppies along the bridge railing and ask for alms. To encourage contributions, or to justify their earning them, they perfunctorily play strident, unmusical tunes on tin whistles. At our first meetings we contributed the requested thousand lire; on subsequent encounters I withheld my donations, and, finally, I told the most insistent beggar that to earn another thousand lire from me he had to perform, at the least, Beethoven's Fifth. Gwen considered this very inappropriate; I replied that I not only was encouraging the young man to get a musical education, but I was also refusing to pay a bridge toll as had been required during the times of Pope Sixtus. Since my request we now cross the bridge undisturbed; once across, a hundred routes are open to us into the cobblestoned, traffic-free Rome, but so are, depending on the nature of our errands, the many paths leading into the noisy chaos of urban traffic.

In that territory, both side-by-side walking and making conversation become arduous. If we have to separate to pursue different goals, I try to distance myself from the hubbub by wearing headphones and listening to music. I wonder if Juvenal, poet, satirist, and Roman, would change his assessment of the Rome of almost two thousand years ago: ". . . most sick men die here for insomnia. . . . The movement of heavy wagons through narrow streets and the oaths of stalled cattle-drivers would break the sleep of a deaf man or of a lazy walrus." He left no prescription for an antidote, but I am glad to have at my disposal a modern-age tool to soften the modern-age blow. To compete with the great cacophony of — not in order of decibel emission — buses, cars, motorcycles, and scooters, a rousing Sousa march should be in order, but a Respighi symphonic poem will do for me and it is, all told, more appropriate.

My tape of *The Fountains of Rome* is by now so worn out that the high notes come with a particular tremolo that, I am quite sure, the maestro did not plan on. But, then, speaking of Roman fountains, my memory of them, just as surely, is somewhat altered by age and usage. When I last splashed my hands in them, more than fountains they were lakes and oceans to discover and to fathom. My friends and I had, then, access to a "circulating library," an old lady's crusade to make us read: a pile of used, donated books, available to us on the "bring-one-back, take-one-home" system. The late 1930s was our era of Jules Verne and of Emilio Salgari, one catering to our curiosity for watery abysses, the other to our thirst for the surface adventures — but just as wet — of "*Sandokan, ed i Pirati della Malesia.*"

The readings inspired us to action, which we brought to the fountain of Villa Borghese, in the eponymous large park in the heart of Rome. The fountain, the one in the park closest to our home, was about a twenty-minute walk, on very young legs. We made up a fleet of three: myself and two other kids, more or less my contemporaries, who lived in my "palazzo," an aggrandizing name for a pseudo-Renaissance apartment building; it had a sizable garden in its central courtyard and also a fountain. Both garden and fountain were off limits to us: the first because our playful noises disturbed the peace of a few childless old biddies; the latter because our marine experiments disturbed the bloated resident goldfish and their protectors, the same old biddies. So we had to take our yelling and our seamanship to the Borghese fountains. Our surface vessels were, technically speaking, nothing exceptional: a piece of board roughly cut in the shape of a hull with one or two masts (sometimes more ambitious with three) with the necessary sails and rigging, a rudder, and a few eightpenny nails stuck under the keel for ballast. These pirate ships, all flying the skull-and-crossbones jack, floated magnificently and went wherever the breeze took them, mostly to the fountain's mossy center island, dominated by the statue of a naked nymph pouring water from an amphora, where they got stuck. But what we were particularly proud of were our submarines. How we came about the blueprints for the ingenious submersibles is hard to say; it was probably the communal improving and perfecting of our individual designs that brought us to the final paragon. All that was needed (and hoarded honestly, as much as possible) was a fifteen-inch length of broom handle, a few inches of tin (canned tomato lids), an eye-screw, a bicycle spoke, two of the nuts (which we called "neeppels") that tied the spoke to the rim, and a good cache of rubber bands knotted together in strings. When all this was whittled, bent, shaped, nailed, and painted (cosmetics), we had our *sottomarini*. Proudly we gave them names worthy of our creations: *Atlantis, Nautilus, Neptune, Thetis, Poseidon*. Give some hundred twists to the rubber bands, release the submarine in the water, and it would silently cruise along the bottom of the fountain to slowly resurface, when its power was spent, at the other side of the basin. Or frequently, like the sailing vessels, among the grassy, mossy growths in the fountain's center. One way to get submarines and sailing vessels dislodged from that Sargasso Sea was to perilously lean over the edge of the fountain and brandish long sticks (never long enough) to poke at the vessels; another was to create great waves in the calm waters of the fountain. The churning would succeed in freeing the boats (sometimes) and in geting us thoroughly wet (always). It also raised the vociferous reproaches of the park guardian. I remember him as a roly-poly, avuncular man wearing a blue-denim smock and a well-worn kepi hat with a chewed-up visor, his brusque manners a cover for his interest in our games and our safety. It was he who showed us the smartest way to salvage our fleet: one boy had to hold the end of a long string (miraculously discovered, among other things, in the guardian's bulging pocket) and another boy, holding the other end, had to walk around the fountain until diagonally opposite the first. The string intersected the ships in distress and brought them back to home port. The gentleman was part of the *Nettezza Urbana*, the corps of people entrusted with keeping the city clean; he was in charge of that particular portion of the park and his inseparable tools were a long broom made of twigs and a three-foot-long, T-shaped metal rod, which I had seen him insert into small manholes in the ground and turn like a key. As he twisted, the water of the fountain would increase, decrease, or shut off altogether. I thought of him as the Lord of the Fountain, in absolute control, able to make it go into a laughter of water, or make it whimper tearfully, or turn it silent and dry — all following his personal mood.

There are, between big and small, about 30 artistic or monumental fountains in the Villa Borghese alone; there are about 450 in all of Rome. "Artistic" differentiates generic, utilitarian fountains from those signed by a recognized artist, the kind of fountains that Respighi elevates into a symphony. Until the mid-1800s there were many *fontane*, large tubs, protected by terra-cotta tiled roofs, that were used for the communal laundry, and also a large number of *abbeveratoi*, troughs for the benefit of urban horses, all of which could hardly be defined as artistic or monumental.

In our recent walks around town, Gwen and I have noticed that some of the artistic fountains spew water, or not, at random hours on random days. I cannot but wonder: how many blue-smocked Lords of the Fountains man the capricious flow? Are they doing so at their whim, or are they following the orders of an overall King of the Fountains? And if so, who and why?

I would not call these questions of mine obsessive, but they surface frequently, especially when I go by a wet, or dry, fountain. To find an answer, I go directly to the source, the *Sovraintendenza ai Beni Culturali del Comune di Roma*, the commission in charge of the administration and preservation of Rome's cultural and artistic domain. I make a phone call, and I get connected with *Dottoressa* Luisa Cardilli, director of medieval and modern monuments. I ask her the questions and, yes, she says, she is — her department is — in charge of, among other things, the *fontane artistiche*, also called *fontane monumentali*. She will gladly see me, but she warns that her jurisdiction stops, so to speak, at the rim of the fountains. As for the management of the fountains' water supply I should talk to the people at ACEA, the agency in charge of bringing water to the fountains. Speak with them first, she suggests, then we can get together. I follow her advice and make an appointment with Signor Campanini, at the press office of ACEA, *Agenzia Comunale Elettricità e Acque*, once a municipal agency, today an independent one at the service of the *Comune*.

In sight of the old bricks and stones of historic Porta San Paolo, one of the gates on the Aurelian Wall, the main offices of ACEA are housed in a modern, attractive, steel-and-glass building; in its front yard are a massive sculpted rock from which flows, as if from a luxuriant spring, a heavy curtain of water, and, closer to the main door, a fountain made by a system of spouts that pour water into descending troughs. There is no mistaking the meaning of this building's watery welcome: in here, our business is water. The large entrance hall is busy with people, yet uncannily quiet; the light filtered and reflected by the walls' and ceiling's glass gives me a feeling (but it could just be a case of autosuggestion) of being underwater. The information clerk assigns me a visitor ID number and a magnetic card; clip the ID to the lapel, slide the card in a turnstile: it clicks open; an elevator whisks me up to the fourth floor; Signor Campanini is waiting for me on the landing. This is, I tell myself, new-age efficiency. Signor Campanini is young, perfectly coifed, elegantly dressed, and has impeccable manners, the image of what my mother always wished me to be. The gentleman is also so thoroughly informed about Rome and water that it takes me some time to navigate among the sea of information. Our meeting turns into a morning-long conversation, and I leave with abundant notes, written and recorded, two informative books, and one beautiful coffee-table book with the pictorial history of ACEA. Jokingly I comment that with all the information and some discipline, I could now write a treatise on the past, present, and future of the waters of Rome. Just as jokingly, he tells me not to bother: there are already entire libraries on the subject.

I spend considerable time sifting through all that information and come up with a reasonable digest.

The question of who turns the fountains on or off is dismissed quite rapidly: yes, ACEA supplies the water; no, there are no men in blue smocks handling the faucets, not anymore. Today the Lord of the Fountains is a microchip. A central station of *telecontrollo*, an electronic brain, controls all the waters of Rome. It takes care of the drinking and all hygienic needs of about three million people within the twenty districts. This water-supply network is one of the largest in the world, and, even considering the recent urban expansion, makes available to every citizen about one hundred gallons of potable water a day. Inside the city alone, the distribution is accomplished by a thirty-five-hundred-mile system of conduits and thirty-five water tanks or towers. These are enclosed by structures designed to fit in aesthetically with their particular urban environment.

Water is supplied by six main aqueducts, fed by five natural springs, one lake, and several underground reservoirs. Many of the aqueducts are still fed by the old springs and still follow the ancient routes; some even use the actual ancient structures — which, naturally, have been fixed, restored, and brought up to today's needs.

As a historical parenthesis, at the time of Emperor Claudius, in A.D. 52, there were eight operating aqueducts, and water-rich Rome acquired the name *Regina Aquarum*, Queen of the Waters. Its many fountains not only fulfilled utilitarian and decorative functions, but were also used to show off the great availability of water, which in those times was equated with power. By A.D. 226 the aqueducts numbered eleven, bringing to the city the waters of many more springs, of a sizable river, and of a lake, for a total volume of water that far exceeded the actual needs of the citizenry. Such abundance, historians say, was never seen before or since. The great surge of water was to fill the needs brought about by the "Cult of the Baths," which was to reach fantastic proportions by the end of the empire. The Romans, previously reluctant bathers, developed a taste for hot baths in simple bathhouses where even the poorest people could relax and forget their worries. These simple establishments developed into a full range of affairs: artificial lakes in the middle of gardens replete with statues and fountains surrounded the spa proper, with libraries, restaurants, gyms with hot and cold baths and showers, steam and massage rooms. The eleven great aqueducts fed 1,212 fountains, 926 public baths, and eleven great imperial *thermae*, the palatial spas. Such wealth of water induced Pliny the Elder to write:

> If anyone will note the abundance of water skillfully brought into the city, for public use, for baths, for public basins, for houses, for brooks, suburban gardens and villas; if he will note the high aqueducts

required for maintaining the proper elevation; the mountains which had to be pierced for the same reason; and the valleys it was necessary to fill up; he will consider then that the whole world offers nothing more marvelous.

By the way, the vaunted Roman aqueducts, built so sturdily that they remain an evident part of the landscape, were indeed a feat of engineering, yet they also leaked like sieves. Some leaks were due to normal structural causes, but many were man-made, for the benefit of the nearby landowners. The water department was under the direction of a *curator aquarum*, a chief water commissioner, who presided over a cohort of architects, clerks, inspectors, artisans, and plumbers, down to the *aquarii*, watermen, slaves to the on-the-spot upkeep of the aqueducts. It seems that the probity of the whole water department, especially of the *aquarii* (first in the line for landowners' bribes), also had great ethical leaks and was open to wide corruption. *Nihil novum sub solem*.

All this came to an end with the first sack of Rome in A.D. 410 by the Goths. That triumph of hydraulic engineering and the hedonistic lifestyle disappeared and was further turned into ruins by the subsequent barbarian invasions. More than a thousand years had to pass for Rome's rebirth from the ashes, and with the beginning of the Roman Renaissance and the advent of the Rome of the Popes, water was on its way to being plentiful again. Various popes saw to the restoration of the old and the birth of new aqueducts, with each point of arrival in the city marked by a *mostra*, a show-piece, a monumental fountain. The *mostra* of the Aqua Virgo is the famous Fontana di Trevi; the Acqua Pia Marcia's *mostra* is the Fontana delle Naiadi; of the Acqua Paola is the Fontanone on the Gianicolo.

Fontana Giulia at dawn, Fontana del Tritone in the morning, Fontana di Trevi in the afternoon, Fontana di Villa Medici at sunset: of these Ottorino Respighi sings, choosing for each the

time of day when, according to his judgment or inspiration, it is at
its best. To these and to all the other hundreds, the ACEA delivers
the water twenty-four hours a day. Water that is filtered, decanted,
analyzed, and delivered pure and deliciously drinkable to all the
households of central Rome and all of its suburbia, and to the
2,350 *fontanelle*, the small fountains that enrich almost every
corner of Rome with their perpetual gurgling. Officially known as
nasoni (big noses, for the bent spout protruding from the four-foot
cast-iron column), they pour water night and day, perfect for
chilling a bunch of grapes or rinsing a bowl of fruit, for refreshing
hands and face, for cleaning a child's ice-creamed face or skinned
knee, or simply to quench a summer thirst. Many foreigners
search for a nonexisting faucet to turn them off, considering the
perennial free flow a waste. Actually, in addition to all their pleasantly useful functions, the *nasoni* serve as pressure valves for the
water supply and, with their constant flow, keep the sewer system
lubricated and clean. The ACEA also takes care of the very complex sewer system (complex because, in Rome, as soon as you go
a few feet below the surface, you are guaranteed historical, archaeological, and technical complications) and also of the
sewage purification, which, I am told, is one of the largest, most
efficient, and most modern systems in Europe.

Looking back at all my accumulated notes, books, and charts,
I feel reasonably prepared to meet with *Dottoressa* Cardilli.

The *Sovraintendenza ai Beni Culturali del Comune di Roma* is
housed in a little medieval building cheek by jowl with the Portico d'Ottavia, at the southern edge of the Ghetto, and practically
on the grounds of the Teatro di Marcello; both sites are landmarks
of the Rome of the Caesars. To reach the entrance of *Sovraintendenza* one has to walk over a kind of temporary catwalk that
bridges current archaeological excavations: down under your feet
you can see old walls define what were once rooms, and arches,
and bits of columns and truncated pieces of ancient pipes and
conduits, and, closer to the surface, more modern tubes and even
what look like electric cables. It reminds me of when, as a callow

guest of a medical student friend, I looked down at the network of veins, arteries, and bones of a postmortem operation; I now look down into the guts of an alive and powerful city.

Signora Luisa Cardilli has a doctorate in history and archaeology and is a handsome woman, wearing sedate business clothes. Her black hair and dark eyes, tanned complexion, and, above all, her accent, reveal her as a Roman. The French doors of her corner office open onto a little balcony, flowering with geraniums, and a view of the Teatro di Marcello. The whole setup is so exceptional that I cannot resist asking Doctor Cardilli if she pays the *Comune* for the privilege of working in that office. She admits that I am not the first to ask; she adds that it has taken her twenty-five years to conquer this *ufficio* (I assume she means real estate as well as position). Which, given her youthful looks, is hard to believe. Pleasantries over, I tell her of the information I collected at ACEA, and that now I am ready to hear from her. She speaks in a free-flow manner, underlining with a chuckle the passages that she thinks more humorous.

She explains that the fountains are the property of the *Comune*. Following an edict of Pope Pius IX in 1849, all the fountains, all the walls, all the monuments, all the functioning elements of the city were transferred from the authority of the Vatican to that of the *Municipio di Roma*. When it came to the fountains, their management was split between the hydraulics department and the fine arts department. Until about twenty years ago the ordinary maintenance — taking care of the plumbing systems, normal cleaning of the basins of mosses, leaves, papers, coins, and whatnot — was under the care of the ACEA, then still a municipal agency. The maintenance of the fountains' structure was done by her *Sovraintendenza*.

"As you can imagine, the artistic fountains get dirty pretty fast; they are, like statues, left in the open and subjected to urban dirt *plus* the effect of the water. It is not a new thing: a good example is *la Fontana delle Tartarughe*, the Fountain of the Turtles, one of the few cast in bronze. It seems it was getting dirty very fast. We have documents about its cleaning — and about other fountains, too — dating from the 1600s and 1700s, and at a time they did not even have any chlorine in the water."

Doctor Cardilli wants to impress on me — and I sense a parental attitude, as if she were speaking of her children —that each fountain needs its particular care and attention; they are not all the same. Bronze fountains need a substantially different treatment from marble fountains. Years back, some of the fountains' waterworks were transformed into closed circuits in which the water is treated and recycled. But only in some, she specifies, because the system is very expensive, and also, in her opinion, quite difficult to control. Yet, she adds, it saves a lot of water. Still, if the water chemistry is not properly balanced it could do more harm than good. At one time, the waters of the different aqueducts were kept separate and distinct, each with its own qualities and properties: it was simpler to devise individual treatments.

Doctor Cardilli hints at the necessity for the two departments — the plumbers and the artists, she says jokingly — to work together, a cooperation that's not easily achieved. Today, for reasons of distribution, the waters are mixed together in a general network, a kind of chemically complex cocktail.

"In the closed circuits," she says, "we have attempted to install water filters to avoid calcium encrustations." With a sort of embarrassed smile, she adds: "It was an idea of mine, but then I had to backtrack because it did not work. Actually it worked too well. It sounds like a paradox: too much calcium is bad, too little is worse. A slight encrustation on the fountain's surface serves as a protection, but it is not a beauty treatment."

I tell her that it all reminds me of taking care of a beautiful lady's complexion with rubbing of creams, brushings of powder puffs.

"Not really, but close," she smiles. "It is really a delicate affair. For example, the Fountain of the Naiadi, that beautiful, monumental splendor, had the bad experience — an accident, really, like too much cream and powder — that it began to look, where it was not wet, as if it were made of marble instead of bronze. The calcium deposit was a bit too heavy. But it saved the bronze underneath."

I had to agree with her: thank God the beauty of the fountain is intact. The fountain, the Acqua Pia Marcia's *mostra*, is a showpiece indeed: at the end of Via Nazionale, the fountain is the centerpiece of Piazza della Repubblica; around its seventy-five-foot circular marble basin four bronze nymphs are showered by jets of water, seemingly indifferent to the powerfully built figure at the fountain's center. The large, masculine sea god, a shiny display of bulging muscles, is wrestling a fish; the beast shoots a white column of water from its mouth high into the sky. The unashamedly naked nymphs, the Naiadi, their luscious full bodies reclined over the symbols of their domains (a sea horse for the oceans, a swan for the lakes, a water snake for the rivers, and a reptile for the subterranean springs), were inspired by the same model. The sculptor, Mario Rutelli, was the great-grandfather of today's mayor, Francesco Rutelli, Doctor Cardilli's boss. She smiles when telling me how, at the fountain's inauguration in 1901, the abundant nudity provoked an indignant outcry. An army of prudes up in arms: an assault to the civic morals! An abomination! Artistically disreputable! A threat to the chastity of our children! But that reaction was soon forgotten, and the fountain is now considered one of the great fountains of Rome. It is even more spectacular at night: hidden floodlights turn Naiadi, sea god, water sprays, and the tall central water jet into a glowing, silvery display.

Dr. Cardilli comments that it took a lot of work and a long time to clean and scrub the bronze of its calcium encrustation (also quite a lot of bickering between the various departments — matters of jurisdiction, she says confidentially, sotto voce, the usual time-consuming squabbles, the infighting and overcoming the inertia of many bureaucrats; sometimes things get terribly tiring . . .), but "we finally made it," she says jubilantly. Going back to the subject of having to face different problems for different fountains, she continues:

"The ideal, in general, is to arrive at a slight veil of encrustation. The experts have told us that water with no calcium at all will corrode. At the opposite end we have too much deposit, as happened to the Fountain of the Triton in Piazza Barberini. Bernini chose to sculpt the triton in travertine marble, perhaps more susceptible to the attack of sediments; with the growth of mosses and lichens it had become all green and yellowish, perhaps fascinating and romantic like a fountain in an enchanted garden, but so encrusted you could hardly see its form. One eye had disappeared completely under fifteen centimeters of deposits; it all happened in forty-two years, from 1936 to 1978. We've had to clean it another three times in the last twenty-two years. Now things are under control, and we clean all the fountains on a regular basis, instead of intervening only when things get really bad. The actual work is done by the Department of Public Works under our direction. We follow a predetermined calendar for cleaning the various fountains."

I tell her about my childhood experience with the man in the blue smock working the fountain. Who, today, is in charge of turning a fountain on and off? Who gives the order?

"There is still a man who manually turns the valves. But he is not your old man in a blue smock, he is a technician, actually more than one, employed by the company hired to do the cleaning under a three-year contract with the *Comune*. On rotation, they start with one, pull the plugs, and while that one is draining — it alway takes some time, depending on its size — move to another, and so on. Then they go back and clean and scrub the first one, let it fill again, and keep going. Sometimes the pipes or the drains need special attention, but generally a fountain is never empty for more than a day, perhaps two. And that is when you saw the water now on, now off . . ."

She goes on to explain that some are more complicated and get dirtier than the others. The grandiose complex of the three fountains of Piazza Navona was a major work of rehabilitation. The two at each end of the square were done in the open, but the central one, Bernini's masterpiece, La Fontana dei Fiumi, with its four massive statues supporting the tall Egyptian obelisk, required extra care and was done under a curtain of scaffolding and plastic tarpaulin.

"It took months," she says, "but now all three fountains are immaculately clean. The Fontana di Trevi is also huge. We had to scrub it from head to toe totally under wraps. A lot of people came to Rome to see one of its most famous sights, and all they saw was a wall of shiny pipes and plastic. I felt sorry for them, but believe it or not, they still threw coins at it, all of which landed on the street!

"This business of the coins could seem like an innocent, symbolic gesture, but it can make physical and chemical problems for the fountain. Some people get really enthusiastic and pitch the coins so hard that they hit the statuary. I once participated in a restoration there myself and got hit on the head by a coin, and I tell you, it really hurt. When the coins hit the marble they nick it and make it more susceptible to decay. Chemically, some of the coins' alloys react with the water, and that too can cause problems. Copper oxidizes and makes ugly stains. We found out that some Japanese coins have a high nickel component, which is even more damaging than copper, and especially the ones with a hole in the middle that act like an electric battery, producing acid."

Speaking of coins, I tell her that in my childhood, from the vantage point of my uncle's apartment just above the fountain, I could watch bands of urchins fighting to retrieve the coins, some fishing them out with a magnet tied to a string, or, in the summer — and I envied them — boldly walking fully clothed into the water and diving for the money. And how they would scatter like a flock of pigeons at the appearance of the *pizzardoni*, the municipal guards.

"The boys with the magnets still show up, mostly at night, when the crowds of tourists are gone. Some, they tell me, make their living that way. But they have to compete with the official cleaners, who collect the coins. They give the Italian coins to the *Comune*, the foreign ones to the Red Cross. It is an old tradition, this of the coins."

It reminds me, I tell her, of when my children were very young and I gave them some coins to pitch over their shoulder into the fountain. "Why?" they asked, much preferring to hold on to their pennies. "It's for good luck," I told them. "Why?" they insisted. I had to admit that really I did not know, and I still don't.

"Neither did I, until recently," Doctor Cardilli comments with a chuckle. "An archaeologist friend of mine told me that in 1852 the Jesuits owned a warm spring near Lake Bracciano; it silted up and they sent some workmen to clean it. The workmen found a layer of bronze and silver coins from the fourth century A.D. at the bottom of the well, and beneath that gold and silver coins of the imperial period, and farther down they found coins of the republican era. Still deeper they found objects predating coins, arrowheads and stone objects, the offerings of prehistoric people to propitiate the spirits of the spring, paying homage to water as source of life, of well-being, a stream that ties the past with the prosperity of the future. For the Fontana di Trevi, this friend of mine ties the beginning of the tradition with an Austrian *liceum*, a school, located in Rome around 1880. The students, before going back to Austria, were encouraged to make the symbolic gesture as a payment — or bribe, if you wish — to the water spirit of the fountain so that she would bring them back to Rome."

I have to tell *Dottoressa* Cardilli that the coin-throwing tradition has really taken hold in the United States. Sparkling on the bottom of any man-made body of water, public or private — but especially in shopping malls — one can see an abundance of coins, pitched there for — to me — unknown reasons.

"You Americans!" she says, "You don't need a reason. You just love to throw money away!"

I Pini di Roma follows the *Fontane* on my tape of Respighi's symphonic poems; they do so in my thoughts as well. And as in the four movements, the first to fill the air are the pines of Villa Borghese. The park — the word *villa* has the double meaning of "park/garden" and "building" — is one of the largest in Rome, definitely the most central, and has been long described as *il pol-mone verde di Roma*, Rome's green lung. The anatomical metaphor for the park's function is indeed correct: it is, for Rome, the deepest breath, one so deep that it hurts the lungs, a surge of oxygen as invigorating as it is intoxicating. After many years of benign neglect from authorities in charge and citizens alike, the park now has been restored to its original beauty. Its enormous, ancient pines tower over the landscape, now carefully trimmed and healthy. There are also oaks, plane trees, horse chestnuts, and cedars and palms. The whole conglomerate of woods is what gives Villa Borghese its face. Some trees are three hundred years old, silent witnesses of a splinter of Roman history. Some barely made it through the darkest days of the dark years of World War II, when the park had become the residence of homeless squatters, the war's disinherited, pushed to Rome like flotsam ahead of the murderous wave; and by bandits, common criminals, and deserters chased by the law to Villa Borghese, like human jetsam. Nights were not safe, and days not much better. The park resonated with the activity of improvised lumberjacks chipping away at trees, wood posts, fences, and park benches, scavenging for anything that would burn, substitutes for heating and cooking with gas. As for cooking, swans, ducks, squirrels, even the carp and goldfish in the fountains disappeared. The final blow came toward the end of the war, when the American Fifth Army liberated Rome and camped in Villa Borghese with their jeeps, trucks, tanks, and field kitchens. It was a vision for us Romans — a return of hope for a more serene future — to see the young, healthy, handsome, cheerful Americans throw at each other for interminable hours, over an implausible distance, a ball as hard as a stone, and catch it with a thud in a huge clownlike leather glove. They, officers and soldiers, were clad alike in sleeveless olive-green T-shirts and roamed at ease around tents as big as palaces, stood in line together at "ciao time," each wolfing down amounts of food that could have fed our family for a month. It all astonished us. Well! we said. That's democracy! That's what we want to be. But when they moved out, Villa Borghese was left with the scars of their youthful enthusiasms. The tracks of the jeeps' gymkhana, the ruts of the heavy trucks and tanks, the refuse pits, gave the coup de grâce to the paths among the myrtle bushes, to the meadows and flower beds. It was a long time before nannies and toddlers, pensioners and lovers ventured back to the park.

Villa Borghese is unique among the parks because it is a compendium of articulated places; each offers an absolutely different landscape, a different atmosphere and mood, yet each joins the other in elegant flow. High grounds and valleys, meadows, playing grounds, little streams, ponds, fountains: they all have a character, they all have a name. From the high point of Porta Pinciana's entrance pillars, on the left is the Galoppatoio, on the right is Piazza di Siena, ahead is Giardin del Lago, and then Valle Giulia and Parco dei Daini and Belvedere del Pincio. One can add statistics: the park's highest point is 150 feet above sea level; it covers 231 acres, with a perimeter of 6 miles; there are 32 miles of avenues, lined by 4,000 shade trees; water flows from 30 monumental fountains and 10 minor ones; one new — and little-used — underground garage contains 1,200 parking spaces. Art comes in with the paintings and sculptures in the Museo Borghese and in the Galleria d'Arte Moderna; there is one major zoo.

But names and statistics cannot evoke the feelings a Roman — of my vintage — has for Villa Borghese. It was where the nannies would keep an eye on their charges and an ear open to the flirting of soldiers at liberty; it was where, any day after school, by virtue of a pair of old shoes and a just-as-scuffed leather ball, one could get in a pickup game of soccer; it was there that a student who played hooky would meet and, forgetting schools' antagonisms for a day, become friends with other students; it was there you took your sweetheart to hold hands and perhaps steal a kiss — a Villa Borghese adventure that in the telling became of epic sexual proportions. It meant being fascinated by the *orologio ad acqua*, the water clock, watching it fragment time in a seesaw of cups of water — splash, tick tock, splash. What a marvel to see the ingenious turning of wheels, all enclosed in a fifteen-foot tower of cast iron and glass, perform the wedding of two fluids beyond grasp: water and time!

The centrality of Villa Borghese, once its great virtue, now is its downfall. Today's traffic makes it arduous to reach the again-pristine and manicured Villa from any corner of the city. The laughter and singsong chanting of children's games do not enrich the air anymore; the many families who once enjoyed the out-doors together have left the place to a few joggers, a few dog walkers, a few bicycle riders. Mostly one encounters tourists taking pictures of each other, and the few Romans around are quiet and subdued, as if they were making a perfunctory visit to an old aunt — one who is a bit too persnickety, clean, and boring.

Two men in blue overalls are pulling on ropes that rise up high into the tall branches of an ancient pine, as if tethering it to Earth, keeping it from flying away like a balloon. The buzz of a chain saw gives away a third worker hidden in the umbrella-like crown of the tree; a big sawed-off dead branch crashes down and makes the ground shake. People in the park ignore the event: I am the only interested spectator, the only one to hear the noise of a tree branch falling in the forest.

Villa Borghese is only one among the many parks of the city. Rome has, at this count, 8,450 acres of *verde*, green space. And for the last five years, by desire of the mayor, it is expanding at a rate of almost 10 percent per year in order to reach the municipal optimum of ten square yards of green space per citizen.

The planning and maintenance of all the *verde* is done by the *Comune di Roma's* Tenth Department, Dipartimento delle Politiche Ambientali e Agricole, and by its Servizio Giardini, which is in charge of the many operative departments needed for the job. Keeping Rome "green" is a huge, complicated, and expensive job. And at the same time it has to be subtle: success is obtained when the appearance of parks, gardens, and tree-lined avenues seems natural. All the *verde*, even in the most formal displays, should appear in perfect harmony with its location, and not a bit contrived or conspicuous. The headquarters, nurseries, and warehouses of Servizio Giardini are located just inside the ancient Roman walls, near Porta Metronia, one of its old gates. For a gardener, or a gardening lover, entering the grounds of the Servizio is like entering the gates of Paradise: its grounds — about ten acres — are a fertile valley of flower beds and greenhouses that slope up to the Colle Celio, one of the Seven Hills of Rome. At walking distance, the Colosseum, the Palatine Hill, and the Baths of Caracalla add the scent of history to the greenery's aroma. The nursery's high grounds are reserved for big trees, and it does not take much to imagine the work and sweat needed to transplant one of these fifty-foot giants. In the flat land below are hundreds and hundreds of decorative potted plants, with three or four gardeners fussing about. These plants, I surmise, must be the ones that go to decorate special events, such as the rich floral displays that welcome foreign dignitaries or simply embellish the city on a special day. From now on my job of watering the houseplants will seem ridiculously insignificant; I will never complain again.

Sprinkled around the grounds, hidden by trees and greenery, are several cottages. Each has a botanical name; they house the different departments of Servizio Giardini. The landscape design and planning office is in Casina delle Azalee, and there I meet with landscape architect Maria Grazia Forte, one of the executive officers in charge of the *verde*. I realize that *verde* covers everything from an official windowbox to the centennial pines of the Gianicolo, from a local postcard-sized children's park to Villa Borghese. It is a big job, indeed, and *architetto* Forte explains how the whole operation is subdivided and organized into several subdepartments. The *Verde Storico*, the great parks — Villa Pamphili, Villa Borghese, Villa Sciarra, Villa Torlonia, Villa Ada, and gardens of extraordinary importance such as Castel Sant'Angelo's or Parco degli Eroi at the Gianicolo — require special attention. They are all managed in cooperation with the *Sovraintendenza ai Beni Culturali*.

"Not a plant or a tree can be planted or moved as one wishes: the historical value of the places has to be respected. So in these places our work is mostly of restoration and maintenance. Even so it is not simple. For example, we had to replace an old, dying tree in the Castel Sant'Angelo's garden. We moved the largest one we could from the nursery, but once in place near the others it looked almost like a dwarf. We tried our best to plant it so that the perspective was little altered, to keep the general feel, if not the appearance, unchanged. We have to integrate the new with the old." She goes on to say that this is much easier to accomplish with mortar and bricks than with living plants.

After the "historical green" come the new green spaces in the new *quartieri*. Most of these areas were built helter-skelter, and *verde* was of the least concern. In these new spaces the Servizio Giardini can be more free with landscape design — but only up to a point.

"Rome is a beautiful city, it is unique," Forte says. "Rome lives on its history, above- and underground. The latter especially," she is quick to add, "is of great national value, but it is also a great headache. Look," she says, pointing to some archaeological artifacts on her desk, "we found these a few days ago. We found them not even a foot underground. So anytime we dig and find anything, we have to alert an archaeologist from *Sovraintendenza* to come and check the stuff out. A few months ago, very close to the surface, we found a sarcophagus. It led to another, and that to a full necropolis. There was no budget available for it anywhere, so we were told to cover it up again, to preserve it. Now it will have to wait underground a few more years until funds are found. So you can see how the great archaeological wealth beneath our feet restricts what we can plant and what we cannot: obviously we could not plant deep-rooted trees above that necropolis; we redesigned the area with shallow-rooted myrtle bushes. It will be different from what we originally had in mind, but it will be a good job anyway. It keeps our creativity exercised. And tested!"

Apropos of archaeological wealth, after receiving her promise of not denouncing me, I tell her of my — actually my children's — archaeological experience. When living in Rome in the mid-1960s, practically every Sunday I took the whole family for an alfresco lunch at *Ar Montarozzo*. It was a simple *osteria*, not much more than a shack with a few tables under a pergola of grapevines, and it served great food. At the very beginning of the Appian Way, barely outside the Aurelian Walls, it took its name from the hillock on which it was built. In Roman slang *montarozzo* means "a bump on the landscape, a heap of dirt." If the good and affordable food was the main attraction for the grown-ups, for our four children (ranging in age from six to twelve) the big deal was that, lunch over, they could play tag on the field just outside the *osteria* and trip over shards of old pottery. I encouraged them to retrieve them; amphora's mouths and broken handles, terra-cotta cups without bottoms and bottoms without cups, all went into shoe boxes for their antiques collection. I convinced them they were thousands of years old and invaluable finds, and when I suggested they number each piece and give it a date (like we had seen in museums) they dutifully inscribed the potsherds with impressive numbers full of zeros, and with the date they had found them. I believe they still treasure their archaeological shoe boxes. I still nurse the guilt of not having dutifully declared the troves to the *Sovraintendenza*, and of having turned my innocent children into history's thieves.

Architetto Forte assures she will not denounce me, nor ask my children to return their treasures. Moreover, she comforts me, there are a great number of *montarozzi* just outside the Roman walls, the sites of ancient dumps full of thousand-year-old valueless (she whispers) broken pottery. Recently I went back to *Ar Montarozzo* for dinner, a personal pilgrimage. It is now a fashionable, upscale establishment, with uniformed valets to park your Ferrari or Rolls. *Sic crescit gloria montis.*

Roman green space is divided into zones, each zone with its specific character and needs. One general, overall director oversees the people in charge of the zones. There is now a project afoot to make the zones independent, let each one design and take care of its *verde* — when not bigger than ten thousand square yards — with its own maintenance people and gardeners. Or perhaps — as Paris and other cities have done — contract a private company to do the job, under the Servizio Giardini's direction and advice.

"We have about a thousand gardeners working for us now, but they are not enough." Architetto Forte makes the point that the Servizio Giardini has a school for botanists and gardeners, but they are not sufficient to fill the needs. Once, she explains, a lot of people with dirt under their fingernails left the farms for the city, and they loved the work and made wonderful gardeners. Now everybody is looking for clean, high-tech jobs. And hiring lumberjacks, tree surgeons, tree trimmers, qualified people to take care of trees, is even more difficult.

It brings me back to the subject of *Pini di Roma*. Architetto Forte informs me that the *Comune*'s Tenth Department has an office for *censimento del verde*, a tree census, and if I call there, I can get more information. I thank her, and the next day I make my call.

An approximate count gives greater Rome 400,000 trees and 800,000 *piante arboree*, shrub and bushes. As for pines: 17,000 are lining streets; 68,000 are in public parks and villas. It was not clear, neither to me nor to the young lady on the phone, if the pines were included in the overall tree count. She was good humored about it; it was a question she had never asked herself before. She would look into it, or, we decided, one day when we had the time we could go and count them ourselves. And if it were as beautiful a day as today, we could round up a few friends and have a picnic, too.

XII

Death of the Sweet Life

Cinecittà

*B*ERNINI'S FOUNTAIN in Piazza Barberini shoots its jet of white water into the air as festive as a flag, rejoicing at the lively traffic that swirls around it. Like a lung timed by traffic lights, the square inhales and exhales cars and buses from the seven streets that open into it. Actually there are six busy, commercial streets that seem ancillary to the seventh: Via Veneto. *The* Via Veneto. By all rights, for its majestic Parisian size, it should be called *viale*, avenue. It moves uphill, stately, in a large reversed S under an imposing canopy of horse chestnut trees, going by a few multistarred hotels on the left, the noble and huge Palazzo Margherita — the American embassy — on the right. The courtly, hushed feeling (in musical terms it could be defined a largo) of this quarter of a mile ends when it crosses Via Boncompagni: here Via Veneto straightens and, its style and pace now more mundane and frivolous, heads directly for the Aurelian Wall's Porta Pinciana and, across from it, to Villa Borghese. Via Veneto begins at a famous Roman fountain and ends at the solemn Roman pines: a hyphen between two Roman mythical symbols, a myth itself, the cradle of *La Dolce Vita*. The city of Rome has put a plaque at

the very end of Via Veneto dedicated to Federico Fellini, who created the street's myth with his film. Federico Fellini is now gone
and, much before his demise, so had *la dolce vita* and what it
stood for. The glamor is gone; its sidewalks' night-till-dawn theatrical ebullience is gone; the stars, the starlets, the directors, the
paparazzi are gone; the eccentric exhibitionists, the seekers of the
one moment of fame are gone; the style is gone. What is left is another elegant avenue, a little stale, a tourist's must-see, overworked in its attempt to live up to its old reputation, an aged
cancan girl with smudged makeup living off the memory of the
high-kick times. The Café Doney, the Café de Paris, and a few
others are still there, but most of the sidewalk tables are gone, replaced by gazebo-like glass enclosures, sad, nearly empty aquar-
iums from which the lonely fish inside ogle the ones on the
outside, both hoping resignedly to spot a celebrity. Lots of money
is being spent by financial interests in trying to revive the old *dolce
vita*, but by 11 P.M. the lights are out and the life, *dolce* or otherwise, is off to bed. No kind of money, no kind of effort can bring
back those glossy days of the cinema, of which *la dolce vita* was
nothing but a public-shocking expression, some authentic, much
contrived for tabloid consumption.

Two major financial reasons coincided with and contributed to
the launching on the international scene of the Roman cinema of
the 1950s and 1960s. The funds of American film production and
distribution companies that had been frozen in Italy during the
World War II years were finally released, with the two governments' mutual agreement that the funds be spent and used in
Italy. It was a considerable amount of money that brought to
Rome's Cinecittà — the capital of Italian film production, and
much cheaper than Hollywood —big historical potboilers with
big American stars, directors, and camp followers. Thousands of
Roman extras cheered Charlton Heston racing his chariot in *Ben
Hur*, paid homage with Richard Burton's Anthony to Elizabeth
Taylor's Cleopatra, joined Kirk Douglas's slave rebellion in *Spar-*

tacus, were easy prey to Steve (Mr. Universe) Reeves in *Hercules* and its many sequels, followed Audrey Hepburn and Gregory Peck's scooter in *Roman Holiday*. The made-in-Italy movie boom also attracted a few valuable non-American productions, such as David Lean's Oscar-winning *Summertime*, with Katharine Hepburn and Rossano Brazzi.

In addition to the funds released after the war, the fact that Americans residing abroad for six months or more did not have to pay U.S. taxes on their foreign earnings boosted Rome's allure. Many Hollywood stars — and crowds of aspiring actors and starlets — took residence in Rome, making it the "Hollywood on the Tiber." They gravitated to the night spots of the Via Veneto, and people, simple people with ordinary uneventful lives, came to watch Ava Gardner's shenanigans, to witness Anna Magnani throwing a Roman tantrum, or to see if Liz came out of Brick Top with Richard, or out of George's without. It was a crowd of onlookers waiting hours till dawn for a vicarious moment of excitement, a receptive audience for the extrovert thespians. The intrusive, arrogant tabloid photographers — the paparazzi — came to record for the world at large, and in many cases provoke, the prurient "news-making" events of the glamorous people, a pseudodiary of the intricate sex lives and love entanglements — and street fights — of the sweet life's *Who's Who*.

Ironically, Fellini's *La Dolce Vita* was not a paean, but his acrid, melancholy depiction of the decadent life of wealthy Roman aristocrats, the sad, fashionably meaningless lives of celebrities. In the provincial Italy of the late 1960s, the film was considered offensive, and the Vatican's daily *L'Osservatore Romano* called the film *La Schifosa Vita* (The Disgusting Life). Others considered it an "affront to the virtue and rectitude of the Roman population," and Catholic activists demanded that Fellini be indicted for costuming his star, Anita Ekberg, in sexy, tight-fitting clerical robes. Despite these intellectualized negative reactions, or perhaps exactly for that reason, the film drew crowds of viewers in Italy and abroad and the scene of superbosomy Anita's night dip in the Trevi Fountain became the worldwide poster image of Rome's *dolce vita*. Ironically, the golden moment of Hollywood on the Tiber was soon over, and with it the real or imagined sweet life. Paradoxically, the very presence of the throngs of Japanese and American tourists who came to witness it gave it the coup de grâce, and finally smothered Via Veneto to death.

The beginning of a myth, *La Dolce Vita* was also the end of an epoch. The resurgence of Italian moviemaking — the cradle of *Neo-realismo* — was similarly suffocated by crass overproduction. Oodles of film producers, directors, actors appeared overnight to get on the filmmaking bandwagon. It was not only for the social prestige of "being in movies," but also for the easy money. The Italian government, to stimulate the rebirth of the war-destroyed Italian movie industry, offered subsidies toward film production. Aspiring producers submitted the script and budget of a proposed film to a government judging board. This board, composed of representatives of all the hues of the political spectrum (at one time it had forty members, but it has recently been reduced to seven — naturally with the governing party's representative holding the make-or-break final vote), on the basis of the proposed film's artistic, cultural, or social relevance, would approve or deny the subsidy/loan. The money was to be repaid with the future film's distribution earnings.

On one level, the scheme worked beautifully: on a yearly basis, Rome produced more films than Hollywood. The movie industry became, after the government, Rome's second-largest employer and the second-largest source of revenue. Technically, it grew to be one of the most sophisticated in the world, developing new, modern equipment and cadres of technicians, artists, and artisans of unparalleled skills. But artistically and financially the subsidies didn't work: of the hundreds of films produced, only a very few captivated international audiences and money. Most of the rest were cheap overnight productions, using regional comedic, vernacular talents, or exploiting regional dramatic events, with a formula that appealed exclusively to local audi-

ences. Seldom did they make enough money to repay the sub-
sidy/loan: none was left after the producer larded his pockets, ap-
portioning what was left, if any, to the director, artists, crew, and
the commissioners who authorized the subsidy in the first place.
In many cases, the producers — because of either inexperience or
dishonesty — mismanaged the funds, running out of money altogether halfway through the production. They had to borrow
money to finish — in the meantime paying whoever was involved
in the film with promissory notes. Film equipment rental companies, film processing labs, sound studios, actors, and crews were
left holding the bag. The many IOUs floating around (they came
to be called *farfalloni*, butterflies, for their ephemeral, flitting nature) provoked periodic "film industry crises," subsequently resolved with government bailouts.

The era of the *farfalloni* affected me directly; it coincided with
the beginning of my career as a cinematographer, the marriage of
my love for technology and photography. It also coincided with
the launching of my family, a fact that was hardly compatible with
being paid in IOUs. The last film I worked on was announced
with colorful posters — as big as the side of a barn — for weeks,
and finally saw the light in a few Roman theaters. After two show-
ings the theaters' lights went out to make room, reputedly, for the
latest Abbot and Costello. And I was left with a drawerful of promissory notes. As consolation, the producer invited me, my wife,
and my infant son to the weekend inauguration of his new seaside
villa. This, plus the empty promises of the *farfalloni*, spurred me
to test the waters on the other side of the ocean, and I was lucky:
my career as director of cinematography at WGBH TV in Boston
bloomed, and so did my family. Boston became our "temporarily
permanent" home.

Paradoxically, the very few good films that surfaced out of the sea of
negligible ones made the international reputation of "Italian film,"
of its directors and actors. Films such as *Roma Città Aperta, Ladri
di Biciclette, Paisà, Sciuscià, La Terra Trema, Umberto D, Divorzio*

all'Italiana; directors, besides Fellini, such as Rossellini, De Sica, Zampa, Germi, De Santis, Visconti, Antonioni; and actors such as Anna Magnani, Marcello Mastroianni, Sofia Loren, Aldo Fabrizi, Virna Lisi, Rossano Brazzi, Gina Lollobrigida became the darlings of the film intelligentsia, of the film clubs and art houses. More paradoxically yet, most of these same films were at first not much appreciated by Italian audiences, accepted on the rebound only after they received international acclaim and imprimatur.

To keep abreast of today's situation, I listen to Peppino Mariani. A way-back-then friend and colleague, he began as gofer to a self-made, blustering film producer, the epitome of all that was unhealthy in the Hollywood on the Tiber. With particular foresight, Peppino left the producer and, with a few other refugees from the film industry, opened a production house that made commercials for the newborn Italian TV. It turned into steady work with steady money — and lots of both; work, money, and exposure to a national audience were provided for a lot of big-name actors and directors who were recruited for the commercials. The spots had a golden age: about four minutes in length, they were real minifilms with a developed plot, shown by Italian national television in groups of five or six in a program called *Carosello*. They made up the only on-air advertising and were the most popular prime-time daily show. Before bedtime, children were allowed or denied permission to watch *Carosello* depending on their day's behavior.

Mariani is now retired and has time for his two hobbies: writing bedtime stories for his grandchild, and film history. Specifically, Italian film history.

"Do we want to talk about Italian cinema?" is Peppino's rhetorical opening question.

"There is no Italian cinema," he answers himself. "There is a ghost of a cinema. I was talking with a friend just yesterday and he asked me what I felt about the current situation. I said that it feels like being betrayed by a lover. No, he said, it's more like being at the funeral of a dear relative. This is the opinion we have of our cinema."

I have to tell him that that is not the opinion held abroad. As a matter of fact, Italian movies have had a great reputation in America, a reputation that I undeservedly carried with me and was perhaps the reason for my modest success there. Even now, I try to continue, but Peppino interrupts me:

"There was a terrific era of Italian cinema, but that was forty, fifty years ago. . . . We were making some — mark my word: *some* — films that worked, we had profits, we had good actors, we had directors of exceptional value. We had a lot of screenwriters, solid, literate, truly intelligent writers; now we have nobody. . . . Once in a while, now, out of vaudeville, comes someone who passes himself off as actor and filmmaker, makes a purely parochial sophomoric movie, sometimes with a semblance of success, a meteor streaking in the desert; then, nothing else. We still have the unfortunate state subsidy system, practically a state-run cinema, that finances films for as much as fourteen to sixteen million dollars that do not make a dime. The latest film was financed for seventeen million and earned forty thousand. There are many others with even more ridiculous returns. And yet there are production companies that are working continuously, making films nobody has ever heard of. Evidently they have access to the state subsidies, and if the films are shown or not isn't the least bit important. Take the money and run, and then come back for more. The state ends up owning the films, a pile of celluloid not even good for recycling. In this way the Italian cinema, as a serious industry, will never make a comeback. We do not have any worthwhile directors, screenwriters, actors: how can you set the foundations for a solid cinema with that? And following this trend of state financing, we do not have a single real entrepreneur left. We are not able to produce films good enough to be exported; they aren't even good enough to compete in our own theaters with foreign films. Italian audiences simply do not go to see Italian films: they are tired of seeing themselves in the mirror, of seeing their life, Italian life, interpreted through the stupid jokes of

grimacing comedians in baggy pants, of seeing themselves as sim-
pletons or clowns. They are bored with poorly made "tits and ass"
B-movies; even a good joke becomes stale after a while. The Italian
public is even deserting movies made by experienced Italian film-
makers, people with excellent reputations: in Italian theaters, the
Italian label is the kiss of death."

I mention to him that I saw on recent op-ed pages and on TV
commentaries that there is a big debate about the Hollywood colonization of Italian screens. Just to see what that was all about, I
checked the entertainment pages, and I saw that of the ten first-
run movies showing in Rome, eight were American, one was
Spanish, and one Italian.

"That's not colonization, that's surrender. The reason is
simple: the American, the foreign movies, even the worst, are professional products made by professionals with the purpose of en-
tertaining, enlightening, inspiring — whatever is their purpose —
they have something to say; hence they bring people to the theaters and make money. On the other hand, the great majority of
Italian movies have nothing to say; at best they are crass vaudeville acts with the deranged ambition of being films."

I try to douse his negative fire by telling him that I have witnessed abroad Italian movies of great success and a renewed interest in Italian cinema. I find it quite promising.

"Yes," is his quick reply, "we have had a few — mark my word:
few — successful films in the last few years, made by young, good
directors, films that have made the international market —
Cinema Paradiso, Il Postino, La Vita è Bella, and five or six more.
But they all happen to be only partly Italian; they are coproduc-
tions with foreign companies, companies that contributed their
professional behavior and experience."

His fire somewhat doused, he now seems resigned, sad. I ask
him, "If you had a crystal ball, what would you forecast for the
Italian movie industry's future?"

"You do not need to be a clairvoyant to see it: it's a blank ball,
a blank screen. Which actually would be a step forward, more en-

lightening than a screen full of idiocy. To have a future, we have to start from the beginning. We have to have schools for directors, actors, editors. Create a new class of intelligent professionals, as in America. The state should give scholarships to deserving people to study in America, do their internships there. The state money would be well spent that way, instead of subsidizing junk at a loss. The subsidy law should be abolished: moviemaking should be like any other industry, survive and prosper by its own merit. It is an expensive industry, so it should be geared not only for a national audience, but also for foreign consumption. Otherwise we have to resign ourselves to colonization."

We reminisce for a moment about old friends and colleagues, the enthusiasm and the pride we had *a fare il cinema*, when we could say: I've been filming at Cinecittà!

"Actually our pride, Cinecittà, is already practically colonized." Peppino is matter-of-fact, now: "To survive it had to sell out to television and foreign film productions. . . . There are rumors abroad that Cinecittà could be made profitable by plowing it under and turning it into a residential development. But that's only a rumor . . ."

I leave Peppino's place — a sumptuous penthouse duplex — with a sour taste in my mouth, especially since he assures me that his views are not pessimistic assumptions but realistic observations. And, after all, Cinecittà was, in a way, my alma mater.

"Movie City" was built in the mid-1930s, by Mussolini, as a functional showpiece of Italian modernity. It was the forge for a booming film industry, producing historic films of true artistic value, many *commedie all'italiana*, most, if not all, with the subliminal propaganda message that Italian heroism, morals, values, and lifestyle were there with the best in the world, thanks to ethnic heritage and Fascism. Many films fell under the category of *i telefoni bianchi*, white telephones — the epitome of modern sophistication, the certificate of Italy's graduation from backwater provincialism — which would invariably appear on the scene.

Look! — the films meant to say — not only do we have an army, a navy, and an air force, we even have *telefoni bianchi!*

Cinecittà, at the time of its creation, was quite a way from urban Rome. Now, with the city's expansion, it is an integral part of it, one of its populous *quartieri*. It can be reached by subway from the underground hub of Stazione Termini in about thirty minutes; the names of the stops on the way sound like a reading of Rome's ancient history: Re di Roma, Furio Camillo, Arco di Travertino, Numidio, Lucio Sestio, Giulio Agricola. Finally, incongruously, Cinecittà. I took Gwen there for a nostalgic visit; we walked under the entrance arch with a sense of reverence: immaculately clean streets are edged with manicured flower beds; tree-shaded avenues lead to the five major sound studios — one of which, #5, is huge — and to the sizable back lot, big enough to house a Roman circus set. There is hardly a person walking around; the quiet is absolute, weird. In one of the studios a large, gaudy set for a television game show is empty at the moment; in another, also empty, is a realistic reconstruction of a police station, with dog-eared telephone books, used pencils and dossiers on desks, chipped file cabinets along the walls; in another is a set, now empty, for a children's television show. The only sign of life is a few lights in a corner of the cavernous #5: five or six people are huddled, filming a commercial, the whole action consisting of a stagehand pouring mineral water into a glass. This is the studio where entire city streets were built and filmed, where in its enormous sunken water tank sea battles were fought. On the back lot we promenade around a Renaissance Venice, a perfect illusion but for its waterless canals. Huge monster heads, reliquiae of Fellini's movies, sprout from the ground, their faux marble chipped, revealing the plaster underneath.

The young guide who accompanies us explains that Cinecittà has been privatized, most of its activity the weekly television shows. Its income is derived from studio rental: production companies can move in and find all that is needed, from the most sophisticated equipment to the last nail for the sets, from processing labs to editing rooms. The studios have not seen much film action recently. There are at the moment plans to re-create New York waterfronts of 1908 in studio #5; work should start soon. He agrees that it is extremely expensive to keep the enterprise going, but with the injection of private funds and energetic, imaginative leadership there are high hopes for the future.

Before leaving we stop at the cafeteria for a bun and a coffee; it is about noon, and there are three other people conversing softly. I tell Gwen that I still remember the feel of the long, smooth mahogany counter, the taste of the bun, the aroma of the espresso: it is all exactly the same. Missing are the throngs of people, the anonymous and the famous, the costumed extras, the gladiators and the French *soubrettes*, the loud and lively everybody . . . now the experience is quite melancholy.

We walk back to the subway station, hoping that its name, Cinecittà, will not become just another in the history of ancient Rome.

XIII

Getting Around

"*R*OME IS LIKE an open, illuminated book. Each street, each square is a beautiful page to read, to savor. It is difficult to find another city that has been able to preserve so well the beauty and the flavor of times gone by. Beautiful pages of a beautiful book."

I have come to the main office of ATAC looking for hard figures and data from a technocrat, and I find a romantic poet instead. ATAC (Azienda Tranvie Autobus Comune) and COTRAL (Consorzio Trasporti Lazio) are the Roman agencies in charge of above- and below-ground public transportation, and Gianni Puddu, my interlocutor, is the executive volunteered by the agency to satisfy some of my curiosity. He is a smiling, middle-aged gentleman dressed in a business suit tending more toward practicality than elegance; he wears glasses low on his nose that give him a benevolent, Benjamin Franklin appearance. His office is in Via Volturno, at the corner of the enormous Piazza dei Cinquecento, where all the buses of Rome seem to congregate; from their terminals there, they spread toward the cardinal points of the city. The eastern side of the square has been taken over by the modern, steel-and-glass facade of Stazione Termini, the central railroad station. On the opposite side of the square are the well-preserved seventeen-hundred-year-old Baths of Diocletian, the largest of all ancient Roman baths. Signor Puddu's window looks over them.

"I agree about the beautiful pages of a beautiful book," I tell him, "but some pages one can walk to, others are too far."

"That's where we come in. We take you there. We definitely try our best."

But it is not a simple job, Signor Puddu emphasizes, no matter how you look at Rome. Most of the beautiful pages are in the *centro*, the Rome inside the Aurelian Walls. The core of the city was never planned for motorized transportation; actually most of it was never planned at all, but grew helter-skelter, and the portions that were planned were made for the horse and carriage, for a population that was a small fraction of today's. As for the Rome outside the walls, it has exploded almost as helter-skelter as the pre-medieval town, its transportation lines expanding like spokes emanating from a hub, not growing like a spiderweb with radials connected by concentric threads. If one wishes to go by public transportation from a new *quartiere* to an adjoining one, say from Tor Marancia to Centocelle, one has to go from the first toward the center of town and then back outward to the second. This is one, just one, of the reasons why a great number of people erroneously use their cars. It is faster, they think, to go by the Grande Raccordo Anulare (GRA), the highway that circles the city, stitching together all the bordering neighborhoods. They are mistaken, because everybody converges on the GRA and gets stuck there. As for the center, it is a maze; there are a few wide, straight major avenues — Via Nazionale, Via del Tritone, Corso Vittorio, the Lungotevere along the Tiber — but most just speed traffic to a few bottlenecks, like Piazza Venezia, or around Piazzale Flaminio, or Ponte Vittorio. Pompeii died of asphyxia, buried by ashes; the city of Rome will also suffocate, buried by cars. Add to the everyday traffic the nearly everyday demonstrations, strikes, parades, processions, visiting foreign dignitaries and their corteges and one can scarcely imagine the mess that Roman transportation has become.

Given all this, Signor Puddu still declares: "I think we are doing a great job; we do move a lot of people around. And we make continuous efforts to do better. We have proclaimed a *Carta dei Servizi*, like a Magna Carta, that specifies our duties toward the passengers."

He says this with a ducal tone and hands me a pamphlet, the *Carta dei Servizi*. ATAC-COTRAL guarantees: A) *Equalità* — accessibility to its services to all passengers, without distinction of nationality, sex, language, religion, or political belief; B) *Imparzialità* — absolute observance of the principles of objectivity, justice, and impartiality; C) *Continuità* — to assure continuous and regular service, and to hold this as the primary objective; D) *Partecipazione* — to encourage the passengers' participation, recognizing their right to suggest solutions and their right to complain . . . and so on with E, F, et cetera.

"We try to keep in sight not only the technical aspects of transportation," says Signor Puddu, "but also its contribution to the quality, the good quality, of life in the city."

ATAC-COTRAL is trying to cut down on pollution by using electric minibuses, on an experimental basis, on a few routes in the very center of town, but the buses are very small and move few people. They are also planning the use of buses with hybrid electric-diesel engines, and engines fueled by an emulsion of water and diesel oil to further reduce environmental decay. To speed up circulation, they have tried to be more agile by using smaller buses with more frequent trips, but that did not really work. So on major arteries they have created special lanes for public transportation only, and that has helped a great deal. They have reinstated routes and put down new tracks for the new ultramodern trolley cars: the use of the trolley was considered a step backward, but the new tracks–new cars combination makes for a very smooth, vibrationless ride. It is also pollution-free, and articulated cars have a large capacity. More comfort, also more safety: the conductor can monitor all the cars via security cameras. There have been complaints about the tracks taking public space away

from private cars, but that is, ultimately, the purpose: to encourage people to leave their cars at home, to take the tram.
There are also new, modern buses with very low platforms, easier
to get in and out of, with cleaner lines inside: passengers should
like them. But "Take the bus, leave the driving to us" has not really caught on. It is a battle, Signor Puddu says, and I agree.

"Buses in Rome are like whales amid schools of rushing,
dashing minnows. Our drivers have to be like flies: one hundred
eyes open all the time."

I tell Signor Puddu that once, to get a better view of the city, of
one of the "beautiful pages," I took a seat up front near the driver.
That one experience was enough for me: in the tight, narrow
streets of downtown, pedestrians jumped off sidewalks and onto
the street, ignoring the oncoming bus, motor scooters appeared
from nowhere, cars came within a hair's breadth of collision. I envied the driver's coolness, his steely nerves: in ten minutes mine
were shattered. "If I had been the whale," I told him, "I would
have swallowed all the minnows in a rage."

"We have drivers who can take it and some who cannot," says
Puddu, "so we have antistress measures. Short shifts for the hard
routes, longer for the softer ones. We alternate personnel, give a
ten-minute rest between runs. But even so, everybody reacts differently; some drivers get exhausted and sluggish, some exuberant
and racy, they want to rush to keep up with the schedules, they get
impatient with passengers who are slow to get on or to get off, they
snap at passengers who get impatient with them . . . tempers
flare."

It's not easy to stay calm, I have to agree. It is a stressful situation.

"The whole city is stressed. Somehow we have to go back to
being a city with human dimensions. Rome is a city made for a
leisurely pace."

Signor Puddu now becomes rhapsodic, eyes semiclosed, his
voice a narration of the images his mind sees. The images are of a
Rome that becomes Rome again on those Sundays when, to alleviate pollution, only public transportation may be used — no pri-

vate cars, no motorcycles. People can walk and hear again the voices of people walking and talking on the other side of the street; people are bicycling; people are laughing: the city is breathing again. It's alive. One does not need to *see* its beauty, one *feels* it.

"For me," he says, "it is an experience similar to being on a beach on a still, early morning, and being able to hear in the distance, without seeing them, the noise of oars stirring the sea."

I mention that on one of those motor-barren Sundays, I heard people not only talking, but complaining loudly about not having the use of their *macchina*.

"Have you ever heard of a for-the-common-good solution resulting in unified applause? Without a protest rising from somewhere? A warming, comforting fire without smoke? There are solutions to social problems that become restrictions for some individuals. Romans, as you probably know, are individualists. Sometimes it is hard to explain that a problem, for example the problem of pollution, has larger repercussions here in Rome than in other places. Here not only our lungs are at risk but our cultural wealth, our monuments, our treasures, our very soul."

It is known that Rome has already lost, or is in the process of losing, some of her finest bronze and marble statues and monuments to the slow gnawing of pollution. Some traffic was detoured away from valuable sites because of damaging vibrations, and a lot of people complained. In Rome there is a definite split in the population, even among intellectuals. One faction is for preserving everything, no matter how small its intrinsic value; the other says "Don't we have enough ruins? Should we allow a few more old stones to impede progress? Are we making a living museum or a modern city? Past or future: which?" Just recently — following a great clamoring for more parking spaces — it was finally decided to build an underground garage beneath the Gianicolo Hill. During its construction, a backhoe dug into the first century A.D. and the beautifully preserved house of Agrippina, Caesar Germanicus's wife. The work had to be stopped, the past-or-future question came up again, and after long arguments the whole works had to be redesigned and restarted. Some of the house was safely moved away, some skirted around, and after much delay both past and future were saved. The work is now finished: it is a beautiful public underground garage. Ironically, nobody is using it yet. A fifteen-minute walk — or even less — from the heart of downtown, obviously considered too far by the driving public.

"We have had to face the ancient-versus-modern conundrum with our subway system," says Gianni Puddu, now in a no-nonsense tone, "and we still do when we plan to enlarge it. The subway is the only instrument that can alleviate the traffic congestion of a modern city. But it is not easy to reconcile the needs of a modern city with the duty to preserve an old one. How many ruins can you drill through, how many can you skirt?"

After many years of planning — the idea of a Roman subway started in the 1950s — Rome now has two lines, the Red and the Blue, that roughly crisscross the city, with the fulcrum at the central Termini railroad station. The system took much longer to complete than was estimated because at every step along the way ruins or catacombs were found. There are layers of ruins, in some places six or seven, and hundreds of miles of catacombs under the city, some still unexplored. The only way was to go below them all. But then another problem arose: water. Rome is blessed with an abundance of water both aboveground and underground. Dig a bit and water gushes out. And when tunnels are dug, the diggers have to make sure that water does not seep inside: that would be a problem. When the first *metropolitana* line was inaugurated, in 1958, some journalist spoke of the marvels he had seen while underground, including a magnificent lake fed by the Tiber. There are no lakes; the subway goes under the Tiber. It turned out to be a large puddle, blown into a lake in the writer's imagination. There are plans to expand the subway lines, especially in the outlying suburbs, but it is not easy. Not only physically but socially as well.

"Socially," says Puddu, reinforcing what Uccio Pizzuti had called the *Mordi e Fuggi*, Bite and Run, syndrome, "because by subway many people come from the suburbs to the center of town for a feel of place, in search of entertainment, in search of an identity, to feel Roman. Many of the suburbs have a name but, paradoxically, are anonymous: have no face, have no soul. By subway they can get to the *centro* in ten minutes. It has changed the social structure of old Rome: a great influx of people come in like a tide, fill downtown, roam awhile and then wane, leaving the city empty and dirty, caring little for its beauty.

Signor Puddu speaks about it all with a proprietary tone, and also — but this could be my interpretation — with mixed feelings: if it were up to him, I think, he would cross out of the *Carta* the bit about equality, and leave the riffraff out. His voice is solemn and low, with a faint accent from his native Sardinia. He has been in Rome for thirty years.

"It is very hard to make people feel that we are a link in a long chain. To make them understand that our present is a link between past and future, and it is up to us to pass on the past in as good a shape as we found it. It is true for anywhere, but here in Rome it is essential. Because she is unique. I have been to the Pincio a hundred, two hundred times; I see Rome at my feet and I am still left breathless. I have been in Saint Peter's Square a hundred, two hundred times and I still marvel at its beauty. There I feel like I am levitating; I get a mystical sense of a God, a superior being able to inspire humans to create such a work."

Puddu proceeds to take me vicariously along in his reveries about the sights of Rome, telling of his emotional experiences, grateful for the past that has been preserved, fearful of the damages the future may bring. I am convinced now of his ambivalent feelings: his work is to sell a modern, fast, efficient Rome, ready and set to navigate quickly and expertly above- and below ground for the next few centuries. Yet his heart is in the past, when Rome was made for walking or, if you were rich and in a hurry, to speed about in a horse and buggy.

Somehow, I feel the same way. I take my leave without asking for the numbers I initially sought: how many buses, how many trolleys, how many subway cars, how many passengers, how many miles. That information, now, seems absolutely unimportant. It also seems unimportant to tell him that for this protracted Roman stay, Gwen and I have elected to do without a car, and that with his buses and his subways — and the addition of short, enjoyable walks — we can go almost door to door anywhere in Rome.

Since it was a beautiful day, I walk the few miles back home, seeing Rome through the sensitive, devoted eyes of Signor Puddu. Like looking anew at a beautifully illuminated page.

To return to Trastevere, I cross the Tiber at Ponte Sisto. I have done that a hundred, two hundred times, and each time I stop to admire the view and the elegance of the bridge itself. Today my attention focuses on the river: it must have rained up north, because the water level is much higher than usual, the current swift, and the water muddier — practically brown — carrying branches and uprooted bushes. The ancient Romans called it *Flavus Tiberis*, the Blond Tiber, the color of the fertile earth — Tuscan earth, Umbrian earth — gouged by the river on its way to Rome and the sea.

The story of the Tiber is the history of Rome since its legendary inception: the infants Romulus and Remus floated on it in a basket and, stopped by a wild fig tree branch hanging low over the current, were rescued from the river's left bank; later, on the same bank, Romulus built his city. The river was the city's bloodline, a fluid highway that brought supplies from the lands up north and from the sea down south. At its *ostium*, mouth, fifteen miles away on the shore of the Tyrrhenian Sea, the port of Ostia channeled goods and food up to the city. The Tiber was Rome's arm into the Mediterranean world. It fulfilled this function through the centuries of Monarchic Rome, of Republican Rome, of Imperial Rome; but the rapport between Rome and its river became closer, almost intimate, when at the end of the 1300s, after the empire's fall and the many dark years of decadence, Rome, the Rome of the Popes, began its own *rinascimento*, its rebirth.

The aqueducts had been deteriorating for centuries; the people who lived in the *rioni* stretched along the Tiber's banks satisfied their water needs directly from the river, giving birth to one of the oldest medieval Roman guilds, the *acquaroli*, porters and sellers of water. Near the river and on the river a great number of activities took place, many of which persisted until our modern era: mills milled grains, presses forged iron, carding mills carded wool; all took advantage of the Tiber's power. Leather tanneries and dyeing plants kept close to the river — wash, rinse, and dump; the main slaughterhouse remained in Testaccio for centuries, close to the left bank at the end of town. The river also took most of the city's sewage. (Around 200 B.C., Rome was the first city with covered, sometimes underground sewers: its main conduit, the *Cloaca Maxima*, spewed into the Tiber. The large orifice, now in use as a water drain, can still be seen on the left bank, near the Isola Tiberina.) Even so, the river was alive with fish, and many were the fishermen and fishmongers who made a living out of it. Stonecutters cut the millstones for the mills, carpenters built boats for the boatmen who shuttled goods across, up, and down the river; mule drivers and cart drivers, their stables also close by the river, took the wares and delivered them all over town. Upriver landings and ports, both large and small, took care of the commerce between the city and the central Italian regions; larger downriver ports attended to the sea traffic coming from Ostia. Warehouses crowded the banks, giving work to scores of stevedores and teamsters. From the fifteenth century on, Rome expanded — commercially, economically, politically — and so continually augmented its needs. Most of its supplies came by river, and many of its *porti fluviali* specialized in the handling of a particular ware. Porto di Ripetta handled wood, construction timber; Ripa di Borgo received all the marble and construction material for the great Renaissance and baroque buildings, including Saint Peter's church and its colonnades. The whole complex of ports and their associated activities was an essential part of the Roman economy. The old river created and gave life to a world of tradesmen, artisans, and merchants who became the template of the *Romano de Roma*, the Roman of Rome. Trastevere still cherishes that *Romano de Roma* aura, even if the arrival of railroads and the industrial revolution managed to make obsolete many of the blue-collar activities tied directly to the river.

Together with its gifts, the Tiber also carried a great menace: floods. The river swelled yearly, threatening the low-lying quarters and thrice every hundred years, on the average, punishing the city with destructive, cataclysmic floods. The mood of the river and its floods is officially classified as "ordinary" when the water level rises to thirty to thirty-six feet above normal, "extraordinary" from thirty-six to forty-eight feet, and "exceptional" above forty-eight feet. Historical records report a long list of exceptional floods, going back to ancient Rome, all with tragic consequences. One can frequently find marble plaques on the walls of ancient buildings: a chiseled horizontal line, with a date underneath, marks the water level of a flood; many are higher than a tall man can reach with a raised hand. The flood of 1530 was reportedly responsible for more deaths and more damage than the dreadful Lanskenechts mercenaries' sack of Rome in 1527. Extremely serious floods occurred in 1180, 1310, 1379, 1422, 1476, 1495, 1514, 1557, 1589, 1598, 1601, 1637, 1647, 1660, 1686, 1805, 1846, and 1870. It was with the *innondazione* of 1870 (the Italian state had just taken Rome from the pope by force, and some of his followers declared the flood a sign of God's displeasure) that plans were made to solve the recurring problem: a massive work to corral the periodically wild river in its urban tract was initiated in 1877; construction lasted several decades. The riverbed was brought to a unified, three-hundred-foot width, some curves were smoothed, and fifty-foot-tall brick-and-marble ramparts were erected to replace the natural banks. The whole operation was necessary, but it changed forever the relationship between Rome and its river. To make room for the new structures, some valuable constructions and artistic buildings were — by necessity — wiped out. One such case was the port of Ripetta, considered an architectural masterwork, the most beautiful of river ports. There was great protestation, especially from the *Papalini*'s side, accusing the new bureaucrats of disrespect for the past. There was probably some truth in it: the new liberal government, with a good dose of backward thinking, was anxious to build a new Rome, a Rome worthy to be the capital of a newly united Italy, even if it meant building over the Rome of the Popes and, in some cases, the Rome of the Emperors.

The tall walls gentrified the proletarian Tiber. The right and left Lungoteveri, the wide, tree-shaded avenues flanking the river, became romantic five-mile-long promenades, the favorite rendezvous of lovers. A popular song warned people not to go there unless they were in love; but that was yesterday. Today, the avenues have become racetracks for cars, buses, and motorcycles; frequent traffic jams turn them into five-mile-long lines of raging, seething, honking vehicles: noise and fumes enough to kill any romantic feelings. Yet the Lungoteveri are still beautiful: Gwen and I take long walks along them, but only after midnight, when things calm down a bit.

Unconsciously, the new *muraglioni*, the ramparts, supplied Rome with superb, most visible blackboards. Anybody with a brush, a can of paint, and a need to vent (and I suppose a very tall ladder, judging by the ten-foot-tall script) writes it on the *muraglioni* for everybody to see. The graffiti reflect the various eras, mostly political. In the 1930s, at the time of the Ethiopian War, huge letters proclaimed "Italy wants its empire!" or "Stalin Murderer," and the ubiquitous, repeated ad infinitum, "Viva il Duce. Viva il Duce. Viva il Duce. Viva il . . ." Then came "Death to Albion," "Churchill is a pig," "Americani Gangsters Assassini," and so on to "Viva la Repubblica," "Vota Democristiano," "Viva Falce e Martello," "Yankee Go Home," "No to NATO," as well as more mundane expressions for the local soccer teams, such as "Viva la Lazio" crossed over and replaced with "Viva la Roma," crossed over and replaced by "Viva la Lazio," and so on until someone ran out of paint. But then, to mark the spirit of the times, there are also more personal declarations. In fluorescent paint the population at large was informed that "Luciana Ti Amo Follemente," signed by a love-smitten "Carlo." Later, perhaps after the lady had joined the Municipal Police Corps, we were told that "Luciana Anche In Divisa Sei Bellissima" or that, in Carlo's eyes, the mentioned lady was beautiful even when wearing her uniform. Naturally, writing on the walls is absolutely forbidden by the law; it remains a mystery to me how anybody can perform, at any time of day or night, such feats of calligraphy — considering the perfect alignment and execution of the huge letters, it must take hours to complete — without being caught in the act and punished.

Along with the corralling of the river and the smoothing of its current, another development took place. In a few spots along its urban course, minibeaches were left for the enjoyment of bathers; they were named *polverini*, a name essentially describing what the beaches were made of: a mixture of coarse *polvere*, dust, and river sand — a city substitute for a real sandy beach. They were frequented by a self-styled fraternity of men of all ages who took the name of *fiumaroli*, rivermen, but river-rats would be more affectionately appropriate. Now a disappearing race, they could be distinguished by their minuscule *triangolo*, a triangular bathing suit smaller than a loincloth, and by their deep, nut-brown tans, both evident even in the coldest winter. To be a *fiumarolo* was to be the most macho Roman in an already macho society. Sun worshipers more than swimmers — the Blond Tiber then being swimmable, risky only in time of epidemics — heroic rescues of the inept were common; a New Year's communal swim was a baptism and a requirement for the valiant.

Similarly, pulling oars on the Tiber turned from the working necessity of the *barcaroli* into a sport for the *canottieri*, rowers. Many club boathouses were tied to the banks, repositories of sleek skiffs and river kayaks, populated by a fraternity of oarsmen with a strong kinship to the river-rats. In most cases it was a very democratic, casual association of people with the same interest, namely to row alone, in twos, or in fours on a fragile scull up and down the Tiber. My father was one of them, and a most dedicated one. Practically every day of the year, generally at lunchtime, he went to the *galleggiante* — the floating boathouse — and went out for an hour's row. He did this until shortly before his death, in his midseventies. I think the rowing was only part of the enjoyment: the camaraderie, the joking and jesting with friends of all social strata and conditions made up the rest. When I was a child he frequently took me along, giving me the incredible honor of being his helmsman and letting me help dock the scull, wash it, and sponge it dry. He also taught me how to swim; his coaching was basic: he tied a rope around my chest like a leash and threw me in the river. He followed my floating and splashing with the current for the length of the boathouse, pulling on the leash only when I went under and swallowed more water than admissible. I understood immediately the meaning of *sink or swim* and, saying it as humbly as my pride allows, I later became a champion swimmer.

And now, after so many years, looking down from the bridge at the swollen river I can still taste its earthy flavor, the grittiness of silt on teeth.

And again I feel, like Rome, a strong kinship with my *Biondo Tevere*.

THE SUITCASES have been carefully packed and are lined up in the hallway awaiting the descent to the street, down the staircase's seventy-two steps. They are packed with clothes — fall, winter, spring, old and new — books, notes, and a lot of memories. It is Sunday again; it is a blue, clear day again. It is a Roman day again: we have just been informed that our departure has been delayed several hours or until the strike of some key airport personnel is called off. The news has been divulged by my sister, and she insists that she herself will pick us up and take us to the airport. She wants to make sure, she says, that we get safely there and away and, she adds with a tear and a laugh, finally out of her hair. In the meantime relax, she says nervously, you have all morning at least.

So we will take a last stroll in town, wishing for a crystal ball to tell us when our next will be. Down the stairs we go, then uphill on Vicolo del Cedro. The usual residue of the dog walks, their abundant morning gifts to Rome, greet us. We skip over them and smile: will we be missing them, once we leave?

But then, we ask ourselves, what else will we miss?

The trips to the museums, to find them closed tight, contrary to all posted timetables?

Standing in line at the post office to pay gas, electricity, and telephone bills?

The ATM machine that, after taking your card, keeps it and flashes, "Sorry, not today, not for you"?

Having to pass by a bank's heavily armed guard, made to step into a glass, bulletproof cubicle, be locked into it, then, if deemed harmless, released into the bank proper to stand in line and, when finally your turn comes, be told by an uninterested employee that the money-exchange person is out having an espresso?

Be given in record time by a most courteous bureaucrat the requested family's certificates — streamlined, computerized, officially stamped — but with wrong birthdates on the wrong names?

Having your ears shattered, your very life endangered by possessed motorcyclists?

Hurdling over the worthless trinkets displayed for blocks on the pavement by insistent peddlers?

We walk and we make a list of all the things, the paradoxical things, big or small, important or trivial, that we will — will we? — miss once we leave. We know it is a game we play with ourselves to soften the departure's blow. After all, *partire è un po' morire*: leaving is a bit like dying. We list the corrupt politics, the shady economy, the selfish *menefreghismo*, the endemic *nepotismo*, the anachronistic *machismo*, the widespread *mammismo*. We challenge each other to search for still more negative *-ismos*. But by now we have reached the Gianicolo's terrace, the air fragrant of flowers and pine trees, few people there to share our space. A gentle breeze has swept away the city's haze and all Rome is there to be seen, a living postcard, with all the roofs, all the cupolas, all the bell towers sharply defined in the clear air. How Roman of Rome, we tell each other: just when one is bent on reviling her, on censuring all her defects and ugliness, here she is like a peacock displaying her incredible plumage. All the warts are gone; only the iridescent colors are there to be admired. "Here I am, this is what I am," she is saying. "Take me as I am. Do not try to change me. Nobody can."

It is magic. Or a puzzle. Perhaps a magic puzzle: as soon as you think you have the solution, almost all pieces in place, the last element will not fit and the whole charade's meaning is obscure again.

On our left, a small assembly of toddlers, in their Sunday best and on best behavior, is watching — entranced, mouths agape — a puppet show. The tiny canvas-and-wood theater has been on this same place, this same pebbled sidewalk, for generations; the wooden actors are the same Pulcinella, the same carabiniere, the same Angelina, the same devil . . . offering the same moral plays that the accompanying parents saw when they were children. It is a charming sight, a magic promise of a gentler world. But then you notice, just below the proscenium, a sign in bold letters: BAMBINI, NON TIRATE I SASSI. Children, do not throw stones. Is it a plea? Is it an order? What prompted it? Could it be that these angel-faced toddlers . . . ? A puzzle, a Roman puzzle.

In the center of the Gianicolo, in a position to see — and be seen by — all of Rome, the equestrian statue of Garibaldi supervises everything. At the base of the monument there is an inscription in bold, bronze letters: ROMA O MORTE, Rome or Death. Read in the heroic, historic context it has a clear meaning. But suppose one takes it at face value, Gwen and I speculate, suppose an alien should read it. Would he take it as a choice, either/or? Would he take it as a mathematical equation: one equals the other? Or would he take it as a syllogism: Death is eternal . . . so must be Rome. That much we knew, that much we had been told. We know also that if the alien should come back in another thousand, two thousand years, he would find the same Rome, the same Eternal Rome, the same eternal, mesmerizing, magic puzzle. The eternal paradox.

It is Sunday, it is noon. The howitzer's blast shatters our speculations. Birds take wing, more from habit than from fear, and circle in the air, giving body to the sound of the church bells of Rome. We decide that it is all for us, the one-gun salute, the flight of birds, the pealing bells.

Rome is saying good-bye.